-- BIKING WITH THE WIND --

Bicycling Day Trips in Minnesota and Wisconsin
Within Reach of the Twin Cities

by

Dixen-Seed-Wilson

Cartographers -- Van Johnson
and Sharon Ketelsen

Published by:
DSW, Inc.
906 N. 4th Street
Stillwater, MN 55082

Printed by:
Print-It-Plus
990 Lone Oak Road, #110
Eagan, MN 55121

2nd Ed. Dec. 1993
Copyright 1993
All rights reserved.

ISBN: 0-9622744-1-0

Library of Congress Card #90-93593

Contents

Page

Introduction i
Legend for Maps iv
Acknowledgement v

Tours
Within 50 miles of the Twin Cities

	Distance from Twin Cities	Page
Stillwater Mini Tours	25 Miles	1
Cannon River Valley Tours	35 Miles	39
River Falls, WI. Tours	35 Miles	61
Spring Valley, WI. Tours	40 Miles	85
Osceola, WI. Tours	45 Miles	105
Taylors Falls History Tours	45 Miles	121
Mantorville - Douglas Trail Tours	50 Miles	131

Within 100 miles of the Twin Cities

	Distance from Twin Cities	Page
Annandale Lakes Tours	60 Miles	137
Menomonie, WI. Tours	65 Miles	145
Lake Pepin East Tours	65 Miles	169
Lake Pepin West Tours	70 Miles	185
Waterville--Sakatah Tours	70 Miles	201
Hinckley/Moose Lake Fire Trail Tours	75-105 Miles	211

Within 140 miles of the Twin Cities

	Distance from Twin Cities	Page
Lanesboro Tours	115 Miles	235
Mississippi River Bluff Country Tours	120 Miles	261
Carlton County -- Munger Trail Tours	130 Miles	281
Trempealeau, WI. Tours	140 Miles	289

Page

Appendix

Rides by Distance	303
Buying a Bicycle	307
Custom Gearing	309
Bicycle Maintenance	311
Transporting Bicycles	313
Packing for a Trip	315
Hints for Better Biking	318

INTRODUCTION

Welcome to enjoyable bicycling! Within easy reach of the Twin Cities are some of the best bicycling day trips in the Midwest. This book describes more than 60 such tours. Each tour is designed for bicyclists who like to explore the small towns and back roads of Minnesota and Wisconsin at a leisurely pace.

The inspiration for this book comes from a shared love of bicycling and a deep-seated frustration over the lack of a really good bicycling guide for the area. Our small group of biking friends has thrived on a diet of interesting bike rides over the years. We wanted to share with you the problem solving we have done for ourselves. We have carefully reconnoitered each of the tours in this book and the options given with them. We hope others will enjoy the tours as we have. They should appeal to families with small children, fast-paced teenagers, and person of all ages who enjoy some exercise and share a love of the outdoors.

The tours are grouped in various areas to allow for one or more bicycling trips on the same day or over the weekend and for sightseeing if desired. The routes steer clear of heavily traveled roads (with some noted exceptions) and use some state trails. In most cases, we describe nearby camping and lodging facilities, places to eat, picnic spots, points of interest, and other lore that may enhance the trip. Omission of any eating or lodging spot does not imply disapproval; merely that we did not discover that place. Toilet facilities are noted, and most routes begin where such necessary facilities are available. We also identify basics such as highway numbers, street names, point-to-point mileage, terrain (with significant hills noted), and location of trailhead. The term "roller-coaster" is used as both a noun and a verb to describe certain roads that no other word fits.

Note that a number of our tours pass by or close to state parks. Admission to these parks is always free for cyclists in both Minnesota and Wisconsin. There is a charge, however, for camping.

The routes vary from approximately 10 miles to 60 miles. As in most recreational cycling groups, individuals in our group range from type A riders, who like to ride fast and long, to type C riders, who like a nice slow 15 to 20 mile jaunt. Problems may arise when a type A rider is married to a type C rider. In that case, try to find a group of riders to bicycle with, as that often gives everyone, someone to ride with. Flexibility may be achieved by designating meeting points along the way or by using the different options. Adaptability is necessary.

A number of our routes make use of off-the-road state trails. In all but one case, the Munger (Carlton-Duluth) State trail, the trails are connected with other roads to allow for a circular route in place of repeating a trail. Road repairs are a part of summer, and we do not guarantee freedom from those hazards (although in 1993, our routes were free from those obstacles).

The format of each chapter in the book starts with a map of the routes, followed by a narrative containing "how to get there," historical, lodging, and sightseeing information about the area. And then for each tour, we have included a brief description of the trip (trailhead, distance, terrain, highlights, and minimal route information); and a mileage log showing turns, significant hills (up and down), landmarks, and points of interest. The cities which provide trailheads for each chapter are:

Chapter	City
Stillwater, Mini Tours	Stillwater/Scandia, Mn./Somerset, Wisc.
Cannon River Valley Tours	Cannon Falls/Red Wing, Mn.
River Falls, Wisc. Tours	River Falls/Trimbelle, Wisc./ Red Wing, Mn.
Spring Valley, Wisc. Tours	Spring Valley/Hatchville, Wisc.
Osceola, Wisc. Tours	Osceola/St. Croix Falls, Wisc.
Taylors Falls History Tours	Taylors Falls, Mn.
Mantorville-Douglas Trail Tours	Mantorville/Pine Island, Mn.
Annandale Lake Tours	Annandale, Mn.
Menomonie, Wisc. Tours	Menomonie, Wisc.
Lake Pepin East Tours	Maiden Rock/Pepin/Stockholm, Wisc.
Lake Pepin West Tours	Lake City/Red Wing
Waterville–Sakatah Tours	Waterville, Mn.
Hinckley/Moose Lake Fire Tours	Hinckley/Moose Lake, Mn.

Lanesboro Tours	Lanesboro, Mn.
Mississippi River Bluffs Tours	Winona, Mn./Stockholm, Wisc.
Carleton County–Munger Trail Tours	Carleton, Mn.
Trempealeau, Wisc. Tours	Trempealeau, Wisc.

The map on the cover locates most of these cities.

In the appendix, we supply all sorts of information -- a list of all tours, including options organized by length of trip; tips on buying, maintaining, and transporting a bicycle; technical insights into custom gearing; and practical suggestions on packing for a bicycle trip and better biking. Great reading for a rainy day.

The authors of this book are an airline pilot-farmer, a public finance lawyer, and an ex-teacher-librarian. With the help of spouses and friends, we have struggled to provide in this book the planning that is necessary for enjoyable bicycling. Although we have tried to update all information in this book, we are aware that telephone numbers change, businesses close or open, roads undergo construction and even highway numbers change. (The recent conversion in Wisconsin of long-standing road names to numbered avenues (east/west) and streets (north/south) has been particularly disconcerting.) We hope that any such instances not caught by the authors are few. Any comments or suggestions may be sent to DSW, Inc., 906 North Fourth Street, Stillwater, Minnesota, 55082.

(IMPORTANT NOTICE)

Needless to say, neither the authors nor DSW, Inc. can warrant the safety of the routes recommended. Most of the roads on the tour have no special provisions for bicyclists. You must assume the responsibilities and risks for your own safety when cycling on the recommended routes. There, the lawyer-author has spoken. Now go and have a good time.

———	**Bicycle Route**
═══	**Optional Bicycle Route**
- - - -	**Off Road Bicycle Trail**
— — —	**State Trail**
❯	**Hill**
❯❯	**Steeper Hill**
❯❮	**Roller Coaster Hill**
■	**Trailhead**
✱	**Point of Interest**
⌂	**Interstate**
⌂	**Highway**
☐ ○	**County Road**

ACKNOWLEDGEMENT

The authors are the first to admit that they could never have produced this book without the unstinting support and advice of others. Foremost are our spouses, Susan Dixen, Linda Seed, and Viktor Wilson. Without question, however, the key contributors to the book are our cartographers, Van Johnson and Sharon Ketelsen (whose maps make this book sing), and our editor, Jill Schmidt (whose writing and formatting skills helped make this book readable) and our word processor, Pat Semborski (who endured countless and at times indecipherable changes). We are forever indebted to them. Other persons who have helped us produce this book are too many to list. Suffice it to say that their goodwill and enthusiasm lifted our spirits and kept us going.

- David Dixen
- Peter Seed
- Nancy Wilson

NOTES

STILLWATER MINI TOURS

The historic town of Stillwater makes a convenient and interesting starting point for a number of short bicycle trips close to the Twin Cities. Starting points vary depending upon the specific route, but we have tried to begin the tours at places that eliminate the steep uphill climb from downtown Stillwater. The Minnesota routes are nearly level. The Wisconsin routes vary from rolling hills to quite hilly.

Tour 1: Stillwater to White Bear Lake -- 22 or 24 miles
Tour 2: White Bear Lake Circle Tour -- 14 miles
Tour 3: Houlton -- Willow River State Park -- 25 or 28 miles
Tour 4: Somerset Route -- 18 miles
Tour 5: Stillwater to Withrow -- 16 miles
Tour 6: Scandia -- Marine -- 14 or 16 miles
Tour 7: Stillwater -- Lake Demontreville -- Lake Elmo -- 24 miles
Tour 8: Afton - 23 miles
Tour 9: High Bridge Circle Tour -- 16, 22, or 29 miles
Tour 10: Stillwater to Marine -- 27 miles

About the Area

How to Get There: About 25 miles and 30 minutes east of the Twin Cities on Mn. Hwy. 36.

Nestled in the hills on the banks of the St. Croix River, Stillwater retains the look and atmosphere of by-gone days. As the oldest official town site in Minnesota, Stillwater was the queen of the lumbering era and home of the territorial convention. Today, it is the year-round home to about 13,000 residents and hundreds of tourists on weekends. Nineteenth-century architecture and church spires reaching high above the city are part of the charm of Stillwater.

The St. Croix River is designated as one of the nation's National Scenic Waterways, and the National Park Service Visitor Center are on Main Street. Several excursion boats are available for visitors. Contact the Chamber of Commerce at 612/439-7700. On occasion, log-rolling contests are held here, and sometimes participants may be seen practicing in the pond along the route of Tour 1 or Tour 5.

In 1848, the Territorial Convention was held in Stillwater, and a plaque on Main Street commemorates that fact. The Historical Museum at the north end of Main Street in the old prison warden's house gives a good picture of the early days. It is open from May 1 to November 1 on Tuesdays, Thursdays, Saturdays, and Sundays from 2:00 p.m. to 5:00 p.m. Special tours can be arranged for groups by phoning 612/439-5956 or by calling the Stillwater Chamber of Commerce.

The homes of lumber barons and prosperous business people as well as every day homes of 1850-1900 are still occupied by Stillwater residents. The Chamber of Commerce is located in the Brick Alley building on South Main Street, where pamphlets describing a walking, bicycling, or driving tour around town are available. A dinner train, the Minnesota Zephyr, leaves from north Main Street for evening dinner trips through the valley (612/430-3000). A newly constructed depot with railroad memorabilia is now home for the Zephyr.

Solid long-time businesses like Simonet's Furniture are housed in buildings that have stood on Main Street for more than 100 years. New shops ranging from sporting goods to art work are in mini-malls such as the Grand Garage, Brick Alley, Old Post Office Shops, Main Street Square, and the River Exchange Building. Antique shoppers could spend a day in Stillwater just moving from antique store to antique store. Staples Mill on north Main Street has 50 dealers on four levels under the same roof.

St. Croix Bicycle and Skate just off Mn. 36 behind the Cub Foods Store has bicycles, parts, and expertise in repairs.

Eating in Stillwater ranges from river-view restaurants, such as the Dock and the Freight House, to ethnic restaurants such as Vittorios, Estebans, and Silver Lake, to the renowned Lowell Inn. For good hometown cooking, try Cat Ballou's, The Main Cafe, or Brines, a turn of the century establishment, with restaurant, bar, and party area on 3 floors. A number of coffee shops and candy stores are also located downtown.

Lodging choices have grown from the early days of boarding houses. The Lowell Inn (612/439-1100) is nationally rated and offers deluxe accommodations while the Stillwater Inn Motel (612/430-1300) and the Super 8 Motel (612/430-3990) offer comfort on the south edge of town. Bed and breakfast accommodations are found in town at the

Rivertown Inn (612/430-2955), the William Sauntry Mansion (612/430-2653), the Battle Hollow (612/430-8001), James A. Mulvey (612/430-8008), Ann Bean House (612/430-0355), The Brunswick Inn (612/430-2653), the Heirloom Inn (612/430-2289), The Elephant Walk Bed and Breakfast (612/430-0359), and Laurel Street Inn (612/351-0031).

Other bed and breakfasts in the vicinity include: Shady Ridge Farm (on Tour 3, 715/549-6258) five miles east of Stillwater in Wisconsin; the Outing Lodge at Pine Point (on Tour 5, 612/439-9747) three miles northwest of Stillwater; the Asa Parker House (on Tour 6, 612/433-5248) 10 miles north of Stillwater in Marine on St. Croix; and Afton Country B&B (On Tour 8, 612/436-6964) 6 miles southwest of Stillwater in Afton. In downtown Afton is The Historic Afton House Inn (612-436-8883), a renovated 1867 inn, with both food and lodging accommodations. Within walking distance of downtown Afton is Mulberry Pond on the River Road (612/436-8086), with two bedrooms, each having a private bath and whirlpool.

Camping is available at William O'Brien State Park (612/433-0500), 12 miles north of Stillwater, and at Willow River State Park (715/386-5931), nine miles southeast of Stillwater in Wisconsin or at Afton State Park (612/436-5391), 12 miles south of Stillwater.

Special Note: The map shows a dual treadway bicycle/horseback trail on the abandoned Soo Line railroad line. The bicycle trail is paved. It intersects the routes for Tours 1 and 5 at three points and offers a tempting scenic diversion. The state acquired the right-of-way as the "Gateway" segment of the Willard Munger State Trail that will someday connect St. Paul with Duluth. This part of the state trail is seventeen miles long. It starts about 1½ miles west of Phalen Park in St. Paul, thus providing residents in a large part of Washington and Ramsey Counties easy bicycle access to the Stillwater Mini-Tours.

TOUR 1: *Stillwater to White Bear Lake*

Trailhead:	Parking lot two miles west of downtown Stillwater on Myrtle Street. On the corner of Myrtle (Co. 12) and Northland Ave. Park by the tennis courts on south side of road. Toilet facilities available.
Distance:	Option A: 22 miles Option B: 24 miles (<u>Plus</u>: 10 mile Bald Eagle Lake side trip)
Terrain:	Level to slightly rolling.
Highlights:	White Bear Lake, attractive lake homes, rural residential countryside, and Gasthaus Bavarian Hunter.
Route:	(0.0) West on Co. 12; (5.4) **Willernie/Mahtomedi**--North on Mahtomedi Avenue; Cross Mn. 244 and West on Frontage Road; (6.0) North on Co. 29 (Birchwood Avenue); (6.5) North on Wildwood Avenue; (8.5) North on Co. Line Road which becomes South Shore Boulevard; (10.2) North on Lakeview Avenue; (10.3) North on Cottage Park Road; (10.7) Northwest on Old White Bear Avenue -- **White Bear Lake**; (11.1) North on Mn. 61; (11.2) Northeast on Lake Avenue North; (12.7) East on Mn. 96; (18.5) Southeast on Co. 64; (20.0) South on Co. 15; (21.0) East on Co. 12; (22.0) Trailhead.

A good tour for an afternoon with easy bicycling, attractive residential areas, and the fascinating White Bear Lake to view. Make a side trip to Aamodt's Apple Farm, to Bald Eagle Lake, or to Pine Tree Orchards for added interest.

Log

0.0 From the parking lot at corner of Co. 12 and Northland Avenue, HEAD WEST ON SEPARATE BIKE PATH on the south side of Co. 12. Initially, climb a little followed by four miles of rolling rural-residential countryside.

1.0 Cross Co. 15. Continue west on bike path. Aamodt's Apple Farm is 1.5 miles south on west side of Co. 15. Apples, gifts, and food are available. The bike trail rises and dips a little but nothing too steep.

2.0 Pass Co. 17 coming in from your left. Coast down gradual hill, pass Co. 63 (Kimbro Avenue) coming in from your right at mile 2.5, and then climb uphill reaching top at mile 3.0. (For a shortcut, turn right (north) on Co. 63. Pass Grant Town Hall on your left (rest room facilities for bicyclists). At T-intersection, turn right (east) on 88 Street for 1.1 mile on gravel road and rejoin main route at mile 19.2).

4.0 Begin easy climb, cross state trail at mile 4.2, reach top at mile 4.4, and then begin gradual downhill at mile 5.1 passing Co. 36, which comes in from your left and joins Co. 13 heading west.

5.4 Approaching the edge of Willernie/Mahtomedi. The trail ends, but continue west on the road to the junction with Mahtomedi Ave. (Phillips 66 is on northeast corner). Several shops and restaurants (including Big Bens) are located here. TURN RIGHT (NORTH) ON MAHTOMEDI AVE. AND AT END OF BLOCK WHERE STREET ENTERS MN. 244, CROSS THE HIGHWAY TO ASH ST. AND TURN LEFT (WEST) IMMEDIATELY ONTO THE SERVICE ROAD which parallels Mn. 244. (Across Mn. 244 to the south is Co. 79 which leads to Wildwood Park 0.2 miles away where there are picnic tables overlooking a small lake.)

6.0 TURN RIGHT (NORTH) ON CO. 29 (BIRCHWOOD ROAD). A slough with birds and other wildlife is on your left. The road winds through the bedroom community of Birchwood.

6.5	TURN RIGHT (NORTH) ON WILDWOOD AVE. A slightly rolling road.
8.5	TURN RIGHT (NORTH) ON COUNTY LINE ROAD (CO. 27), with White Bear Lake soon coming into view as the road begins to hug the shoreline. (Paved bicycle shoulder for most of the next 10 miles.) A nice view of the lake on your right. As the road turns left, it becomes South Shore Boulevard.
9.0	Bellaire Park is on your right. Picnic grounds and swimming beach here. This road continues to give nice view of the lake.
10.2	TURN RIGHT (NORTH) ON LAKEVIEW AVENUE. Nice view of the lake as road turns left (west).
10.3	TURN RIGHT (NORTH) ON COTTAGE PARK ROAD (Just before Old White Bear Avenue).
10.4	TAKE THE RIGHT FORK ON COTTAGE PARK ROAD. Pretty houses line both sides of the road.
10.7	TURN RIGHT (NORTHWEST) ON OLD WHITE BEAR AVENUE. Lions Club Park (picnic and toilet facilities) soon appears on your right next to the lake. Pass a shopping center on your left with a nice view of the lake on the right. Pass docking area strewn with boats on your right.
11.0	VFW 1782 on the right. Good place for a snack and a drink.
11.1	TURN RIGHT (NORTH) ONTO MN. 61. Stay on the sidewalk!
11.2	TURN RIGHT (NORTHEAST) ONTO LAKE AVENUE NORTH. Follow the bike path along the lake for the next 1.5 miles. Beautiful lakeside houses along this one-way road.
11.9	Morehead Street comes in from your left. Fillebrown House, a restored 1876 lake cottage, is on the corner. Sunday afternoon tours available during the summer.
12.0	Fourth Street comes in from your left. Turn off for downtown White Bear Lake and Country Home, a cafe and bakery, 0.3

mile west on Fourth Street and Kenwood Cyclery, a bicycle store on Third Street.

12.1 Octagonal gazebo set in Matoska Park on your right just before turn off to Manitou Island. Coming up is Eighth Street which leads east to the Depot Museum.

12.5 Street terminates, and separate bicycle trail begins. At this point, CONTINUE ON BIKE TRAIL past condominium development on your left. Eleventh Street leads west to McDonald's.

12.6 White Bear Lake Park with swimming beach, toilets, picnic area, and refreshments.

12.7 EXIT ONTO MN. 96, TURN RIGHT AND HEAD EAST along a four-foot paved shoulder with nice views of the lake.

13.2 Pass Northwestern Avenue coming in on your left. (At this point, you may want to add 9.7 miles to your trip by biking over to Bald Eagle Lake for a beautiful ride around the lake and back again. Turn left (north) on Northwestern Avenue. After 0.6 mile, turn left (west) at T-intersection on Buffalo Street, cross Mn. 61, and continue east to T-intersection with lake at mile 1.2. Turn left (south) on Bald Eagle Boulevard and follow road around the lake clockwise until you reach Lakeview Inn -- a small establishment at the north end of the lake (mile 5.3) where pop, beer, ice cream, and microwave food are sold. Continue clockwise around the lake until mile 6.5, at which point the road heads east from the lake and becomes 120th Street. Follow this road east to Mn. 61.

Option: Either (1) turn right (south) on Falcon Avenue, stop at the Bald Eagle Regional Park 0.6 miles away for a swim and a picnic break, rejoin Buffalo Street, and retrace route or (2) cross Mn. 61. If you cross Mn. 61, the road becomes Portland Avenue (when it turns south) and takes you back to Mn. 96 and White Bear Lake at mile 9.7, just 0.1 mile further east from where you first left Mn. 96 for the side trip.)

13.5	Dellwood Avenue comes in from your right. Continue east on Mn. 96 as the road begins to climb and dip a little past White Bear Lake Yacht Club and Dellwood Hills Country Club and through lots of tree cover.
14.2	Apple Orchard Road (leading to Pine Tree Apple Orchards 1.6 miles away) comes in from your left. This road goes through expensive residential areas and lovely woods.
15.1	Co. 62 (Quail Road) comes in from your right. After a gentle climb, the road breaks out into a more open rural/residential landscape of farmland dotted with large acre homesites.
15.8	Pass North Port on your right, Grant Township's own (nearly defunct) airport, an important training facility in World War II.
18.5	TURN RIGHT (SOUTHEAST) ON CO. 64, through pleasant wooded areas and past Sawmill Golf Course.
19.2	Pass 88th Street coming in from your right.
19.5	To your right is the road to Gasthaus Bavarian Hunter, an excellent German restaurant. It has an outdoor porch in a park-like setting. Bicyclists welcomed.
20.0	Junction with Co. 15.

Option A: Turn right (south) on Co. 15 (wide paved shoulder), go one mile, and, at junction with Co. 12, turn left (east) onto the bicycle path on the south side of Co. 12 and return to the trailhead one mile away for a 22-mile trip.

Option B - McKusick Alternative Route: Continue east on McKusick Road (Co. 64) and take alternative route described below. |
| 21.1 | Ride south near the pretty Oak Glen Development and golf course on the outskirts of Stillwater. The road here is very narrow and sometimes busy. |

21.9	Pass Lake McKusick on your right.
22.6	TURN RIGHT (SOUTH) ON CO. 5 (NORTH OWENS STREET) AND RIGHT AGAIN (EAST) A BLOCK LATER ON WEST LINDEN STREET.
23.0	TURN LEFT (SOUTH) ON BIRCHWOOD DRIVE.
23.3	Junction with Co. 12 -- Myrtle Street. CROSS STREET AND TURN RIGHT (EAST) ONTO BICYCLE TRAIL on south side of road.
23.6	Climb hill and, after reaching top at mile 23.9, coast down to trailhead at mile 24.2.
24.2	Turn left (south) into parking lot for trailhead.

TOUR 2: *White Bear Lake Circle Tour*

Trailhead:	Mahtomedi High School parking lot. North side of Co. 12, one mile east of Mahtomedi and six miles west of Stillwater.
Distance:	14 miles
Terrain:	Slightly rolling
Highlights:	White Bear Lake and residential areas
Route:	(0.0) West on Co. 12; (0.5) **Mahtomedi/ Willernie** -- North on Mahtomedi Avenue; Cross Mn. 244 and West on Frontage Road; (1.1) North on Co. 29 (Birchwood Avenue); (1.6) North on Wildwood Avenue; (3.6) North on Co. Line Road which becomes South Shore Boulevard; (5.3) North on Lakeview Avenue; (5.4) North on Cottage Park Road; (5.8) Northwest on Old White Bear Avenue -- **White Bear Lake;** (6.2) North on Mn. 61; (6.3) Northeast on Lake Avenue North; (7.8) East on Mn. 96; (10.2) South on Co. 62 (Quail Road); (11.4) East on Briarwood Avenue; (11.7) South on Griffin Avenue; (12.3) East on Juniper Street; (12.5) South on East Avenue; (13.4) East on Co. 12; (13.6) Trailhead.

A shorter version of the White Bear Lake trip, this tour still includes the area around the lake and some attractive residential sections.

Log

0.0   From Mahtomedi High School parking lot, HEAD WEST ON THE PAVED BICYCLE TRAIL which parallels Co. 12.

0.5   The trail ends. Continue west on Co. 12 into Mahtomedi/Willernie and TURN RIGHT (NORTH) ON MAHTOMEDI AVENUE (Phillips 66 is on northeast corner). WHERE ROAD ENTERS MN. 244, CROSS THE STREET TO ASH STREET, AND TURN LEFT (WEST) ONTO THE FRONTAGE ROAD which parallels Mn. 244.

Follow directions on Stillwater to White Bear Lake Tour (Tour 1), including optional side trip to Bald Eagle Lake, from mile 5.4 to mile 15.1 [junction of Mn. 96 with Co. 62 (Quail Road)]. Then continue as below.

10.2   Junction of Mn. 96 with Co. 62. TURN RIGHT (SOUTH) ON CO. 62 (QUAIL ROAD). The road dips and winds through an attractive mix of birch trees, sloughs, and residential homes.

11.4   TURN LEFT (EAST) ON BRIARWOOD AVE.

11.7   TURN RIGHT (SOUTH) ON GRIFFIN AVE. as road begins to wind through Mahtomedi residential area.

12.3   TURN LEFT (EAST) ON JUNIPER STREET.

12.5   TURN RIGHT (SOUTH) ON EAST AVE. Continue straight on East Ave. to Co. 12.

13.4   TURN LEFT (EAST) ONTO CO. 12. Pick up bicycle trail and continue back to Mahtomedi High School.

13.6   Mahtomedi High School parking lot.

TOUR 3: *Houlton -- Willow River State Park*

Trailhead: Municipal parking lot in downtown Stillwater at the bridge.

Alternative trailhead: School parking lot on north side of Co. E 1/4 mile east of junction of Wisc. Hwys. 64 and 35 and Co. E on top of the hill in Houlton at B & L Liquors. The alternative trailhead avoids the climb up the hill from the river. When climbing the hill, take the right fork on Co. E if you are driving or like biking steep hills or take the less steep left fork on Wisc. 64 if you are biking and turn right on Wisc. Hwys. 64 and 35.

Distance: 25 or 28 miles (depending on the trailhead used)

Terrain: Rolling hills with some very steep ones

Highlights: Views of wooded valleys and rolling farmland, Base Lake Cheese Factory, Burkhardt, Willow River State Park, and Perch Lake

Route: (0.0) Stillwater--Cross bridge; (1.0) East on Co. E; (4.1) North on Valley View Trail; (7.7) North on Co. I; (8.8) East on 153rd Avenue; (10.7) South on 85th Street; (11.7) West on 140th Avenue; South on 83rd Street; (12.6) West on 132nd Street and South on 80th Street; (13.8) West on Co. 1; (14.4) South on Co. A; (15.7) **Burkhardt**; (16.6) Willow River State Park--turn around; (18.1) West on Co. I; (20.0) West on Perch Lake Road (130th Ave.); (22.5) West on Old Co. E East; (23.0) West on Co. E; (23.2) South on Old Co. E West; (23.8) West on Co. E; (27.0) **Houlton**; (28.0) Stillwater--Trailhead.

A tour of medium distance, this one is hilly enough to give most people a workout. It is such a pretty route, however, that even if you don't like hills you might consider doing it and stopping frequently at viewpoints or snack stops. Plan to stop at Willow River State Park for a picnic if not for overnight camping.

Log

0.0   Leaving downtown Stillwater, cross the bridge to Wisconsin, and ascend hill.

1.0   Junction of Wisc. Hwys. 64 and 35 with Co. E. PROCEED EAST ON CO. E. This is a hilly route and easy road and is a designated bike trail by the State of Wisconsin. Pass Houlton Elementary School (alternative trailhead), which is part of the Hudson, Wisc., school system. Area then opens up to rolling farmland.

1.8   Climb a little reaching top at mile 2.1.

2.7   Begin steep descent, bottom out, and pass the now defunct Birch Park downhill ski area at mile 3. Climb reaching top at mile 3.2.

3.4   Cross Co. V. Continue straight ahead on Co. E.

4.1   TURN LEFT (NORTH) ON VALLEY VIEW TRAIL. This is a delightful hilly road that winds and climbs through wooded areas and provides views of rolling farmland on the way.

6.0   At junction with 50th street, BEAR RIGHT ON VALLEY VIEW TRAIL.

7.0   Bass Lake Cheese Factory. Get your cheese right at the factory. They will also send gift boxes of assorted cheeses for you. Picnic table next to the building. Continue straight ahead (east) on Valley View Trail as road levels off and area opens up to more rolling farmland.

7.7   At T-intersection, TURN LEFT (NORTH) ON CO. I. More rolling farmland interspersed with evergreen or deciduous trees on hillsides.

8.8	TURN RIGHT (EAST) ON 153RD AVE.
9.3	Descend to the north end of Bass Lake where fishing is always good according to the locals. Satellite toilet next to lake at east end.
9.9	Begin climb from lake reaching top and more rolling farmlands at mile 10.5.
10.7	TURN RIGHT (SOUTH) ON 85TH STREET. Gentle rolling hills in the distance with farmlands on both sides.
11.7	TURN RIGHT (WEST) ON 140TH AVE. AND AT MILE 11.9, TURN LEFT (SOUTH) ON 83RD STREET.
12.6	TURN RIGHT (WEST) ON 132ND STREET, AND LEFT (SOUTH) ON 80TH STREET.
13.8	At stop sign, TURN RIGHT (WEST) ON CO. A. Co. E comes in from left and joins Co. A at mile 14.
14.4	TURN LEFT (SOUTH) ON CO. A. (Co. E goes straight.) Road gradually descends into tree-covered area drained by the Willow River.
15.2	Junction with Co. Roads A and I. Follow Co. A across Willow River, which is a beautiful spot to stop and rest. You will see people fishing, canoeing, and simply relaxing here.
15.7	Enter village of Burkhardt. The Willow River Inn, Rustic Hut, Town Mart Burkhardt Co-Op, and a few houses make up the town. The movie Rachel River, released in 1988, was filmed in this area using some of the buildings, the countryside, and the river near here. At this point, you can turn around and continue the tour or take the two-mile trip to Willow River State Park before doubling back.
16.6	Entrance to Willow River State Park. This park has all facilities -- camping, swimming, fishing, hiking, and shelters. It is about one mile from the road into the park itself. This would make a nice stop for an easy two-day trip with overnight

camping in the park. When you leave the park, head back north on Co. Road A.

18.1   At junction with Co. Roads A and I, TURN LEFT ON CO. I going west and north. This is a designated bike route. Pass Mill Pond wetlands on your left and then 115th Avenue (River Road) coming in from your left at mile 18.6. Stay on Co. I (right-hand fork) and begin long climb up a wooded defile.

18.8   Cross Co. E and keep climbing on Co. I.

20.0   Top is reached. TURN LEFT (WEST) ON PERCH LAKE ROAD (130th AVE.). Nice views as road clings to the high ground for the next 0.5 miles.

20.7   At stop sign, cross 60th Street and a block later begin steep roller coaster descent back into the woods to Perch Lake.

21.5   A turn off here leads north to a dead end road which circles Perch Lake to a privately run swimming area. The lake's water is clear, deep, and cold. Continue east as road follows the lake's south shore and at mile 21.7 begin a steep 0.2 mile ascent as road turns south away from the lake.

22.5   Junction with Co. E. CROSS DIRECTLY OVER CO. E ONTO OLD CO. E EAST. At this point, the road makes a loop behind a hill and comes back to Co. E.

23.0   TURN LEFT (NORTHWEST) BACK ON CO. E. Shady Ridge Farm B&B on your right a block Northeast on Highland View Drive. Check out the llamas, antiques and artwork by local artists for sale.

23.2   TURN LEFT (SOUTHWEST) OFF CO. E ONTO OLD CO. E (WEST), which again takes you behind the hills and through the woods for a look at the back country and then back to Co. E at mile 23.8.

26.8   Back at school parking lot.

28.0   Back at Stillwater parking lot.

TOUR 4: *Somerset Route*

Trailhead:	The north edge of the River's Edge Restaurant at the River's Edge tubing area (two miles southeast of Somerset, Wisc.) where the sign says one-lane bridge.
Distance:	18 miles
Terrain:	Level along the river but hilly on the return trip.
Highlights:	Apple River views and pastoral scenes.
Route:	(0.0) North on Co. C; (4.0) North on Co. CC; (6.5) East on Co. H; (9.0) South on Co. C; (11.0) West on Co. C; (13.0) South on 110th Street; (14.5) West on 192nd Avenue; (18.0) River's Edge.

A short tour but long on scenery, this route follows the Apple River and the hills and valleys north of Somerset, Wisconsin. In the summer, combine this tour with a day of tubing on the Apple River. In the fall, you will find less traffic and spectacular tree colors.

Take Wisc. Hwys. 64 and 35 east from Stillwater across the bridge to Wisconsin and follow it nine miles to Somerset. Somerset has a number of campgrounds and recreational facilities mostly dealing with tubing down the Apple River. All the campgrounds provide pick-up or drop-off for tubers.

The Treadmill Sporting Goods Store in Somerset is handy for bicycle parts and other bicycling, camping, and sporting needs. Somerset has a Dairy Queen, several restaurants, and a number of bars.

From downtown Somerset, continue east on Wisc. 64 for two miles to the River's Edge tubing area, which is one of the many drop-off points for tubers. Also located here are the Jellystone Park

Campground, a water slide, ample parking, the Galway Sidewalk Cafe and Pub, and the River's Edge Restaurant and Lounge, known for its high quality meals.

Log

0.0   From River's Edge, head past the north edge of the restaurant, where the sign says one-lane bridge. Cross the bridge and TURN RIGHT IMMEDIATELY ONTO CO. C. The road, level at this point, follows the west bank of the Apple River on your right with wooded areas and some homes. Pass a dam on the river.

2.2   Entrance to Riverdale Campground on your right. Slightly rolling terrain.

4.0   Junction with Co. CC and Safari Bar (open every day with a Friday night fish fry). TURN LEFT (NORTH) ON CO. CC just before the Safari.

5.8   Pass the entrance to Cedar Lake Speedway, a popular spot on Saturday nights for auto racing fans.

6.5   TURN RIGHT (EAST) ON CO. H. The area is wooded with slightly rolling terrain. Pass Cedar Lake with cabins and homes along its edge. This area is called Huntington.

8.7   Cedar Creek Inn. Cross the Apple River again.

9.0   TURN RIGHT (SOUTH) ON CO. C. (Town of Star Prairie is 0.75 mile further east on Co. H. A friendly tavern in the town.) Huntington Farm Pottery. This is a slightly rolling road with farms on both sides.

11.0 Junction with CC. TURN RIGHT (WEST) ON Co. C.

13.0 TURN LEFT (SOUTH) ON 110TH STREET.

13.5 Climb part way up the hill but just before the trees, stop and rest on the side of the road and enjoy the view of the Apple River over the hills and backwater. A beautiful pastoral scene.

This is a winding road with some hills and woods but nothing too steep.

14.5 At the stop sign, TURN RIGHT (WEST) ON 192ND AVE. This area is hilly.

16.5 The road curves to the south, west, and then south again.

17.5 You are now heading south on the east side on the Apple River.

18.0 You can see the band shell, water slide, and facilities at the River's Edge. TURN RIGHT AT THE FIRST ROAD, which takes you back to the parking lot.

TOUR 5: *Stillwater to Withrow*

Trailhead:	Pioneer Park. On North 2nd Street six blocks north of downtown Stillwater. Beautiful views north and south of the St. Croix River. Parking, shelters, and toilets.
Distance:	16 miles
Terrain:	Level
Highlights:	Pioneer Park and pleasant countryside
Route:	(0.0) West on Laurel Street; (0.3) North on 5th Street; (0.6) West on West Wilkins Street; (1.0) North on Co. 5 (Owen Street); (2.0) North on Co. 55 (Norell Avenue); (4.0) West on Co. 61; (6.5) North on Co. 15; (7.0) West on Co. 7; (8.0) South

> on Co. 8 -- **Withrow**; (11.0) South on Co. 15; (11.1) East on Mendell Road East; (13.0) East on Mn. 96; (13.1) South on Neal Avenue; (13.5) East on Oak Glen Trail and South on Heifort Court; (14.0) East on McKusick Road; S(15.5) East on Laurel Street; (16.0) Pioneer Park.

This is the perfect tour for a morning or an afternoon. The easy riding, pleasant countryside, and short distance allow you to relax or to combine it with another tour in the area.

Log

0.0   Begin at Pioneer Park. GO WEST ON LAUREL STREET for three blocks.

0.3   TURN RIGHT (NORTH) ON 5TH STREET for four blocks. Note the house called the "Alhambra" on the corner of 5th and Maple. It was the "playhouse" for the mansion just behind it and contained a ballroom, bowling alley, and pool. It is now a private home.

0.6   At T-intersection, TURN LEFT AND GO WEST ON WEST WILKINS STREET for four blocks.

1.0   Junction of West Wilkins Street and Owen Street (also Co. 5). Food and Fuel store on the corner has groceries and a deli. TURN RIGHT (NORTH) ONTO CO. 5. In two blocks, a separate bicycle path begins on the east side of the road. On the left is Oak Glen Golf Course and on the right is the Stillwater Golf Course. Check the small pond on your right to see if the log rollers are practicing.

2.0   CROSS MN. 96 AND CONTINUE NORTH ON NORELL AVENUE (CO. 55). Bike trail is on the wide shoulder and is marked as such. Otto Berg Memorial Park, Stillwater Township Hall, and VITA course are on your right. Slightly rolling rural, residential countryside.

4.0   TURN LEFT (WEST) ON CO. 61. The sign points to Washington Co. Highway Dept.

5.0	Highway Department on your left and The Outing Lodge at Pine Point on your right. The Outing Lodge at Pine Point is a bed and breakfast and provides gourmet dinners by reservation.
5.5	At T-intersection, TURN LEFT (WEST) FOLLOWING CO. 61 (120TH STREET N.).
6.5	Stop sign. TURN RIGHT (NORTH) ONTO CO. 15 (MANNING TRAIL). Wide shoulder, marked bike route.
7.0	TURN LEFT (WEST) ON CO. 7. Signs say to Withrow. Wide paved shoulder continues.
8.0	TURN LEFT (SOUTH) ON CO. 8 INTO WITHROW. Pass the Withrow Ballroom, which is noted for its live music on weekends. Pass the old Withrow Depot, the Keystone Bar & Lounge, a few more houses and that is the end of Withrow. Continue south and east on Co. 8. Level, winding, and picturesque road.
11.0	At T-intersection, TURN RIGHT (SOUTH) ON CO. 15.
11.1	TURN LEFT (EAST) ON MENDELL ROAD EAST.
12.5	Pass North Twin Lake on your left.
13.0	TURN LEFT (EAST) ON MN. 96. Busy road but a short distance on paved shoulder.
13.1	TURN RIGHT (SOUTH) ON NEAL AVE. Gravel for less than 0.5 mile.
12.5	TURN LEFT (EAST) ON OAK GLEN TRAIL, THEN TAKE FIRST RIGHT (SOUTH) ON HEIFORT COURT.
14.0	TURN LEFT (EAST) ON MCKUSICK ROAD. This can sometimes be busy, so be alert.
15.0	Pass Oak Glen Country Club and Golf Course. The club house and course are open to the public. McKusick Lake is on your right.

15.5 Junction with Co. 5 (Owen Street). Gannons Body Shop is on your left. Look for classic cars being restored. CONTINUE STRAIGHT AHEAD ON LAUREL STREET, which is a marked bicycle path.

16.0 Return to Pioneer Park.

TOUR 6: *Scandia to Marine*

Trailhead:	Begin in Scandia, 12 miles north of Stillwater. Take Mn. 95 to Mn. 97 to Scandia or go the "back" way taking Co. Roads 55, 7, 4, and 3. Parking is on the street.
Distance:	Option A: 16 miles Option B: 14 miles
Terrain:	Level to slightly rolling.
Highlights:	Scandia, Gammelgarden Museum, Hay Lake Museum, Marine-on-St. Croix, and William O'Brien State Park.
Route:	(0.0) South on Co. 3; (4.5) East on Co. 4; (8.5) **Marine-on-St. Croix** -- North on Judd Street; East on Oak Street; North on 2nd Street; East on Elm Street; (9.0) Marine Landing -- return to Mn. 95; (9.5) North on Mn. 95; (12.0) **Copas** -- **Option A:** North on Co. 53 (Quinnel Avenue North); (13.3) North on Mn. 95; (13.7) West on Mn. 97; (15.0) South on Co. 3; (15.5) Trailhead. **Option B:** North on Mn. 95; (13.0) West on Co. 52; (14.0) Trailhead.

A short tour, which could be called "the eating tour," as it passes two ice cream spots and three good restaurants. Easy bicycling with nice countryside views along the way.

Log

0.0   At the corner by the Elim Lutheran Church, HEAD SOUTH ON CO. 3. Get an ice cream cone from Swenson's Grocery to prepare for the ride or be sure to stop when you return as you won't want to miss these BIG cones.

0.5   Gammelgarden Museum. Swedish immigrant setting with homes, church, barn, and gift shop. Open May to mid-October, Friday and Saturday -- 1:00 p.m. to 4:00 p.m.; Sunday -- 12:30 p.m. to 4:00 p.m. Other times by arrangement. Small fee requested.

3.0   Pass Hay Lake School Museum. This old school is furnished as it was when the early Swedish settlers attended. The old log cabin is authentically furnished, too. Hours are from May 1 to September 30 on Saturdays and Sundays from 1:30 p.m. to 4:30 p.m. Special tours can be arranged for groups by calling 612/433-2762.

4.5   TURN LEFT (EAST) ON CO. 4 (170TH STREET). Look for swans on the pond to your left. Wooded areas ahead. Watch for deer.

7.0   Begin downhill into St. Croix River valley. Go through railroad tunnel. Woods.

8.0   At T-intersection, TURN LEFT (EAST) ON CO. 4 and resume descent into river valley. Follow Co. 4 into downtown Marine-on-the-St. Croix. This side of Mn. 95 is known as Upper Marine. Pass picturesque Christ Lutheran Church.

8.5   CROSS MN. 95 into Lower Marine. Marine General Store (prototype for Prairie Home Companion's Pretty Good Grocery Store) is on your right. The Voyageur Cafe and the Old Lumberyard Shops, which include the Village Scoop and Scandinavian Imports, are on your left. The Voyager Cafe is highly recommended for fresh, wholesome, well-cooked foods and the Village Scoop has a wide variety of ice cream flavors. The village green with an old-fashioned gazebo is a nice resting spot. The town hall, the library, and the Brookside Bar and Grill are on your right. TURN LEFT (NORTH) ON JUDD STREET. TURN RIGHT (EAST) ON OAK STREET TOWARD THE RIVER TO SECOND STREET. TURN LEFT AND FOLLOW SECOND STREET AND THEN RIGHT ON ELM STREET TO MARINE LANDING. River is on your right.

9.0   Marine Landing. Canoe and boat Launching and rental. Restaurant open for breakfast and lunch during the summer. Sit back on their pleasant deck and relax and eat while looking out over the river.

Retrace the road back to the highway, going STRAIGHT ON OAK STREET TO MN. 95.

9.5   TURN RIGHT (NORTH) ON MN. 95 on the paved shoulder and climb a little. Pass Asa Parker Bed and Breakfast on your left. A separate bicycle trail begins soon on the west side of the highway. CROSS OVER AND PICK UP THE TRAIL.

11.0 William O'Brien State Park. Camping, hiking, swimming, canoeing, interpretive programs, and skiing trails. Full facilities. Continue north on bike path.

11.7 Bicycle trail crosses to east side of the road just before village of Copas.

12.0 **Copas.** Crabtree Kitchens and Crabtree's School House Antiques are located here. Try their apple pie or other desserts. **Decision point:**

Option A: Turn right on Co. 53 (Quinnel Avenue N.) going northeast through deep woods.

Option B: Stay on Mn. 95 climbing for one mile to Co. 52. Turn left (west) on Co. 52, climb a little more and enter Scandia from the west at approximately mile 14. (Llama farm on your right at mile 12.3). Option B shortens the route by 1.5 miles but misses the lovely Quinnel Avenue section.

The rest of the log describes Option A.

13.3 At T-intersection TURN RIGHT (NORTH) ON MN. 95. There is a separate bike path on the east side.

13.7 Junction of Mn. 95 and Mn. 97. Signs say to Forest Lake. TURN LEFT (WEST) ON MN. 97 and climb 0.6 mile.

15.0 Enter village of **Scandia**. TURN LEFT (SOUTH) ON CO. 3.

15.5 Kaffe Stuga Restaurant and Swenson's Grocery with the great ice cream cones. Natural foods at the "Naturally Good Market" across from the restaurant.

TOUR 7: *Stillwater -- Lake Demontreville -- Lake Elmo*

Trailhead:	Tennis courts and park two miles west of Stillwater on Myrtle Street (Co. 12) at the corner of Northland Avenue. The park has parking and toilet facilities. A bicycle path is on the south side of Co. 12.
Distance:	24 miles (or 17-mile shortened route)
Terrain:	Mostly level.
Highlights:	Lake Demontreville, Lake Elmo, and Lake Elmo Park Reserve.

> **Route:** (0.0) West on Co. 12; (2.0) South on Co. 17; (3.5) West on frontage road of Mn. 36; (6.0) South on Demontreville Trail (Co. 13); (12.5) East on Co. 70 (10th Street); (15.0) North on Co. 17; (17.5) **Lake Elmo**; (18.0) Southwest on Mn. 5 and North on Co. 17; (20.5) East on frontage road on Mn. 36; (21.5) North on Co. 15; (23.0) East on Co. 12; (24.0) Trailhead.

This ride is a pleasant, easy one through an attractive residential area and around Lake Demontreville and Lake Elmo. The new Lake Elmo Park Reserve is a possible stopping place. A shortcut at mile 9.1 bypasses Lake Elmo and substitutes Lake Jane.

Log

0.0   Beginning at the bicycle trail on the corner of Co. 12 and Northland Avenue, GO WEST ON THE BIKE PATH. Climb a little.

1.0   Cross Co. 15. Continue straight ahead on Co. 12 bike path. (Aamodt's Apple Farm is located 1.5 miles south on Co. 15. See mile 21.5).

2.0   TURN LEFT (SOUTH) ON CO. 17.

3.5   TURN RIGHT (WEST) ON THE FRONTAGE ROAD FOR MN. 36 on the north side of the highway.

6.0   Stop sign. Marked bike route. TURN LEFT (SOUTH) AND CROSS BUSY MN. 36 ONTO DEMONTREVILLE TRAIL CO. 13). A gentle glide down to the lakes soon begins. On the way pass the turn-off on your left to the Jesuit Retreat House. Follow winding road along Lake Demontreville shoreline and past Olson Lake on your left.

8.0	TURN LEFT (SOUTH) ON OLSON LAKE ROAD. Still on Co. 13.
9.1	Pass Lake Jane Trail coming in from your left. (For a shortcut, turn left (east) on Lake Jane Trail, follow the trail east, and turn north 1.7 miles later. Turn east along Lake Jane, pick up 42nd Street, and continue east up a slight hill into wide open countryside. Finally, after passing Keats coming in from your left, turn right (north) 0.5 mile further at a T-intersection on Kimbro. The road eventually rejoins the main route at mile 18.7. The shortcut bypasses Lake Elmo and saves 6.5 miles.)
9.5	CROSS MN. 5 AND CONTINUE SOUTH ON CO. 13. Open fields replace the residential scene.
10.0	At T-intersection, TURN LEFT (EAST) ON CO. 13, which joins Co. 6.
10.5	TURN RIGHT (SOUTH) ON CO. 13.
12.5	Stop sign. TURN LEFT (EAST) ON CO. 70 (10TH STREET).
14.0	Entrance to Lake Elmo Park Reserve on your left. Park has bike trail, picnic facilities, swimming area, and toilets. Road into park is approximately one mile.
15.0	TURN LEFT (NORTH) ON CO. 17. (Lake Elmo Avenue N.). Road follows Lake Elmo shoreline on your left for approximately one mile. Road to 3M Tartan Park comes in from your right.
17.5	**Village of Lake Elmo.** Lake Elmo Inn on your left. Nice outdoor patio. One of the top-rated restaurants in the area.
18.0	Junction with Mn. 5. TURN LEFT (SOUTHWEST) ON MN. 5 for one block. White Hat Restaurant is on your left. Lake Elmo Elementary school is on your right. Just past the elementary school, TURN RIGHT (NORTH) ON CO. 17.

18.7   Pass Kimbro Road coming in from your left.

20.5   CROSS MN. 36 AND TURN RIGHT (EAST) ON THE FRONTAGE ROAD (60TH STREET N.).

21.5   TURN LEFT (NORTH) ON CO. 15 (MANNING AVENUE). Pass Aamodt's Apple Farm on your left. Apples, fresh pies, cider, and gifts in an atmospheric barn. Live music and hay rides are often featured on weekends in the fall.

23.0   TURN RIGHT (EAST) ON CO. 12 on the separate bike path on the south side of the road.

24.0   Northland Avenue. Tennis courts, parking where we began. Additional two miles (east) to downtown Stillwater.

TOUR 8: *Stillwater to Afton*

Trailhead:	Southeast corner of the St. Croix Mall (behind the stores) located at the junction of Mn. 36 and Osgood Avenue on the southern edge of Stillwater. Plenty of parking and public toilets in the mall. Several restaurants are located in this area and also some fast food stops.
Distance:	23 miles
Terrain:	Level to slightly rolling. No steep hills.
Highlights:	Afton, hills, valleys, and Belwin Nature Center.

Route: (0.0) South on Oren Avenue, East on Upper 56th Street North, and South on Osgood Avenue; (1.5) East on Co. 14; (2.0) South on Co. 21 (Stagecoach Trail North); (10.5) South on Mn. 95 and Co. 21; (11.0) **Afton** -- return north on Mn. 95; (16.0) Northeast on Rivercrest Road; (17.0) North on Mn. 95; (20.0) **Bayport** -- West on 5th Avenue; (21.0) South on Co. 21 (Stagecoach Trail North); (21.2) West on Co. 14; (21.7) North on Osgood Avenue; (22.7) West on Upper 56th Street North and North on Oren Avenue; (23.0) Trailhead.

This tour takes in some of the best of the St. Croix Valley. Hills, valleys, woods, and river are typical of the area. For the first 6.5 miles, the tour follows a wide paved shoulder, passing first through a small residential area and then into the open countryside along a broad plateau of farmland hemmed in by the St. Croix River to the east and a chain of low lying hills to the west. After crossing U.S. 94, the paved shoulder ends and soon the route begins a long, gradual descent through woods and past hobby farms to Afton -- a little town tucked between the bluffs and the river.

The return trip follows a paved bicycle trail which parallels Mn. 95 through a canopy of overhanging trees eventually giving way to an open right-of-way that terminates at U.S. 94. The route then tracks the St. Croix River to Bayport either on a paved shoulder along Mn. 95 or on a quiet access street for riverfront homes. At Bayport, you climb out of the river valley and rejoin the first part of the tour at mile 2 for the return trip to the trailhead.

Log

0.0   From the southeast corner of the mall parking area, TAKE THE SMALL STREET (OREN AVENUE) SOUTH FOR TWO BLOCKS TO UPPER 56TH STREET N. TURN LEFT (EAST) FOR ONE BLOCK TO THE STOP SIGN ON

OSGOOD AVENUE. TURN RIGHT (SOUTH) ON OSGOOD AVENUE. Pass Valley View Park on your left, which has picnic facilities, and the Minnesota Correctional Facility -- Maximum Security Prison, which is built mostly underground.

1.5   TURN LEFT (EAST) ON CO. 14 (47TH STREET N.). Level road, wooded area, and nice views.

2.0   At T-intersection, TURN RIGHT (SOUTH) ON CO. 21 (STAGECOACH TRAIL N.). Nice open countryside for next 4.5 miles.

6.5   CROSS I-94. CONTINUE SOUTH ON CO. 21 (STAGECOACH TRAIL N.) Dee's Bed and Breakfast is 1 mile west on frontage road.

7.5   Downhill, winding road through wooded area.

8.5   Pass Belwin Nature Center on your left. Open to the public with interesting nature trails.

10.5 Stop sign at St. Croix Trail South (Mn. 95). TURN RIGHT (SOUTH) ON MN. 95 AND CO. 21 into the village of Afton (staying on Co. 21 instead of turning west on Mn. 95 just short of the town center). Pass Afton Historical Museum on your left. (Open Sundays from 2:00 p.m. to 5:00 p.m., Memorial Day to mid-October). Find Afton Antiques, Selma's for ice cream, Lerk's Bar for "Lerkburgers," Riverside Deli, the 1867 Afton House Restaurant and the Catfish Saloon, the Afton Toy Shop, and the Little Red Store gifts and antiques. The old-fashioned Afton town park has picnic tables and shelters. A sign above the window in front of Selma's Ice Cream Parlor commemorates the high water mark from 1965. Spend a day browsing in this tiny 19th century village, named by its founder after the line from a poem by Robert Burns that reads "Flow gently, sweet Afton."

WHEN LEAVING, GO NORTH ON MN. 95 FROM AFTON. Just past the lumber company, a separate bicycle trail begins on the east side of the road. The large building on your left was once a schoolhouse but is now a private home.

	Pass Lake St. Croix Beach, St. Mary's Point, and Lakeland -- all bedroom communities.
13.5	Valley Trail Cafe on your right. Cozy spot for breakfast or lunch.
14.0	Lakeland Plaza shopping center.
15.0	Bike trail ends. CROSS I-94. CONTINUE NORTH ON WIDE SHOULDER OF MN. 95.
16.0	TURN RIGHT (NORTHEAST) ON RIVERCREST ROAD, just past the Bungalow. The Bungalow often has live music on weekends. St. Croix River on your right. The town you see across the river is Hudson, Wisc.
17.0	REJOIN MN. 95. GO RIGHT (NORTH) on the wide shoulder.
18.0	Beautiful views of Lake St. Croix and Wisconsin. Long downhill.
19.0	Enter Bayport. Bayport Marina and Clyde's Restaurant on your right. Clyde's is open to the public. Bayport has several restaurants, stores, and useful services.
20.0	Junction with 5th Avenue in downtown Bayport. TURN LEFT (WEST) ON 5TH AVENUE. Broken In Sports (bicycle store) on your right. Continue west on 5th Avenue (which becomes Co. 14) past Barkers Alps park with satellite toilet on your left and past the minimum security prison farm on your right.
21.0	TURN LEFT (SOUTH) ON CO. 21 (STAGECOACH TRAIL) and climb for 0.2 mile on Co. 21.
21.2	TURN RIGHT (WEST) ON CO. 14. You have returned to mile 2 on the log.
21.7	TURN RIGHT (NORTH) ON CO. 67 (OSGOOD AVENUE) and climb a little.

22.7   TURN LEFT (WEST) ON UPPER 56TH STREET N. AND RETRACE STEPS from beginning of ride back to St. Croix Mall parking lot.

23.0   St. Croix Mall.

TOUR 9: *High Bridge Circle Trip*

Trailhead:	North end of River's Edge Restaurant at River's Edge tubing area (two miles southeast of Somerset, Wisc.) where sign says one-way bridge.
Distance:	16, 22, or 29 miles.
Terrain:	Mostly level to slightly rolling with some hills (one steep hill).
Highlights:	High Bridge, Pine and Bass Lakes, rolling farmland, and Apple River.
Route:	(0.0) Southwest on Co. C; (0.4) West on Wisc. 64; (1.0) Northwest on unmarked road; (1.6) **Somerset** -- Southwest on Wisc. Hwys. 35 and 64; (2.6) Northwest on 180th Avenue; (4.4) North on 38th Street and West on 180th Avenue, which becomes 37th Street and then 192nd Avenue; (7.7) North on Co. I; (11.1) North on 50th Street; (12.9) East on 232nd Avenue; (13.9) South on Co. I; (14.2) East on 230th Avenue, which becomes Co. H; (16.3) South on 80th Street East; (18.8) East on 205th Avenue; (19.9) South on 90th Street; (20.5) Southwest on Co. C; (22.4) East on bridge to trailhead.

This tour begins at the same starting place as Tour 4 -- River's Edge. This route, however, turns west and heads through Somerset toward the St. Croix River. After an eye-filling stop at the High

Bridge, with spectacular river views, the route circles back on a northerly arch through rolling farmland. The Apple River guides you back to the trailhead.

Log

0.0   Head past the north end of the Apple River Restaurant where the sign says one-way bridge. Cross the bridge and TURN LEFT (SOUTHWEST) ON CO. C.

0.4   TURN RIGHT (WEST) ON WISC. 64.

1.0   TURN LEFT (NORTHWEST) ON UNMARKED ROAD.

1.6   TURN LEFT (SOUTHWEST) ON WISC. HWYS. 35 AND 64, cross Apple River, and enter downtown Somerset. Head west out-of-town on paved shoulder.

2.6   TURN RIGHT (NORTHWEST) ON 180TH AVENUE. (Wild River Super Chute is on the left (south) side of Wisc. 64.) Road winds and dips just south of the Soo Line railroad tracks.

4.4   At T-intersection, TURN RIGHT (NORTH) ON 38TH STREET, CROSS RAILROAD TRACKS, AND THEN TURN LEFT (WEST) ON 180TH AVENUE.

5.2   Road turns right (north) at the river and becomes 37th Street. At this point, the High Bridge, a 2,600 foot long bridge, spans the St. Croix River approximately 185 feet above the water. The bridge is on the National Register of Historic Places for the "innovative engineering techniques used in its design, for the length and height of its span, and for the beauty and drama of its structure."

6.6   Road turns right (east) and becomes 192nd Avenue.

7.1   Pass 45th Street coming in from your right.

7.7   TURN LEFT (NORTH) ON CO. I.

8.6	Begin steep descent and climb in and out of gully cut by Apple River.
9.5	Pass 205th Avenue coming in from your right and reach top of hill at mile 9.7.
	For a shortcut which saves 6.3 miles, turn right (east) onto 205th Avenue, go east for three miles to where 80th Street intersects 205th Avenue at mile 18.8 on the log, and pick up main route at that point by continuing east on 205th Avenue.
11.1	GO STRAIGHT (NORTH) ON 50TH STREET instead of turning right on Co. I.
11.4	Begin nice descent and at bottom pass between Pine and Bass Lake, two vest pocket lakes lined with slender reeds and dead trees. Probably teeming with fish. Easy climb follows.
12.9	TURN RIGHT (EAST) on 232ND AVENUE.
13.9	At T-intersection, TURN RIGHT (SOUTH) ON CO. I and climb a little.
14.2	TURN LEFT (EAST) ON 230TH AVENUE. Road roller coasters.
14.8	CROSS WISC. 35 AS ROAD BECOMES CO. H. Lush farmland to the south.
16.3	TURN RIGHT (SOUTH) ON 80TH STREET. (To lengthen the trip 5.5 miles, continue east on Co. H for three miles, turn right (south) on Co. CC, and three miles later turn right on Co. C to join the main route at mile 20.5.)
18.8	TURN LEFT (EAST) ON 205TH AVENUE. Smooth back road with more scenic farmland to the south.
19.9	TURN RIGHT (SOUTH) ON 90TH STREET.
20.5	At T-intersection, TURN RIGHT (SOUTHWEST) ON CO. C. Apple River soon comes into view on your left as road follows river to trailhead.

22.0   Pass dam on your left.

22.4   TURN LEFT (EAST) ON BRIDGE and return to trailhead at River's Edge.

TOUR 10: *Stillwater to Marine*

Trailhead:	Pioneer Park. On North 2nd Street six blocks north of downtown Stillwater. Beautiful views north and south of the St. Croix River. Parking, shelters, and toilets.
Distance:	27 miles
Terrain:	Varied with one challenging hill out of the river valley.
Highlights:	Pioneer Park, pleasant countryside, Marine-on-the-St. Croix, and Square Lake County Park.
Route:	(0.0) West on Laurel Street; (0.3) North on 5th Street; (0.6) West on Wilkins Street; (1.0) North on Co. 5 (Owen Street); (2.0) North on Co. 55 (Norell Avenue); (6.4) East on Co. 7; (7.0) North on Co. 55; (10.4) East on Co. 4; (15.1) **Marine** -- South on Co. 7; (18.8) Square Lake County Park; (19.1) South on Co. 51; (22.0) Southwest on Co. 82 -- Stone Bridge Trail; (25.4) Cross Mn. 96 and South on Co. 5; Stillwater -- return to trailhead at mile 27.4.

This tour should be savored, not hurried. It combines a little city biking in historic Stillwater with a countryside ramble that includes farmland vistas, gentle hills (save one), woods, and shimmering waters. Marine-on-the-St. Croix is nicely positioned for a leisurely lunch break, and Square Lake County Park is a perfect spot for a cooling dip.

Log

0.0 Begin at Pioneer Park and follow the log for Tour 5 as far as the turnoff onto Co. 61 at mile 4.

4.0 CONTINUE NORTH ON CO. 55 on wide paved shoulder, which soon becomes a separate bicycle path. Nice views as countryside opens up. Loon Lake to your right.

5.1 Cross state trail. Just beyond the trail on your left is a parking lot and satellite toilet, and the entrance to Pine Point County Park with hiking and skiing trails. See Narrative.

5.3 Cross railroad tracks. More vistas.

6.4 At T-intersection, TURN RIGHT (EAST) ON CO. 7. Wide paved shoulder.

7.0 TURN LEFT (NORTH) ON CO. 55. The wooded slopes of gently rolling hills soon close in as road dips and climbs.

8.3 Thread between West and East Boot Lakes on gentle roller-coaster ride. A scenic gem in the midst of white birch.

8.8 Pass back entrance to Lee and Rose Warner Nature Center on your right. Admission by appointment only (612/221-9444).

9.7 Cross railroad tracks at right angles and catch glimpses of the marshy Long Lake to the west.

10.4 At T-intersection, TURN RIGHT (EAST) ON CO. 4. You will soon pick up the south end of Tour 6 as the road passes Co. 3 coming in from your left and heads for Marine. Look for swans on the pond to your left. More wooded areas ahead. Watch for deer.

13.3 Begin downhill into St. Croix River valley. Go through railroad tunnel and woods.

14.3	At T-intersection, TURN LEFT (EAST) ON CO. 4 and resume descent into river valley. Follow Co. 4 to the town of Marine-on-the-St. Croix. This side of Mn. 95 is known as Upper Marine. Pass picturesque Christ Lutheran Church.
14.8	CROSS MN. 95 INTO LOWER MARINE. See description of quaint downtown and local attractions in log for Tour 6 at miles 8.5 and 9.0. TURN RIGHT (SOUTH) ON JUDD STREET (CO. 7) as road passes through the residential area of Lower Marine just above the St. Croix River.
15.5	CROSS MN. 95 AND CONTINUE WEST ON CO. 7 up the somewhat steep but shaded Nasson Hill Road reaching a false top at mile 16.2. A gradual climb resumes and crests at mile 16.9. Note the giant Norwegian Pine near the top. Farmland and forests (hiding the Wilder Nature Center) soon open up to the west followed by sweeping views to the east.
18.7	At junction with Co. 59, TURN RIGHT (WEST) ON CO. 7. Reap the reward of your arduous climb out of the river valley and take turnoff to the Square Lake County Park to your right. This lake is one of the clearest in the area, and scuba divers often practice here. Swimming beach, toilets, and picnic grounds. Adjacent to the park on the southwest side is a private campground.
19.1	TURN LEFT (SOUTH) ON CO. 51 (PARTRIDGE ROAD). Climb a little reaching top at mile 19.7. Trees and farms punctuate a rolling landscape for the next three miles.
21.6	Descent begins. Nice view ahead.
22.0	TURN RIGHT (SOUTHWEST) ON CO. 82 (STONE BRIDGE TRAIL) just before reaching Mn. 95. A gradual 0.3 - mile climb along a wooded slope followed by a large lot development of luxury homes.

23.6	Cross Co. 11 and wind and roll through more scenic rural residential countryside.
25.5	CROSS MN. 96, FOLLOW ROAD TO CO. 5, AND THEN TURN LEFT (SOUTH) ON CO. 5. Retrace your route back to the trailhead at mile 27.4.

NOTES

CANNON RIVER VALLEY TOURS

In 1982, the Chicago Northwestern abandoned its railroad right-of-way linking Red Wing to Cannon Falls. Through the timely intervention of dedicated citizens, a "joint powers board" acquired the rights-of-way and developed it as the Cannon Valley Trail, a fully paved, non-motorized recreational trail. The total length of the trail, when combined with a city trail in Cannon Falls, is about 20.2 miles.

Each of the Cannon River Valley Tours (except one) uses the trail as a focal point. The tours range from level routes confined to the trail itself to more varied circle routes which climb out of the river valley to return by way of the trail (or, in one case, along the crest of high farm country). There is a tour to fit every type of bicyclist. Three of the tours originate in Cannon Falls, and the other three tours begin in Red Wing. A daily $2.00 trail fee is charged each bicyclist over 18.

> **Tour 1:** Cannon Falls River Valley Trip -- 9, 21, 41, or 45 miles
> **Tour 2:** Cannon Falls to Welch Circle Trip -- 34 miles
> **Tour 3:** Cannon Falls Back Country Tour -- 28 miles
> **Tour 4:** Red Wing to Welch Circle Trip -- 28 or 32 miles
> **Tour 5:** The Poet's Route -- 19 or 23 miles
> **Tour 6:** Red Wing River Valley Trip -- 20, 24, 41, or 45 miles

About the Area

How to Get There: To Cannon Falls: About 35 miles and 45 minutes southeast of the Twin Cities just off U.S. 52 at Mn. 19 exit. Take Mn. 19 into Cannon Falls.

To Red Wing: About 55 miles and 1 1/4 hours southeast of the Twin Cities. Take either U.S. 61 or U.S. 52 (crossing over to U.S. 61 on Mn. 50).

The Cannon Valley Trail generally follows the Cannon River in a deep valley shaped by glacial meltwater. Literally cut from cliffs along the river valley, the trail provides many views of the river particularly between Cannon Falls and Welch. Other scenic attractions along the trail range from overhanging cliffs and distant hills to farm fields, marshes, and floodplain forests. Nature lovers can enjoy wildlife there, such as the red fox, white-tailed deer, heron, and red tailed hawk. Marsh marigold, prairie plant species, and watercress grow along the way. Remnants of Indian villages and burial mounds are located near the trail. In the cool moist north-facing slopes along the trail are oaks, basswood, maples, and patches of white birch.

The Cannon River Valley was initially settled by Indians who used the river for transportation. It was opened for wheat farming in 1851 and continues to be farmed. Cannon Falls is located within a broad valley at the junction of the Big Cannon and Little Cannon Rivers. Like many other small towns south of the Twin Cities, the city once thrived off its water-powered flour mills. A brochure providing 1, 2 and 3 mile historic walking tours of the city can be secured at most stores.

Some motels can be found on the outskirts of Cannon Falls. Call the Cannon Falls Chamber of Commerce (507/263-2289) for names. Located three blocks from the center of town is a delightful bed and breakfast - the Quill and Quilt (507/263-5507) (four rooms). Two other bed and breakfasts in town are Candlewick Country Inn (507/263-0879) (two rooms) and Hart House (507/263-3617) (two rooms). Also about 10 miles south of town on Tour 3 is Country Quiet Bed and Breakfast (612/258-4406) (2 rooms). There are two nearby campgrounds: Dakota County Park (612/437-6608) on Lake Byllesby, four miles west of Cannon Falls on Highway 88, and Cannon Falls Campground (507/263-3145) located 1.5 miles east of Cannon Falls approximately 0.25 mile off Mn. 19.

Within the city are two recreational parks. Eastside Park has picnic and rest room facilities and is located just north of Mn. 19. Riverside Park has picnic and toilet facilities, is near the municipal swimming pool, and is connected to the city bike trail system. The Goodhue County Park has swimming and picnic facilities and is located along Mn. 19 just west of town. There is a cafe in town. As an alternative, both the Super Valu store and Lorentz Meats have deli departments featuring sandwiches and other picnic items. Just off the trail, in town, is Trail Station Sports, providing bike repair and rental and a 2 bedroom cabin (507/263-0884).

Welch lies midway between Cannon Falls and Red Wing. It is home to the Welch Ski Village in the winter and journey's end for river tubers and canoeists in the summer. The Cannon River Inn at Welch is a friendly tavern serving sandwiches, chili, and soup. A mile west of Welch along the river and trail is Hidden Valley Campground (612/258-4550), a private campground offering campsites along the river bank. Also within five miles of Welch are two other bed and breakfast accommodations: Hungry Point Inn (612/437-3660), a colonial New England style home and separate 100-year-old log building (six rooms) and Hearthwood Bed and Breakfast (612/437-1133) (five rooms). Whole house rental and full country breakfasts are provided.

Red Wing was named after Chief Red Wing of the Dakotah Indians. Red Wing stands out as a prosperous trading center situated in the heart of the Hiawatha Valley along a strategic bend of the Mississippi River. In town, Pottery Place, the state's oldest and largest factory outlet center, has been restored to accommodate 52 commercial establishments.

More than 20 buildings in Red Wing are listed on the National Historic Register. Of these, the jewel is the T.B. Sheldon Auditorium Theatre (612/388-2892), a restored, historical theatre. When T.B. Sheldon, one of Red Wing's most prosperous businessmen, died in 1900, he left half his fortune for a civic purpose. This resulted in the construction of the nation's first municipally owned and operated theatre. Programs at the theatre include world class touring attractions, classic films, and multi-media presentations. The interior alone is worth the price of admission, with its curving stairways and balcony, marble pillars, dancing nymphs painted on the ceiling, and gold leaf decorations. Further insights into the history of the theatre and of Goodhue County can be found at the Goodhue County Historical Society Museum (open 1:00 p.m. to 5:00 p.m., Tuesday through Sunday). The museum is reputed to be one of the finest local historical museums in the state.

Red Wing has several parks. Two parks along Levee Road, Bay Point Park and Levee Park, provide easy bicycle access to comfortable picnic areas overlooking the river. Near Bay Point Park is "Boathouse Village," a mass of boathouses that ride up and down on "gin poles" to adjust to variations in water level. For geology buffs and nature lovers, a hike up Barn Bluff at the south end of town provides panoramic views of the city and river valley below.

Several motels are located in Red Wing. Call the Red Wing Area Chamber of Commerce (612/388-4719) for names. There are also lodgings listed on the National Register of Historic Places. The St. James Hotel (612/388-2846) is an old Victorian hotel dating from the 1870s and restored in 1979. It has 60 guest rooms, each uniquely furnished with antique and antique reproductions of the Victorian era, and three restaurants, from the cozy to the elegant. Pratt-Taber Inn (612/388-5945) is a restored 1876 Italianate mansion providing bed and breakfast (seven guest rooms). Cold lemonade and homemade cookies greet the weary bicyclist at the end of the day, and a sumptuous sit-down breakfast provides a fitting send off in the morning. Two other bed-and-breakfasts are the Candlelight Inn (612/388-8034), an 1877 Victorian home with four bedrooms (whirlpool and private bath) and Golden Lantern Inn (612/388-3315) (4 rooms).

A nearby campground is Hay Creek Valley Campground (612/388-3998), six miles south of Red Wing on Mn. 58, with 80 sites, showers, pool, camp store, laundry, and a state-stocked trout stream. Just across the river off U.S. 63 in Wisconsin is Island Campground (715/792-2502) with showers, groceries, and nice access to the river.

TOUR 1: *Cannon Falls River Valley Trip*

Trailhead:	Public parking lot -- one mile east of U.S. 52 on north side of Mn. 19 in downtown Cannon Falls just east of the Little Cannon River (across the street from the Super Valu store)
Distance:	Option A: 9 miles to Anderson Memorial Rest Area and back Option B: 21 miles to Welch and back Option C: 45 miles to downtown Red Wing and back
Terrain:	Level with a slight downhill grade all the way to Red Wing.
Highlights:	All the sights on the Cannon Valley Trail
Route:	Stay on Cannon Valley Trail going east or west

This tour sticks to the city park trail and Cannon Valley Trail. The tour provides three optional turn around points.

Option A (the first leg of the tour) is perfect for beginners and small children. The trail works its way out of Cannon Falls initially along the river, past a dam and duck pond, and eventually connects with the Cannon Valley Trail. The trail passes through patches of prairie grasses, which harbor many prairie plant species -- such as the spring blooming pasqueflowers, summer monardas and cureflowers, and the fall asters. Soon afterwards, the trail begins to traverse a birch-covered hill sloping to the river below. The intermittent views of the river during this leg of the tour are a special treat. The turn around point for Option A is Anderson Memorial Rest Area (picnic tables and loop trail).

Option B continues east. On this leg of the tour, the views of the river are less frequent as the trail alternates between crossing open farmland and traversing wooded slopes. Welch is the turn around point for Option B (see narrative).

Option C continues east from the turn-off for Welch. After passing the entrance to the Welch Ski Village and cutting through more open fields, the trail crosses a creek and enters the floodplain forests. This closed-in mix of oak, maple, and basswood, interspersed towards the end of the trip with marshlands and patches of open water, stands in sharp contrast to the river run in Option A and the farm fields in Option B. The area is a haven for wildlife and plants as the river fans out before emptying into the Mississippi.

The Cannon Valley Trail ends two miles short of downtown Red Wing. A trip along the Levee Road to the center of town is well worth the extra mileage. Along the way is "boathouse village." See narrative.

OPTIONS A, B, and C -- Log (East to west mileages are in parentheses)

0.0 (20.2)   Trailhead: Public parking lot off Mn. 19 in Cannon Falls just east of Little Cannon River (opposite Super Valu store). HEAD NORTH ON CITY BICYCLE TRAIL along Little Cannon River on west side.

0.3 (19.9)	Pass dam on west side and trout pond fed by artisan well on east side as you TURN EAST AND PASS UNDER BRIDGE.
0.4 (19.8)	Trail reaches 3rd street. TURN LEFT (NORTH) ON TRAIL which parallels road. Continue following trail as it turns east and crosses road. Kiosk and water fountain at mile 0.6 (19.6).
1.1 (19.1)	Trail either goes straight (east) or turns right (south) to Grove Street North. GO STRAIGHT.
2.4 (17.8)	Open area harboring many prairie plant species. See description of tour.
2.8 (17.4)	Pretty stand of birch on south side as trail begins to traverse bluffs leading to river first observed below.
2.9 (17.3)	Milepost 76, the site of the "Big Fill." Originally, a railroad trestle connected the banks of this ravine, only to be removed about 1916 with the gap filled.
3.2 (17.0)	Nice view of river nearly 60 feet below. Favorite stop for river watchers.
3.8 (16.4)	Trail follows river, as it cuts through limestone with overhanging birch. From then on super views of river.
4.4 (15.8)	Anderson Memorial Rest Area (picnic tables on south side just before creek crossing). At this point, a path leads to the creek providing good views of railroad bridge construction and a new half-mile loop. Trail gives direct access to the Cannon River. The loop trail is appropriate for hikers and mountain bikes. Turn around and return to Cannon Falls on same route if Option A is being taken.

OPTIONS B and C -- On to Welch

5.2 (15.0)	Cross wooden bridge with pretty farmhouse to the south.
5.5 (14.7)	Cross gravel road. Satellite toilet on south side.

7.2 (13.0)	Milepost 80 marks the spot of a 1912 train accident. The cargo of granite tombstones can be seen on the hillside between the road and the Cannon River. Nice views of river as both trail and road traverse wooded hill leading to river below.
9.6 (10.6)	Cross gravel road which leads to Hidden Valley Campground on north side.
10.4 (9.8)	Welch Station Access -- with parking lot, artisan well, toilet facilities, benches, information kiosks, and picnic tables in shadow of an old storage building and elevator from railroad days.
10.5 (9.7)	TURN NORTH OFF TRAIL AND PICK UP CO. 7 FOR WELCH which is 0.3 mile away.
10.7 (9.5)	Welch Town Hall on west side. Small playground. Good rest break for antsy children.
10.8 (9.4)	Welch -- Cross Cannon River. Cannon River Inn on right (see narrative). Turn around and return to Cannon Falls on some route if Option B is taken.

OPTION C -- On to Red Wing

Mileage assumes no side trip to Welch

10.9 (9.3)	Entrance to Welch Ski Village area on south side.
11.3 (8.9)	Trail crosses Co. 7 and begins to cut between corn fields with distant views of exposed bluffs to the northeast.
11.9 (8.3)	Belle Creek crossing as trail begins to traverse hillside with floodplain forest on north side. The bridge across the river is the longest bridge on the trail. It's a nice place to stop. Examine the railroad construction, and if you are lucky, spot some wild turkeys. Good turtle viewing on rocks and logs in this area.
15.5 (4.7)	Trail passes under U.S. 61 bridge.

15.6 (4.6)   On south side is tall, narrow iron structure with a cross bar and lines dangling at the top. Known by railroad buffs as a "flycatcher" or "telltale," its purpose is to warn any crew member (or bum) on top of the trail to duck for a tunnel or bridge ahead.

15.9 (4.3)   Cross gravel road (Cannon Buttoms Road). Satellite toilets on north side. Trail opens up a little. Marshland soon begins to appear. Keep a sharp eye for seeps and springs which release cold, clear water. As stated in the *Trail Times:* "Green and tangy watercress covers the surface of the resulting stream as it flows into marshes to the north. There it continues to feed the plants and animals of the wetlands."

16.2 (4.0)   Small slough on south side as trail cuts through floodplain forest.

17.2 (3.0)   Beaver dam on north side as marshland becomes more pronounced.

17.7 (2.5)   Milepost 91 on south side. According to the *Trail Times*:

> Near urban conditions existed at locations near here 1,000 years ago. Discovery and exploration of several known archeological sites has revealed fortified villages, storage pits, evidence of trade with faraway cultures, and numerous burial mounds. Red Wing is the latest of a series of settlements.

Plans are being made to open up as an archeological park some of the sites with direct access to the trail, including a relatively undisturbed Native American village.

18.3 (1.9)   Nice expansive views to the north of marsh, patches of open water, and standing dead trees.

18.5 (1.7)   Trail crosses Cannon River Drive. Red Wing Mall just beyond on the right. Proceed east across Spring Creek. (In alternative, take a left on Cannon River Drive which quickly turns right and becomes Industrial Park Road running parallel to the trail and providing a better view of the marshlands on the left (north). About a mile later the road turns right (south) for you to rejoin the trail.)

18.9 (1.3) Pass spur to Lower A.P. Anderson Park less than 1/2 mile southwest across U.S. 61 (picnic, recreational and toilet facilities).

20.2 (0.0) End of Cannon Valley Trail. Take St. James Hotel **Spur** (described at the end of the chapter) into center of city approximately two miles away.

TOUR 2: *Cannon Falls to Welch Circle Trip*

Trailhead:	Same as Tour 1
Distance:	34 miles
Terrain:	Varied but no difficult hills
Highlights:	Rolling farmland, wildflowers crowding remote country road, wide scenic valley, the Vasa Lutheran Church and Museum, the plunge into Cannon River Valley, and the return trip along the Cannon River
Route:	(0.0) East on Mn. 19; (2.8) South on Co. 8; (9.7) **White Rock** -- East on Co. 1; (13.6) North on Co. 7; (16.9) **Vasa** -- Cross Mn. 19; (20.7) West on trail to trailhead at mile 34.3.

This tour begins at the trailhead for the city park trail, which connects to the Cannon Valley Trail. The tour, however, saves the trail for the end and heads instead for the open roads west out of Cannon Falls. Within a couple of miles, the route turns onto a remote country road which gradually climbs out of the river valley through a swath of yellow wildflowers crowding the edges in season. For the next 12.5

miles, you are treated to a gentle ride through rolling farmland over hill and dale.

At Vasa, the striking Vasa Lutheran Church (a red brick church with a white cupola and steeple) and nearby gazebo and one room museum (Vasa Museum) offer a restful pause before the long descent into the Cannon River Valley and Welch below. At the bottom, the route picks up the Cannon Valley Trail and heads west back to Cannon Falls, which is 12.5 miles away, after perhaps a quick detour into Welch for a break and maybe a wade in the Cannon River.

Log

0.0	Trailhead: Parking lot in downtown Cannon Falls, off Mn. 19 just east of bridge crossing Little Cannon River (across from Super Valu store). GO EAST ON MN. 19.
0.6	Pass First Baptist Church, then East Side Park on your left (toilet facilities, water, picnic area), and next Colvill Memorial Cemetery on your right.
1.7	Pass Oak Lane on your right. It leads to Cannon Falls Campground. (See narrative.)
2.8	TURN RIGHT (SOUTH) ON CO. 8. Road soon begins gradual climb which eases off then resumes through a limestone cut. Watch for yellow wild flowers in season.
5.5	Top is reached. Sheep farm on your left. For next four miles, road dips and winds through a wide scenic valley and rolling farmland.
9.7	**White Rock.** TURN LEFT (EAST) ON CO. 1. No facilities.
10.9	Co. 1 merges with Co. 7 which comes in from the southwest and joins Co. 1 going east. Road climbs gradually for next 2.5 miles.
13.6	Co. 7 turns left (north) while Co. 1 continues east. TURN LEFT (NORTH) ON CO. 7 and climb a little. More open

countryside for next 3.3 miles with one winding roller coaster run beginning at mile 15.

16.9	**Vasa.** Cross Mn. 19 and stay on Co. 7.
17.1	Vasa Lutheran Church on your left. On church grounds are gazebo and Vasa Museum (open Sundays, June through August from 11 a.m. to 5 p.m.). No water or toilets here.
17.3	Follow Co. 7 as it turns left (north) and begins descent into Cannon Falls River valley, a nice two-mile plunge.
20.7	TURN LEFT ON CANNON VALLEY TRAIL. Use the Log for Tour 1 (east to west) starting at mile 8.9 and head east to Cannon Falls trailhead 13.3 miles away.

TOUR 3: *Cannon Falls Back Country Tour*

Trailhead:	Same as Tour 1
Distance:	28 miles
Terrain:	Varied but no killer hills
Highlights:	Rolling farmland, inviting valleys, and sweeping vistas
Route:	(0.0) East on Mn. 18; (2.8) South on Co. 8; (9.7) **White Rock** -- West on Co. Roads 1 and 8; (12.2) South on Co. 8; (14.4) West on Co. 9; (16.7) North on Co. 56; (19.3) Cross Co. 1 and continue North on Co. 25; (27.1) North on Co. 24; (27.5) Downtown Cannon Falls -- West on Co. 19 to parking lot at mile 27.6

This tour offers spectacular back country scenery. It takes the same route as Tour 2 to White Rock. At that point, however, rather than head for the high country and the Cannon River valley beyond, the route turns west and finds yet another more narrow farm valley to explore in the Belle Creek water drainage. Eventually, the route circles back to Cannon Falls on a roller-coaster ride that sticks mostly to the high ground until the descent into town.

Log

0.0   Trailhead: Parking lot off Mn. 19 in Cannon Falls just east of Little Cannon River (opposite Super Valu store). GO EAST ON MN. 19 and follow the same route as Tour 1 to White Rock.

9.7   **White Rock.** TURN RIGHT (WEST) ON CO. ROADS 1 AND 8.

10.0   TURN LEFT (SOUTH) ON CO. 8 and enter another pretty farm valley shaped by Belle Creek. The road follows the west side of this narrow valley for the next four miles, traversing several limestone cuts on the way.

11.2   Belle Creek Store (small general store) on your left.

12.6   Begin gradual climb reaching top at mile 13.

14.1   Cross Belle Creek and begin climb out of valley reaching top at mile 14.4.

14.4   TURN RIGHT (WEST) ON CO. 9 and soon descend hitting bottom and crossing creek at mile 15.

15.5   Begin gradual climb reaching top at mile 16.1.

16.5   Country Quiet Bed and Breakfast on your right on 112th Avenue Way (see narrative).

16.7   TURN RIGHT (NORTH) ON CO. 56 and make gradual rolling climb reaching top at mile 17.6.

17.7	Begin steady winding descent to creek below at mile 18.3 followed by gradual climb, topping off at mile 19.1. Silhouetted to the northwest is the majestic spiral of Green Valley Lutheran Church.
19.3	Cross Co. 1 and continue north on Co. 25. For the next five miles, the road winds and rolls along the highlands with vistas of open farmland and scattered groves of trees.
24.7	Begin long descent reaching bottom at mile 25.6 followed by ascent that tops off at mile 26.1.
26.1	Begin one-mile descent into Cannon Falls.
27.1	At T-intersection, TURN RIGHT (NORTH) ON CO. 24.
27.5	Downtown Cannon Falls. TURN LEFT (WEST) ON CO. 19 and return to parking lot at mile 27.6.

TOUR 4: *Red Wing to Welch Circle Trip*

Trailhead:	Cannon Valley Trailhead is west of the Red Wing downtown area, one block north of U.S. 61 on the Bench Street turn off. Alternative Starting Point: Intersection of Bush and Main Streets with St. James Hotel on northeast corner.
Distance:	28 miles (or 32 miles if starting from center of city)
Terrain:	Varied but with only one significant uphill grade

> **Highlights:** High farm country, Vasa Lutheran Church and Museum, plunge into Cannon River Valley, and teeming marshlands and floodplain forest along Cannon Valley Trail
>
> **Route:** (0.0) South on Bench Street; (0.1) East on U.S. 61; (0.2) South on Bench Street (Co. 1); (11.9) North on Co. 7; (15.4) **Vasa**; (19.0) East on trail to trailhead at mile 27.9

Like the Cannon Falls Circle Trip, this tour saves the Cannon Valley Trail for the end and begins by climbing out of Mississippi River valley. The trip initially heads up a water drainage, which narrows to a tree-covered coulee and then breaks out into relatively flat, wide open farmland. On top, the route passes a barn with a poem inscribed on its side. Eventually, you return to the Cannon Valley Trail by way of Vasa and Welch beyond. (See narrative and description of Tour 1.) At the bottom, the route picks up the trail and heads back to Red Wing. (See Tour 1, Option C, for a description of this part of the trip.)

Log

0.0   Trailhead: Trailhead for Cannon Valley Trail (west end of downtown Red Wing 0.1 mile north of U.S. 61 at Bench Street turnoff). Parking a trailhead. (St. James Hotel Spur adds about 2.1 miles from center of town.) HEAD SOUTH ON BENCH STREET.

0.1   Cross to south side of U.S. 61 with caution. TURN LEFT (EAST) ON U.S. 61.

0.2   TURN RIGHT (SOUTH) ON CO. 1 (BENCH STREET).

1.6   Pass Pioneer Road coming in from your left (east).

2.0   Barn on right. Watch out for wandering guinea hens. Begin gradual climb out of valley with plenty of tree cover.

3.9   Ascent steepens.

4.6	Road breaks out of tree cover into open pasture as climb continues.
5.0	Top is reached with sweeping view of rolling farmland to the right (north).
5.8	Barn on your left (south) with poetic inscription on the side that reads:

> Breathing in leaves --
> The wing's chorus and the tractors'
> Turning over shadows --
> Drawing the harvest inside us.

5.9	Featherstone Town Hall on your left. For next two miles, road rambles through wide open farm country.
8.2	Cross Co. 6. White Farm equipment dealer on northwest corner (pop machine inside).
9.6	Nice pastoral view as road drops about 100 feet.
11.3	Cross Co. 51.
12.0	TURN RIGHT (NORTH) ON CO. 7. AT this point use Log for Tour 2 at mile 13.6 for trip to Cannon Valley Trail.
19.0	TURN RIGHT (EAST) ON CANNON VALLEY TRAIL. (Welch is 1.1 miles further southwest on Co. 7. See narrative.) At this point use the Tour 1 Log (west to east) at mile 11.3 for return trip to Red Wing, which is 8.9 miles away.

TOUR 5: *The Poet's Route*

Trailhead:	Same as Tour 4
Distance:	19 miles (or 23 miles if starting from center of city)
Highlights:	High farm country, poetic inscriptions on barns, winding descent back into valley, and teeming marshlands and floodplain forests along Cannon Valley Trail
Route:	(0.0) South on Bench Street; (0.1) East on U.S. 61; (0.2) South on Bench Street (Co. 1); (7.2) North on Co. 6; (11.5) Northeast on Mn. 19; (14.2) West on U.S. 61; (14.4) North on Cannon Bottom Road; (14.9) East on trail to trailhead at mile 19.2

Poetic inscriptions found on several barns along the route inspired the name of this tour. The tour is a shortened version of Tour 4, providing only a 4.5 mile return trip on the Cannon Valley Trail. The trip begins the same way as Tour 4 by following a water drainage out of the Mississippi River valley to the high farm country above. After passing the first barn with a poem inscribed on its side (see Lot for Tour 4), the ride starts to circle back to the trail. You will soon pass another barn bearing a poetic inscription and then descend on a winding road that follows the Spring Creek drainage past two more posted poems and back to the Cannon Valley Trail. At the bottom, the route picks up the trail for the return trip to Red Wing.

Log

0.0   Trailhead: Same as Tour 4. Use the Tour 4 Log for trip as far as junction of Co. Roads 1 and 6 at mile 7.2

7.2   TURN RIGHT (NORTH) ON CO. 6.

7.8	Barn on your right has inscribed on its side:

> Only wind speaks
> In the empty tree tops --
> The mute farmer draws a fish
> In the March snow.

Panoramic views to the north. |
8.0	Long descent begins as road winds down an expansive valley reaching bottom at mile 10.
11.5	TURN RIGHT (NORTHEAST) ON MN. 19.
11.7	Side of barn on left has half of poem which starts "When walking after the storm" and leaves to the imagination the rest of the poem, which has been covered by new construction.
13.0	One more mystic verse on the barn to your left just beyond Mill Road turnoff:

> Green lit limbs fan glances --
> Shirtless contours in the downpour
> Ancestors folded into valleys --
> Honey in the burning hive. |
14.2	TURN LEFT (WEST) ON U.S. 61 (Information Bureau, food, picnic area 0.1 mile west on north side.)
14.4	TURN RIGHT (NORTH) ON CANNON BOTTOMS ROAD AND LEFT AT T-INTERSECTION AND DESCEND. (Gravel descent to trail.)
14.9	Junction with Cannon Valley Trail (satellite toilet). TURN RIGHT ON TRAIL.
19.2	Red Wing Trailhead reached.

TOUR 6: *Red Wing River Valley Trip*

Trailhead:	Same as Tour 4
Distance:	Option A: 20 miles (or 24 miles if starting from center of city) to Welch and back Option B: 40.5 miles (or 44.5 miles if starting from center of city) to Cannon Falls and back
Terrain:	Flat with a slight uphill grade all the way to Cannon Falls.
Highlights:	All the sights on the Cannon Valley Trail
Route:	Stay on Cannon Valley Trail

This tour is simply the reverse of Tour 1. Use the Log for Tour 1 (east to west) if you are going all the way to Cannon Falls and back (Option B). We think that Option A (Welch and back) is the preferred tour for the lingering nature stalker and archeological buff. For that reason we have repeated that portion of Tour 1 but in reverse to facilitate use.

Log

0.0   Trailhead: Same as Tour 4. HEAD WEST ON TRAIL. Marsh off to the right with bluffs across the river in the distance.

0.9   Cross North Tyler Road (Red Wing Mall just beyond on the left.) (In the alternative, take a right on North Tyler Road which quickly turns left and becomes Industrial Park Road running parallel to the trail and providing a better view of the marshlands on the right. About a mile later the road turns left (south) for you to rejoin the trail.)

1.3   Pass spur to Lower A.P. Anderson Park less than 1/2 mile southwest across U.S. 61 (picnic and recreation facilities).

1.7 Cross Cannon River Drive. (Extension of Industrial Park Road at point where it turns left to cross trail.) Sweeping views to your right of marshlands, standing dead trees, and large patches of open water.

2.5 Milepost 91 on left. According to the *Trail Times*:

> Near urban conditions existed at locations near here 1,000 years ago. Discovery and exploration of several known archeological sites has revealed fortified villages, storage pits, evidence of trade with faraway cultures, and numerous burial mounds. Red Wing is the latest of a series of settlements.

Plans are being made to open up as an archaeological park some of the sites with direct access to the trail, including a relatively undisturbed Native American village.

2.7 Small makeshift pullover and log seat on your right (with similar stop at mile 2.9).

3.0 Beaver dam to your right as the marsh becomes more pronounced.

4.3 Traverse hillside as area opens up. Keep a sharp eye for seeps and springs which release cold, clear water.

4.5 Satellite toilet on your right just before crossing small wooden bridge and Bottoms Road (gravel).

4.8 Pass under bridge (Hwy. 61) with back water on your right. Just before the overpass is an iron structure on your left known by train buffs as the "fly cather." Attached on the top is a cross bar extending across the trail with dangling ropes to alert any crew member (or hobo) on top of the train to duck for a tunnel or bridge ahead.

5.0 Small slough on your left as trail starts to cut through the flood plain forest.

8.6	Creek crossing and trail opens up as it begins to cut through corn fields on both sides with distant views of exposed bluffs to the east.
9.1	Cross Co. 7.
9.5	Entrance to Welch Ski Village on your left.
9.8	TURN RIGHT (NORTH) OFF TRAIL AND PICK UP CO. 7 FOR WELCH WHICH IS 0.3 MILES AWAY.
9.9	Welch Town Hall on your left. Small playground. Good rest place for antsy children.
10.0	**Welch** -- Cross Cannon River. Cannon River Inn on right. (See narrative about Welch.) Turn around and return to Red Wing on same route.

St. James Hotel Spur

0.0	At Red Wing Trailhead, TURN LEFT OUT OF PARKING LOT ONTO WEST MAIN STREET.
0.3	TURN LEFT ON WITHERS HARBOR DRIVE and cross bridge over railroad tracks.
0.5	BEAR RIGHT ON LEVEE ROAD. Nice paved shoulder.
0.9	Water on your left and coal barges.
1.1	Marina on your left.
1.3	Public parking and rest room facilities on your left.

1.4 Boathouse village on your left (Red Wing Yacht Club). See narrative.

1.9 Levee Park on your left. Red Wing Excursion provides boat rides in old-fashioned steam boat. TURN RIGHT. Red Wing Depot on your left. TURN LEFT AND PASS DEPOT.

2.0 TURN RIGHT UP SLIGHT HILL ON BUSH TO WHERE IT INTERSECTS MAIN STREET AT MILE 2.1. The St. James Hotel is on the northeast corner.

NOTES

RIVER FALLS, WISC. TOURS

Less than one hour's drive from the Twin Cities, the area south and east of River Falls, Wisconsin offers wide open country, gentle hills, and restful streams-an ideal locale for bicycling. Two of the tours start in River Falls, a third tour in Ellsworth and a fourth in Trimbelle.

Tour 1: River Falls to Diamond Bluff Circle Trip -- 46 or 51 miles
Tour 2: The Eastern Loop -- 10, 19, 29, 39, 43 or 47 miles
Tour 3: Round Barn Trip -- 23 or 38 miles
Tour 4: Trimbelle Circle Trip -- 24 miles

About the Area

How to Get There: About 45 minutes and 35 miles southeast of the Twin Cities in Wisconsin.

To River Falls: Take I-94 east across the St. Croix. Go south on Wisc. 35.

To Ellsworth: Take U.S. 61 south to U.S. 10 just north of Hastings. Go east on U.S. 10 across the St. Croix river to Ellsworth.

River Falls was first settled in 1848 by Joel Foster and a black indentured servant named Dick. The men were enchanted by the beauty of the woods and the falls. In a letter to his brother, Mr. Foster wrote:

> I think I have found the New England of the northwest, the same pure water, the same speckled trout, the same swamp alder, with a more beautiful formation. It looks as though the Almighty had made this portion of our country first and made a perfect system, piling rocks up in beautiful mounds, spreading over them sufficient soil to dress and make pasture lands out of them, spreading out the farming lands between the mounds, with pure streams of water and beautiful falls, with timber convenient. The great growth of vegetation growing wild told me that the same soil would also grow tame vegetation.

The original reasons for settling in the area were its natural beauty, fertile soil, and churning water to power saw mills and flour mills along the Kinnickinnic River. Although the first mill along the Kinnickinnic opened in Clifton Hollow in 1850, River Falls soon followed suit with a mill in 1852. In fact, Wisconsin's first grist mill to open and last grist mill to close was the Prairie Mill built in River Falls in 1854. It ceased operations in 1950. The Prairie Mill building and wheelhouse have survived and can be seen from the Cedar Street Bridge.

Another vestige of water power is the municipal power plant which still produces electric power for the towns' people. Although most power is now produced by fossil fuels, water power is still used for "peak power" needs.

River Falls is a full-service community. The current economy is mixed, with the University of Wisconsin -- River Falls having the largest payroll. The City is home to several manufacturing plants and is also a service center for the surrounding agriculture community. The newest attraction are the Kansas City Chiefs who train and hold scrimmages for general public viewing. For team information call 800/452-2522. For general information about River Falls, contact the Chamber of Commerce at 715/425-2533.

A bike repair shop is located on 122 South Main -- the Bike Shop (715/425-8684). For custom bike frames and/or lessons in frame building, contact Peterek Frames, Route 2, Box 234, River Falls, Wisc. (715/425-9327).

River Falls has 16 parks, including, many neighborhood parks. Some parks worth a visit include:

- Hoffman Park -- a trailhead and convenient starting point for two of the trips (plus the in-town ride described below). The park has 18 camping spots ($5.00/night with electricity) and plenty of parking. To find Hoffman Park, turn east off Main Street onto East Division Street (also known as Co. M). Then go east 0.7 miles to the park located on the north side of the road.

- Mound Park -- found by walking the Mound Park Trail northwest from Hoffman Park.

- Glenn Park -- an old growth of towering trees and the South Fork Ravine, spanned by a suspension bridge, are this park's scenic attractions. (Playground, toilets, pool, and water.) To find Glenn Park, ride south on Main to West Park Street, turn right (west) on West Park Street and go about two blocks to Glenn Park.

On Tuesday evenings in the summer, free community concerts are given at the outdoor band shell. The band shell is located on the University campus south of Hathorn Hall and east and north from Hunt Area.

There are three motels in River Falls -- Super 8 Motel on 1207 St. Croix Street (715/525-8388), the Best Western at 708 North Main (715/425-6707) and the River Falls Motel at 1300 South Main (715/425-8181). There are also two bed and breakfasts, the Knollwood House (715/425-2555), an 1880s brick farmhouse on 80 acres just south of town on Cemetary Road and Trillium Woods Bed and Breakfast (715/425-2555) a little further south of town on Happy Valley Road (Tours 1 and 2).

Over a dozen restaurants are located in River Falls. Four restaurants on the north end of town have good and reasonably priced salad bars.

In addition to Hoffman Park, camping facilities can be found within striking distance at:

- Kinnickinnic State park -- about 8 miles west of River Falls (715/425-1129) at the mouth of the Kinnickinnic River (boat camping only);

- Island Campground -- just across the Mississippi from Red Wing, Mn. (715/792-2502) (see description of Red Wing Spur at end of log);

- Freedom Park -- about 12 miles southwest of River Falls in Prescott, Wisc. (715/262-5544);

- The county fairgrounds (on emergency basis) at Ellsworth, Wisc. (see log for Tour 2); and

- Campgrounds just south of El Paso on the Rush River (see mile 29.3 for Option D of Tour 3).

River Falls is an ideal town to tour on bicycle. It's too large to walk around and not particularly convenient to auto tour. Ride around town just for the fun of it. The following is a brief guide to River Falls on bicycle:

Trailhead:	Hoffman Park
Distance:	5 to 9 miles depending on your choices
Terrain:	Level unless you ride the ski trails down to the river or go up to the golf course
Highlights:	The parks, University of Wisconsin, outdoor bandshell, the dam, and the Glenn Park suspension bridge
Note:	Directions are general, so feel free to deviate from the recommended tour as it is hard to get lost for more than five minutes in River Falls. If you get lost, just go toward Main Street; then follow it to Division to get back to Hoffman park.

To start, TURN RIGHT (WEST) FROM HOFFMAN PARK ONTO DIVISION.

TURN LEFT (SOUTH) ON NORTH EIGHTH STREET and go one block to get on Cedar. TURN RIGHT (WEST) ON CEDAR. Cross Main and the river on Cedar. From the bridge look north to see the old Prairie Mill Building on the river's east bank. (See narrative.)

TURN LEFT (SOUTH) AS SOON AS YOU CROSS THE RIVER. Cross Maple and continue through the parking lot along the river on the bike/foot path through White Park to the bridge that is just above the dam.

Cross the river, follow the road about one block, and TURN RIGHT ON STATE STREET, where you will see the suspension bridge over the South Fork Ravine. Cross the bridge into Glenn Park. Stop and look down if you dare. On a windy day, the bridge's movement is easily felt.

From Glenn Park proceed south two blocks and east to Main. Cross Main at Dick's IGA and go east by the Hunt Arena on the bike/foot path. This path wanders east and north past the outdoor band shell which has free summer picnic concerts on Tuesday evenings.

Continue north through the University of Wisconsin campus. From any point on campus, head north until reaching Division Street.

Hoffman Park is the end of the in-town tour.

The Pierce County Fairgrounds in Ellsworth provide the first of four round barns featured in Tour 2. You should hurry to see these unique bits of architectural history. They are fast disappearing from the countryside. In researching this tour, we found two fewer round barns in Pierce County than had been counted only 10 years earlier.

Round and polygonal buildings trace back to ancient Greek and Roman times. In the United States, round barns first received considerable attention in the 1850s. They seem to be a regional phenomena, due to the scarcity of carpenters skilled and interested in building round barns. More round barns have been built in Wisconsin than in any other state, most dating back to around the turn of the century. Their primary advantages were efficient feeding, lower costs of construction (in both material and labor, per unit area), and greater strength. The primary disadvantages were inadequate lighting at the center of the barn, poor layout for mechanization, and no easy way to expand the building to house additional livestock.

Just outside of Ellsworth is the David Motel (715/273-4453). In addition to the campgrounds already mentioned, Nugget Lake County Park (715/639-5611) provides a pleasant site about 10 miles east on Wisc. 72 to Wisc. 183, then south on Wisc. 183 for two miles to Co. HH. Follow the signs.

TOUR 1: *River Falls to Diamond Bluff Circle Tour*

Trailhead:	Dick's IGA Store parking lot on west side of Wisc. Highways 29 and 35 about one mile south of the center of town. Alternative trailhead: Hoffman Park at intersection of Wisc. 65 and East Division Street (0.7 miles east of Main Street on north side of Co. M). (Add five miles to trip if alternative trailhead is used.) For Red Wing Spur, see end of this chapter.
Distance:	46 miles (or 51 miles if alternative trailhead is used)
Terrain:	Varied with hills, valleys, and level farmland
Highlights:	Rolling farmland, river bluffs, and glimpses of the Mississippi and meandering Trimbelle River
Route:	(0.0) South on Wisc. Highways 29 and 35; (1.2); West on Co. FF; (6.0) South on Co. QQ; (11.0) East on 620th Avenue (Stirrat Avenue); (14.2) South on Co. E; (17.2) East on Spring Green Drive; (19.2) South on Co. OO; (24.4) West on Wisc. 35; (25.2) South into **Diamond Bluff**; (25.4) West on Lower River Road to Kask's Bar at mile 25.6 -- turn around and go East on Lower River Road; (28.8) West on Wisc. 35 and North on Co. O; (37.0) **Trimbelle** -- West on U.S. 10; (37.2) North on Co. O; (42.0) West on 710th Avenue (Pleasant View Road); (42.5) North on 910th Atreet (Happy Valley Road); (45.2) North on Wisc. Highways 29 and 35 to trailhead at mile 46.5.

This tour has everything. It explores the rolling farmland and the tree-lined hills. It dips down into the Mississippi River valley and in Diamond Bluff. Spectacular views of limestone river bluffs highlight this part of the trip. The climb out of the river valley is barely noticed as the route crisscrosses the meandering Trimbelle River through a snug defile leading to the high farm country above. All in all, this is an invigorating and eye-filling trip with plenty of opportunities for quality stops.

Log

0.0	River Falls: 1 mile south of center of town begin at Dick's IGA Store parking lot on west side of Wisc. Hwys. 29 and 35. HEAD SOUTH ON WISC. HWYS. 29 AND 35.
0.4	Pick up bicycle path on east side of road.
1.2	TURN RIGHT (WEST) ON CO. FF. Some easy climbing for next 3 miles. Scenic farm country soon takes hold.
6.0	TURN LEFT (SOUTH) ON CO. QQ. Town Hall on your right. Neatly kept farm house and flower garden on your left. Gentle rolling farmland interspersed with some forested areas lies ahead.
7.1	Pass Highland Drive (1070th Street) coming in from your right as road winds through lush farmland.
8.3	At T-intersection, TURN LEFT (EAST) ON CO. ROADS MM AND QQ.
8.8	TURN RIGHT (SOUTH) ON CO. QQ (1170TH STREET) and climb a little before descent at mile 9.1.
9.5	At T-intersection, TURN RIGHT (WEST) ON WISC. HWYS. 29 AND 35 AND CO. QQ.
9.8	TURN LEFT (SOUTH) ON CO. QQ (1170th Street) for straight shot through open fields.
11.0	TURN LEFT (EAST) ON 630TH AVENUE (STIRRAT AVENUE) and climb a little.

12.4	Climb again reaching top at mile 12.7 followed immediately by downhill plunge.
14.2	At T-intersection, TURN RIGHT (SOUTH) ON CO. E and soon climb reaching top at mile 14.8.
15.5	Junction with 570th Avenue (Crosstown Road). Perched at top of hill on southwest side is St. Mary's Catholic Church (lovely sanctuary inside). Continue south on Co. E.
16.0	CROSS U.S. 10 and CONTINUE SOUTH ON CO. E for a little more climbing.
16.8	Pass Staiger Avenue coming in from your left. Road roller coasters somewhat.
17.2	TURN LEFT (EAST) ON SPRING GREEN DRIVE. More roller-coaster rides. Sweeping panoramic views ahead.
19.0	At T-intersection, TURN RIGHT (SOUTH) ON CO. OO. Road continues to roller coaster through high farm country.
19.5	Note round barn to your left (east).
22.6	Long descent into Mississippi River bottom begins. Catch view of "Diamond Bluff" to your left on way down.
24.5	At T-intersection, TURN RIGHT (WEST) ON WISC. 35 (used to be Co. E).
25.2	TURN LEFT (SOUTH) FOR TOWN OF DIAMOND BLUFF across railroad tracks. Head all the way to river. Sandy beach straight ahead. (Perfect spot for bocce ball.)
25.4	At T-intersection just before river, TURN RIGHT (WEST) ON LOWER RIVER ROAD to bar and riverside porch.
25.6	Kask's Bar on right (friendly bar, great chile, and cheese burgers). Picnic table on riverside porch opposite bar. TURN AROUND for return trip and head east on same road.

25.8	Pass road you earlier took, coming in from your left. Keep going straight along river on Lower River Road (sandy beach on your right).
26.4	Cemetery on your left.
26.6	Spectacular views of river bluffs to your left. Road soon becomes gravel for 0.3 mile.
28.2	Wind between barn and farmhouse. Antiques and other odds and ends for sale. Nice frontal view of Skidmore Bluff as road turns north.
28.8	Cross railroad tracks and, at T-intersection (the Red Wing Spur joins the route at this junction), TURN LEFT (WEST) ON WISC. 35, THEN RIGHT (NORTH) ON CO. O. This road follows the Trimbelle River and is a pleasant gradual ascent out of the Mississippi River basin with nice interspersed views of the Trimbelle River. The road works its way up the river valley with tree cover and high slopes on your left and some farmland on your right.
31.2	Intermittent river crossings for next 1.5 miles.
35.8	Cross river again and then climb gradually.
36.2	At T-intersection, TURN LEFT (NORTHEAST) ON CO. O (Leghorn Lane goes right). More crisscrossing of river as gradual winding climb is resumed.
37.0	**Trimbelle.** At T-intersection, TURN LEFT (WEST) ON U.S. 10. The "Gaslite" bar is on your left. Nice place for a break. (Trailhead for Tour 4.)
37.2	TURN RIGHT (NORTH) ON CO. O. Vest pocket park (Leonard Park) on your right next to Trimbelle River. Nice spot for a dip. Cross small bridge, climb a little and reenter high farm country.
38.4	Cross Crosstown Road (570th Avenue) and climb some more.

40.5	Finny's Antiques on your right (closed on Sundays).
42.0	TURN LEFT (WEST) ON 710TH AVENUE (PLEASANT VIEW ROAD) along upland terrain.
42.5	TURN RIGHT (NORTH) ON 910TH STREET (HAPPY VALLEY ROAD) and climb a little.
43.0	Nice long descent begins along tree-lined defile. Pass Trillium Woods Bed and Breakfast on way down (see narrative).
44.0	Pass Cady's Lane coming in from your left as road levels off.
45.2	At junction with Wisc. Hwys. 29 and 35, TURN RIGHT (NORTH) ON BICYCLE PATH which parallels highway.
46.1	River Falls and end of bike path. Continue north on Wisc. Hwys. 29 and 35.
46.5	TURN LEFT (WEST) INTO DICK'S IGA PARKING LOT. (Alternative trailhead, Hoffman Park, is another 2.5 miles north and east. To reach this trailhead continue north on Wisc. Hwys. 29 and 35, turn East on Cascade and follow route North on Oak Street, East on Spring Street, North on Third Street and East on Division to alternative trailhead as described for the last 1½ miles of the log for Tour 2.

TOUR 2: *The Eastern Loop*

Trailhead:	Hoffman Park. To find Hoffman Park, drive to the junction Wisc. 65 and East Division Street (0.7 miles east of Main Street on north side of Co. M).
Distance:	Option A: 39 miles or 43 miles with the Red Barn addition Option B: 10 miles Option C: 19 miles Option D: 47 miles with the El Paso Addition Option E: 28 miles with the New Centerville cutoff

Terrain: Fairly level for Wisconsin (i.e., gently rolling terrain with some manageable hills)

Highlights: River Falls, Arabian horse farm, restored 1868 school building, rural churches, fairly open farmland with good views, and some woods and valley riding.

Route: Option A: (0.0) East on East Division Street (Co. M); (1.6) North on Liberty Road; (3.5) East on River Drive; (5.2) North on Co. JJ; (6.4) East on Co. J; (9.5) North on 162nd Street; (10.4) East on Co. N; (14.1) South on Co. Y; (21.9) West on Co. J; (26.2) West on 690th Avenue; (28.5) Southwest on Co. W; (29.6) Northwest on 820th Street (Sleepy Hollow Road); (30.2) West on road which becomes Pleasant View Road; (32.5) North on 910th Street (Happy Valley Road); (36.0) North on Wisc. Highways 29 and 35; (37.7) East on Cascade and stay on Wisc. 29; (37.9) North on Oak Street, East on Spring Street and North on Third Street; (38.9) East on Division Street (Co. M) to trailhead at mile 39.3.

Option B: Take Option A Route to mile 5.2, then South on Co. JJ; (6.9) West on Co. M to trailhead at mile 10.4.

Option C: Take Option A Route to mile 9.2, then South on Co. W; (12.7) West on Co. M to trailhead at mile 18.7.

Option D: Take Option A Route to mile 14.1, then continue east on Co. N; (18.0) South on Co. BB; (28.0) **El Paso**, West on Co. G through **El Paso**; (32.5) North on 530th Street (Rush River Road); (34.5) West on 690th Avenue (Stone Hammer Road, which becomes Morton Corner Road after crossing U.S. 63); resume Option A Route at mile 26.2.

This is a super ride through mixed farmland, over good roads that are for the most part lightly traveled. There are some nice vistas and plenty of opportunities for shortcuts for returning early. The scenery provides a rich tapestry of rolling farmland, wide valleys, woods, hills, rivers, defiles, and highlands. We recommend a lunch break at the Red Barn Cafe (or better yet, to catch the early morning magic of the ride, breakfast).

Log

0.0   Parking lot at Hoffman Park.

0.1   TURN LEFT (EAST) ON DIVISION also known as Co. M and climb a little.

0.7   Ride by the golf course and resume climb to the high ground.

1.6   TURN LEFT (NORTH) ON LIBERTY ROAD and head through some wooded and hilly terrain.

2.2   Enter pretty valley drained by the Kinnickinnic River.

2.8   Pass Rifle Range Road coming in from your right as road beings to parallel a windbreak of giant Norway pines.

3.5   TURN RIGHT (EAST) ON RIVER DRIVE and ride through the McLaughlin Arabian horse farm as road proceeds along flat valley bottom.

5.2   At T-intersection, TURN LEFT (NORTH) ON CO. JJ and climb a little. **Note:** For Option B of 10 miles, turn right (south) instead of Co. JJ and continue south 1 3/4 miles to Co. M, turn right (west) on Co. M, and continue west 3 1/2 miles to Hoffman Park.

6.4   Soon after crossing Kinnickinnic River, TURN RIGHT (EAST) ON CO. J. Note the 1868 white, one-room schoolhouse with the bell tower -- restored and maintained by the Kinnickinnic Historical Association.

7.0   Cross the Kinnickinnic River again and continue east past Pleasant Road with rolling farmland and nice vistas to the north.

8.2   Parker Creek (great trout stream) to your left (north).

9.2   At junction with Co. W, CONTINUE EAST ON 35TH STREET through a small family farm and under an overhanging tree next to the road. Nice views to the south as area opens up. **Note:** For Option C of 19 miles, turn right (south) on Co. W for 3.5 miles to Co. M. Turn right (west) on Co. M and continue 6 miles west to Hoffman Park.

9.5   At T-intersection, TURN LEFT (NORTH) ON 162ND STREET.

10.3   At T-intersection, TURN RIGHT (EAST) ON ST. CROIX CO. N. Road soon begins to roller coaster a little.

12.1   After slight climb, cross Co. T and continue east on Co. N. Nice vistas.

13.4   After short climb, magnificent vista ahead with Peace Lutheran Church in the distance.

14.1   TURN RIGHT (SOUTH) ON CO. Y. Peace Lutheran Church sits on the southeast corner. Great vistas initially to the south and west and then to the west. Continue more or less south on Co. Y for about seven miles as the road snakes through the Rush River drainage area. **Note:** For Option D of 47 miles through El Paso, continue east on Co. N and skip to Option D below.

15.6   Cross Rush River (barely a stream).

16.8   18th Avenue comes in from your right and leads to a bridge over the Rush River just a block away. Nice spot for a snack break by the river.

18.5   Cross Rush River again, turn south past the New Centerville United Methodist Church, and wind through town (no stores).

18.7	TURN LEFT (SOUTH) ON CO. Y WHERE CO. Y IS JOINED BY CO. M and continue weaving course. **Note:** For Option E, a shorter trip of 28 miles, turn right (north) at the curve and continue north then west on Co. M for 9 miles to Hoffman Park.
19.8	The Rush River Lutheran Church. Notice the tall pine woods planted by the congregation in the 1950s to serve as a wind break and break up what was then a desolate setting.
20.1	Junction with Wisc. 29. **Decision Time:** For those who would like to go to the Red Barn antique store, ice cream store, and cafe, turn left (east) on Wisc. 29, go east 1 3/4 miles across Rush River, then turn right (south) on busy U.S. 63/Wisc. 29 for one mile to the Red Barn. To return to the route, simply leave the Red Barn and continue south on U.S. 63 which soon heads west through Martell, past the Martell Methodist Church, and then south again. Turn right (west) on Co. J, picking up the log at mile 21.9. This adds 3.5 miles to your total mileage. Otherwise, cross Wisc. 29, climb a little, and continue south on Co. Y.
21.5	Pass the Martell Methodist Church. Co. Y ends where U.S. 63 comes in from your left. CONTINUE SOUTH ON U.S. 63.
21.9	TURN RIGHT (WEST) ON CO. J and head west past more farmland.
23.0	Cross narrow bridge as trees begin to close in and soon begin climb that cuts through a limestone outcrop.
23.5	Junction with West Martell Road (unmarked) coming in from right (west). BEAR LEFT (SOUTH) and continue on Co. J reaching top at mile 23.8. Nice views to east.
24.6	Pass Hillcrest Road coming in from your right. (Note: Kanten's Circle K Orchards are 0.7 miles north on Hillcrest Road -- opens at noon.) Soon afterwards, road descends into valley. Beautiful view from on top.

26.2	TURN RIGHT (WEST) ON MORTEN CORNER ROAD (690TH AVENUE), pass between hills on both sides, and enter another wide valley drained by the Trimbelle River.
28.5	TURN LEFT (SOUTHWEST) ON CO. W.
29.6	CROSS WISC. 65 AND CONTINUE NORTHWEST ON SLEEPY HOLLOW ROAD (820TH STREET) along west slope of river valley as trees close in.
29.9	Chicken Coop Antiques on your right.
30.2	TURN LEFT (WEST) ON PLEASANTVIEW ROAD (gravel road) up a double-tiered hill topping off initially at mile 30.4 and rising again at mile 30.7 for another 0.2 miles. After one more roller-coaster dip, high farm country is reached.
32.1	Cross Co. O and continue west on Pleasantview Road (710th Avenue, now paved) along upland terrain.
32.6	TURN RIGHT (NORTH) ON HAPPY VALLEY ROAD (910TH STREET). This road climbs a little and then at mile 34.1 plunges northwest down a narrow valley road lined with trees. Pass Trillium Woods Bed and Breakfast on way down (see narrative).
36.0	TURN RIGHT (NORTH) ON THE BIKE PATH that parallels Wisc. Hwys. 29 and 35 into River Falls.
36.8	River Falls and end of bike path. Continue north on Wisc. 29 and 35, Main Street.
37.1	Dick's IGA on your left, an alternate parking spot and a good place to get groceries.
37.5	Pass West Park Street coming in from your left. A block west on Park Street is Glenn Park (see narrative).
37.7	TURN RIGHT (EAST) ON CASCADE (Wisc. Hwys. 29 and 35) instead of heading straight on Main Street.

37.9   TURN LEFT (NORTH) ON OAK STREET, RIGHT (EAST) ON SPRING STREET AND LEFT (NORTH) ON THIRD STREET and continue north to East Division Street.

38.9   TURN RIGHT (EAST) ON EAST DIVISION STREET, continue to Hoffman Park.

39.3   Hoffman Park.

OPTION D: El Paso Addition

14.1   CONTINUE EAST 4 MILES ON CO. N past both Peace Lutheran Churches and across U.S. 63 to Co. BB.

18.0   TURN RIGHT (SOUTH) ON CO. BB. Continue south for 10 miles to Co. G.

28.0   TURN RIGHT (WEST) ON CO. G. Co west down into the historic old town of El Paso. It is now hard to imagine, but this town was once one of the largest towns in Pierce County. Among other businesses were a hotel, shoemaker, clothing store, three grocery stores, blacksmiths, and saw and flour mills. As you get to the bottom of the hill, be sure to note the Log Cabin Bar. The bar is on the Pierce County register of historic buildings. It was built in about 1860 and has been operated since 1937 by Ernie Seifert. A memorable place to stop for a cool one. In town is the Basement Bar next to the river.

29.3   Log Cabin Bar in El Paso. TURN RIGHT (NORTH) ON CO. G at T-intersection. There is a camping spot on the Rush River just a block south of the bar on the dead end road. The cost is $3.00 per tent, no reservations or telephone number.

29.5   TURN LEFT (WEST) ON CO. G and climb the long hill past the St. Thomas Cemetery and Memorial Bell Tower.

32.5   TURN RIGHT (NORTH) ON 530TH STREET (RUSH RIVER ROAD) at Sunny Side School. Go past Our Saviors Lutheran Church, cross Co. N, past the old Our Saviors Memorial Bell Tower.

34.5   TURN LEFT (WEST) ON 690TH AVENUE (STONE HAMMER ROAD). Cross U.S. 63, pass the round barn on what is now called Morton Corner Road and then cross Co. J. Note: At this point join the original log at mile 26.2 and continue west. This side trip adds about 8 miles to the tour.

TOUR 3: *Round Barn Trip*

Trailhead:	The Pierce County Fairgrounds in Ellsworth, Wisc. About 0.5 mile north on Wisc. 65 from junction of U.S. 10 and 63 and Wisc. 65. Parking is available close to the round barn that was built for the dairy exhibits in 1920.
Distance:	38 miles; a shorter route of 23 miles is available
Terrain:	Rolling; there are two valleys to enter and climb out of.
Highlights:	Disappearing round barns, Trimbelle Valley, and mixed farm country.
Route:	(0.0) **Barn** -- West on W. Cairns Street and North on Wisc. 65; (2.7) Northeast on Co. J; (14.2) East on 690th Avenue; (4.6) **Barn**; (7.9) South on 530th Street; (12.0) West on Wisc. 72 and South on 530th Street; (15.4) West on 410th Avenue; (18.5) North on Co. C; (19.5) West on 450th Avenue (Co. K); (23.5) North on 810th Street; (24.3) West on 480th Avenue (Leghorn Lane); (26.1) South on Co. O; (27.8) West on Fairview Lane; (29.3) North on Co. OO; (30.6) **Barn**; (32.8) East on 570th Avenue (Crosstown Road); (37.8) South on Wisc. 65 to trailhead at mile 40.

This tour travels on good roads through mixed farm country with scenic hills, woods, and valleys. The sight of these round barns as historic architecture makes the ride much more interesting. Note the difference continual maintenance makes to wooden buildings.

Log

0.0   Start at the ROUND BARN at the fairgrounds. As you leave the fairground WEST ON W. CAIRNS STREET, TURN RIGHT (NORTH) ON WISC. 65. Ride down into Goose Creek Valley. **Note:** Wisc. 35 in this area was renamed Wisc. 65 in 1989; older maps will show this road as Wisc. 35. This can be a busy road so watch for traffic.

2.7   As road bends left, TURN RIGHT (NORTHEAST) ON CO. J. AT the V in the road, BEAR LEFT (NORTH) ON CO. J and climb a little.

4.0   At some distance to the northeast, you can catch your first glimpse of the next round barn perched on a hill.

4.2   Morton Corner. TURN RIGHT (EAST) ON 690TH AVENUE. There are three fairly challenging roller coaster dips on this segment.

4.6   ROUND BARN on your left. This barn is currently used for young stock. Note the views that allow you to see all the way to Minnesota.

5.9   Cross 610th Street and note the old log building that was the early Morton Corner School.

7.2   CROSS U.S. 63. CONTINUE EAST.

7.9   TURN RIGHT (SOUTH) ON 530TH STREET (RUSH RIVER ROAD). If uncertain, note "Ron Anderson" on the mailbox.

8.3   Pass the old Our Saviors Lutheran Cemetery and Memorial Bell Tower.

8.9   Cross Pierce Co. N. Notice the Our Saviors Lutheran Church. These two congregations are united again after about 100 years of separation. The two groups are said to have separated because of differing beliefs in predestination. Some members actually shot at one another.

10.0 Cross Co. G., pass the Sunny Side School, and continue south.

12.0 Lantz School and junction with Wisc. 72. TURN RIGHT (WEST) ON WISC. 72, GO 0.25 MILE, AND THEN TURN LEFT (SOUTH) ON 530TH STREET. Follow this road through a double jog south, over some small hills, and past the Covenant Cemetery.

15.0 When we first started working on this book there used to be a round barn here on your right. Alas, it was torn down.

15.4 CROSS U.S. 10 ONTO CO. D AND TURN RIGHT (WEST) ON 410TH AVENUE (CLAYFIELD ROAD).

17.4 Road becomes gravel for a mile as it negotiates a small gorge cut by Isabelle Creek. Steep descent. Tough climb.

18.5 TURN RIGHT (NORTH) ON CO. C and go one mile. You are now two miles south of East Ellsworth.

19.5 TURN LEFT (WEST) ON 450TH AVENUE (SLEEPY HALLOW ROAD) (CO. K) and continue west for 1½ mile through this picturesque valley and hill country.

21.0 750th Street (Maple Street). **Decision Time:** For those who would like to return to the Pierce County Fairgrounds, turn north on 750th Street and ride 2.4 miles, through Ellsworth, to the trailhead. For those who wish to continue on this scenic tour, continue west on 450th Avenue (Co. K).

22.5 CROSS U.S. 63.

23.5 TURN RIGHT (NORTH) ON 810TH STREET (APPLE LANE) and pass small private park.

24.3	TURN LEFT (WEST) ON 480TH AVENUE (LEGHORN LANE) and follow this high road until it descends into the Trimbelle River Valley.
26.1	TURN LEFT (SOUTH) ON CO. O and ride along the river for 1.7 miles.
27.8	TURN RIGHT (WEST) ON 450TH AVENUE (FAIRVIEW LANE) and climb.
29.3	TURN RIGHT (NORTH) ON CO. OO and ride along high farm country again.
30.6	ROUND BARN on your right. This barn appears to be in very good condition considering its age.
31.8	CROSS U.S. 10 AND CONTINUE NORTH for one mile.
32.8	TURN RIGHT (EAST) ON 570TH AVENUE (CROSSTOWN ROAD) and continue east for 6 miles through a pretty valley and a scenic climb to the high country and Wisc. 65.
37.8	TURN RIGHT (SOUTH) ON WISC. 65 and go 1/4 mile to the Pierce County Fairgrounds.

TOUR 4: *Trimbelle Circle Trip*

Trailhead:	Parking lot at the "Gaslite" bar located in Trimbelle on south side of U.S. 10 just west of junction with Co. O. Red Wing Spur -- see end of this chapter.
Distance:	24 miles
Terrain:	Varied with river valley, rolling highlands, steep descent, and gradual ascent
Highlights:	Rolling farmland, river bluffs, glimpses of the Mississippi, and meandering Trimbelle River.

> **Route:** (0.0) East on U.S. 10; (0.1) South on Co. O; (0.9) East on 480th Avenue (Leghorn Lane); (2.0) South on Over The Hill Road; (2.6) West on Co. K; (9.0) Northwest on Wisc. 35; (12.0) South to **Diamond Bluff;** (12.2) East on Lower River Road to Diamond Bluff Bar at mile 12.4 -- turn around and head West; (15.6)East on Wisc. 35, then North on Co. O; (23.8) West on U.S. 10 to trailhead at mile 24.

This tour packs a lot of variety into a 24 mile trip. It initially follows the Trimbelle River along a winding pastoral back road. It then ascends to the high rolling farm country that rises above the Mississippi River. The route then plunges into a narrow river valley cut by the Trimbelle River and Little Trimbelle Creek that meet and empty into the Mississippi. And finally, after wandering along the Mississippi with the imposing river bluffs as a backdrop, the route returns to the starting point by way of the Trimbelle River. The return trip is an easygoing, almost imperceptible climb out of the river valley.

Try this trip on a sunny day in November when the leaves have fallen and the views through the trees open up new vistas.

Log

0.0   Starting at the Gaslite bar in Trimbelle HEAD EAST ON U.S. 10 FOR 0.1 MILE. THEN TURN RIGHT (SOUTH) ON CO. O.

0.9   BEAR LEFT (EAST) ON 480TH AVENUE (LEGHORN LANE) instead of following Co. O which turns right (south). Climb reaching top at mile 1.5.

2.0   TURN RIGHT (SOUTH) ON OVER THE HILL ROAD and climb a little. Nice vistas of farrowed fields.

2.4   Test brakes for short roller-coaster descent.

2.6	At T-intersection, TURN RIGHT (WEST) ON CO. K as road levels off (somewhat) for awhile before a more gradual uphill ride.
3.6	Pass Maple Lane coming in from your left as more rolling farmland comes into view.
5.9	Pass Mathew Road coming in from your right. Note to your right the tall antenna on one of the highest elevations in the county.
6.2	Test brakes for fast, steep descent into beautiful valley with possible speeds in excess of 30 miles per hour.
7.4	Pass Nelson Road coming in from your left.
8.3	Note sirens on a tall pole to your right. The sirens sound an alert if an unscheduled "release" should occur at the Prairie Island Nuclear Plant.
8.6	Cross Little Trimbelle Creek. Nice bridge to stop, snack, and view surrounding hillsides. Climb a little.
9.0	TURN RIGHT (NORTHWEST) ON WISC. 35 (used to be Co. E). The Red Wing Spur joins route at this junction.
9.5	Pass Lower River Road coming in from left and Co. O coming in from right. Skidmore bluff looms on the right.
11.3	Pass Co. OO coming in from right. At this point use the log for Tour 1 starting at mile 24.5 and ending at the Gaslite at mile 37.1.

Red Wing Spur

0.0	In Red Wing, start at Bay Point Park, which has playgrounds, boat launching, picnic areas, and a large grass area. The park is located between two marinas and can be found by turning down to the river front, then driving north (upstream) on Levee Street, past the tall grain elevators about one block.

HEAD SOUTH ON LEVEE STREET. TURN RIGHT (WEST) and go past railroad station (still in use), up hill, and across Main Street one block to Third Street. TURN LEFT (SOUTH) ON THIRD and three blocks later TURN LEFT (EAST) ON U.S. 63. Crossing bridge is not too bad. The lanes are wide and traffic is slow.

1.7 Just across bridge, TURN LEFT (SOUTHWEST) ONTO ISLAND ROAD.

2.1 Harbor Bar on your left. This bar features many wood carvings both inside and outside. Notice the totems out on the waterfront. Bar stools are carved to resemble horses and saddles. Proceed upstream on Island Road as it circles back to U.S. 63.

3.6 REJOIN U.S. 63. Gene's Bar on your left. Bar food available.

3.9 Cross channel. This is an unpleasant crossing because of the speed of the traffic. However, you can walk your bike across in safety and be more comfortable. TURN LEFT (NORTHWEST) ON TIMBERLAND ROAD on opposite side of bridge. This is a pretty ride with woods on both sides of the road.

4.3 Road climbs onto floodplain with patches of agricultural land. Trenton Cemetery. About a mile northeast are the high rock cliff banks through which the Mississippi cuts.

4.9 TURN LEFT (WEST) ON CO. K.

5.4 Pass River Ridge Road coming in from your left. Dead end.

5.6 Trenton. No stores. Go on by.

7.2 Junction of Co. K and Wisc. 35. **Decision Point:** If you want to take Tour 4 that proceeds next to Diamond Bluff, pick up log for Tour 4 at mile 9. In any event TURN LEFT (NORTHWEST ON WISC. 35 (used to be Co. E).

7.7 Junction with Lower River Road coming in from your left and, just a little further west, Co. O coming in from your right. **Decision Point:** If you want to take Tour 1 that follows to Trimbelle River, pick up log for Tour 1 at mile 28.8 by heading north on Co. O. Otherwise continue west on Wisc. 35 and stay with Tour 4.

SPRING VALLEY, WISC. TOURS

Spring Valley is a picturesque town located on the Eau Galle River. It is surrounded by tranquil valleys and rolling countryside that characterize the terrain between the Red Cedar River to the east and the Rush River to the west. This chapter features two tours with lots of options which begin in Spring Valley, and a circle tour starting at Hatchville about six miles east of Spring Valley where the boundaries of Dunn, St. Croix, and Pierce Counties meet.

Tour 1: Eau Galle River Valley Loop -- 18, 36, 37 and 44 miles
Tour 2: Rural Church Route -- 10 ,17, 28, 40 and 47 miles
Tour 3: Hatchville and Weston Circle Trip -- 20 miles (although a number of shortcuts may be taken)

About the Area

How to Get There: About 40 miles and one hour east of the Twin Cities. Take I-94 to U.S. 63 and then take U.S. 63 south for about seven miles. At the Red Barn Antique Store, turn left (east) on Wisc. 29 and follow Wisc. 29 for about seven miles to Spring Valley.

Spring Valley is located in a small, steep-sided valley. This feature has contributed to the town's inability to grow as well as its flooding problem. The town's population of approximately 1,000 is almost the same as it was in the 1910s. It is the home of the Midwest's largest earthen dam. The dam was built in 1958 to control the floods that would inundate the town nearly every year. About once every 10 years, a flood would nearly wash away the town. Finally, the U.S. Corps of Engineers built the dam for flood control and recreation. Today the area-wide benefits from the dam are flood control, a swimming and fishing lake (Lake George), and a couple of park-like recreation areas (one with camping) next to the lake.

Spring Valley is fun to explore on bicycle. Of special interest is the old theater on the main street. It comes alive with theater presentations performed several times each year.

There are several establishments serving food in or near Spring Valley. The Crystal Bar offers a salad bar when their garden is in production. The Bowling Alley has bar food. Debby's offers typical small town meat-and-potatoes type of food. These restaurants, however, do not provide a smoke-free environment. A special treat is the Golf and Ski Club Sunday brunch and Friday night fish fry. This restaurant provides excellent food at a reasonable price in an attractive setting. The golf course is considered very good by many golfers and is located in the highlands just west of town. To get there, go west of town about 0.5 mile on Wisc. 29 and then turn right (north) or go west 0.5 mile on Mines Drive (4th Street) and turn left (south), up the hill to the club driveway.

Another local attraction is Crystal Cave (715/778-4414 or 800/236-CAVE), 0.5 mile west of Spring Valley on Wisc. 29. The cave is a good place to cool off on a hot summer day. Bring a jacket as the temperature stays at 48 degrees year-round. A one-hour tour of about 1,800 feet of passageway cost $6.00 per adult and $3.00 per child in 1993.

Elmwood, Wisc., is the home of the future UFO landing site. Because of the large number of UFO sightings in the area, Elmwood has, for several years, celebrated UFO Days with a parade and carnival.

There is no lodging in either Spring Valley or Elmwood. There are, however, camping facilities in the area.

The Eau Galle Recreation Area (715/778-5562) offers camp sites on Lake George. It is accessible from St. Croix Co. N between Co. B and Wisc. 128 about five miles north of Spring Valley. The area has many camp sites, some with electricity, and about five miles of self-guided nature trails.

In Elmwood, Butternut Park (715/639-3792) has campsites. To get to the park, go east four blocks from downtown to Public Street (also Co. P), then straight south. The street becomes Park Street, which ends in the park. This is a nice park with some free camping, water, and toilets.

Nugget Lake County Park (715/639-5611) also provides camping. It is eight miles from Elmwood. Go west three miles on Co. G and then south five miles on Co. S to Popular Hill Drive. After crossing Wisc. 72, continue south as the road becomes South Rock Elm Road, which leads to the park.

TOUR 1: *Eau Galle River Valley Loop*

Trailhead:	The parking lot at the south end of Spring Valley (with the Super Valu store) on the east side of Co. B and McKay Street
Distance:	Option A: 18 miles Option B: 36 or 37 miles Option C: 44 miles
Terrain:	Quite level along the Eau Galle River Valley, which is half of each option. There is at least one major hill to climb in getting from the valley to the highlands. In each case, the return route is mildly rolling.
Highlights:	Scenic Eau Galle River valley, small towns, pretty highlands, and for Options B and C, the Martin Van Canoe factory.
Route:	(0.0) East on Central, South on Sabin, and East on Eau Galle Streets; (0.5) Northeast on Wisc. 29 three blocks and East and South on Wisc. 128; (7.3) **Elmwood** -- East on Wisc. 72; (8.4) Junction with Co. P. Option A: North on P; (8.6) Northwest on 690th Street (Lincoln Road); (12.3) West on 770th Avenue (McKinnly Road); (13.4) West on Wisc. 128; (13.6) West on Hoover Road and one block later, North on 740 Avenue (Washington Road); (14.7) North on Wisc. 128; (17.5) Spring Valley.

> Option B: East on Wisc. 72; (10.2) South on Co. C; (17.2) North on Co. D; (20.5) West on Wisc. 72 and one block later, North on Co. D; (22.3) West on Co. X; (24.5) **Weston;** (28.0) North on Co. P; (30.0):
>
> Option B-1: West on 890th Avenue (Elm); (34.0) Southwest on Wisc. 29; (36.1) Spring Valley.
>
> Option B-2: North on Co. PP; (31.1) West on Wisc. 29; (37.0) Spring Valley.
>
> Option C: East on Wisc. 72; (10.2) South on Co. C; (14.5) North across river and East on 210th Avenue (Bridge Road); (15.4) South on Co. D; (15.9) East on Co. C; (18.4) South on Co. Z; (23.0) West on Co. D -- **Eau Galle;** (26.2) West on Co. C; (26.9) West on 150th Avenue (High Road), which becomes Pleasant Valley Road; (33.1) North on Co. P; (35.6) West on 690th Street (Lincoln Road); (39.3) West on 770th Avenue (McKinnly Road); (40.4) West on Wisc. 128; West on Hoover Road and one block later, North on 740th Avenue (Washington Road); (41.7) North on Wisc. 128; (44.5) Spring Valley.

This is a beautiful route with a great deal of variation on one loop. It ranges from a curving, wooded road to rolling farmland with distant vistas. Fertile valleys and tree-lined hills beckon. Truly an odyssey for the venturesome cyclist.

Log

0.0   Starting from the parking lot, HEAD EAST ON CENTRAL STREET ACROSS THE RIVER AND THEN TURN SOUTH ON SABIN STREET FOR ONE SHORT BLOCK BEFORE HEADING EAST AGAIN ON EAU GALLE STREET.

0.6	TURN LEFT (NORTHEAST) ON WISC. 29. Notice the picturesque white-steepled Lutheran Church in a sea of green grass.
0.8	TURN RIGHT (EAST) ON WISC. 128. Follow Wisc. 128 and look for the picturesque cemetery on your left. You will be riding along the serpentine Eau Galle River through a pretty valley. The road initially hugs the east sloping wooded hills with the river below to your right for the first mile.
1.7	Pass Fillmore Road coming in from your left. Stay on Wisc. 128 all the way to Elmwood.
2.5	Pass Washington Road coming in from your right. Look for the high sandstone cliff just to your left.
3.5	Pass Hoover Road coming in from your right. Look west to the fishing hole on the river. Some people catch good-sized trout here regularly.
4.1	TURN RIGHT (SOUTH) ON WISC. 128 at Spring Lake Church, four corners.
5.7	Look toward the hills to the east. The seven concrete pylons are remnants of a limestone quarry that was mined by hand. The crushed limestone was dumped into railroad cars from a platform on top of these pylons. The railroad was flooded out in 1942.
7.3	Enter **Elmwood, Wisc.** See narrative. TURN LEFT (EAST) ON WISC. 72 and ride through Elmwood staying on Wisc. 72. Downtown on your left, look for the fuel pump atop the gasoline station for gas-guzzling UFOs.
8.4	Junction with Co. P. **Decision Point**: Either (1) turn left (north) for Option A of 17.5 miles back to Spring Valley or (2) continue east on Wisc. 72 for (i) Option B of 36 or 37 miles to Eau Galle, Weston, Hatchville, and Spring Valley, and (ii) Option C of 44.5 miles to Pine View Park. Option A is described first.

OPTION A: Back to Spring Valley

8.4 Junction of Co. P and Wisc. 72. TURN LEFT (NORTH) ON CO. P.

8.6 TURN LEFT (NORTHWEST) ON 690TH STREET (LINCOLN ROAD) and climb. This is a steep but pretty hill. Notice the limestone cliffs and the trees which overhang the road creating a tunnel to give you shade most of the day.

9.4 Crest of the hill.

9.8 Road turns right (north). If you look south, there is access to the abandoned quarry mentioned earlier.

10.8 Lundgren Farm on the south. Magnificent look-back view (southeast) of the Eau Galle River valley in the distance.

11.7 Fred Larson Farm on the west. Check out the maple trees to the east and the valley to the west. This is a stunning ride in the fall.

12.3 TURN LEFT (WEST) ON 770TH AVENUE (MCKINNLY ROAD) and descend. This is the payoff for the earlier climb. It is a quick ride down to the four corners.

13.4 Four corners, go straight across the intersection (WEST) ONTO WISC. 128 AGAIN.

13.6 Junction with Hoover Road where Wisc. 128 turns right (north). TAKE HOOVER ROAD (WEST) ACROSS THE BRIDGE to 740th Avenue (Washington Road) on other side.

13.7 TURN RIGHT (NORTH) ON 740TH AVENUE (WASHINGTON ROAD).

14.7 At T-intersection, TURN LEFT (NORTH) AND REJOIN WISC. 128. Continue north toward Spring Valley.

17.5 Back in downtown Spring Valley.

OPTIONS B and C: Continue East Along Eau Galle

8.4   Junction of Co. P and Wisc. 72. Continue east on Wisc. 72. Ride out of town following the Eau Galle River valley for a fairly level ride.

10.2   TURN RIGHT (SOUTH) ON CO. C just before the bridge crosses the river. This leg provides a lovely, slightly rolling ride along the Eau Galle River. It is lightly traveled. In the fall, a profusion of color highlights the tree-lined hills to the north.

14.5   Junction with Bridge Road coming in from the left. **Decision Point**: Either (1) turn left (north) across Eau Galle River and then right (east) on Bridge Road for Option C of 44.5 miles. This ride takes you past Pine View Park, through Eau Galle and Elmwood, and on a highland route back to Spring Valley; or (3) continue with log for Option B. Option B is described first.

OPTION B: Eau Galle Boat Shop and Beyond

14.5   Continue south on Co. C.

16.8   Eau Galle Boat Shop. This is the home of Martin Van canoes (715/283-4302). Martin will give interested persons a short tour of his shop as time permits. These are really beautiful cedar strip canoes. Water and toilet facilities available.

17.2   At T-intersection, TURN LEFT (NORTH) ON CO. D. (To add 8.5 miles to the trip, turn right (south) on Co. D and head to Eau Galle and Co. Z. Turn left (north) on Co. Z past the Pine View Park to Co. C. Turn west on Co. C to Co. D and rejoin the main route at mile 18.5.)

18.5   Pass Co. C coming in from your right (east).

20.5   TURN LEFT (WEST) ON WISC. 72 FOR 0.1 MILE AND THEN RIGHT (NORTH) ON CO. D.

21.1 Pass Zeiling Drive coming in from your right. Stay on Co. D, which crosses Knights Creek twice, and continue north in this very picturesque valley.

22.3 TURN LEFT (WEST) ON CO. X. Route proceeds through a valley surrounded by steep hills and bluffs.

24.0 TURN LEFT (WEST) TO STAY ON CO. X. Going straight ahead on Decker Road leads you to Hatchville and Spring Valley by a more hilly route. See Tour 3: Hatchville and Weston Circle Trip.

24.5 Cross Knights Creek and pass Weston to your left (south). Weston has a popular bar. Nice stop for a cool drink.

25.0 Long, gentle-hill climb begins. On the north side is one of the longest farm fields in Dunn County (more than a mile). On the south side is a nice woods with a couple of shady spots to stop and cool off or have a snack.

27.0 Top of hill. Look to the north for a log building that looks as good as new. The rest of the trip back to Spring Valley is mostly gently rolling countryside.

28.0 TURN RIGHT (NORTH) ON CO. P past the Evangelical Lutheran Church.

30.0 Hatchville Creamery and Cheese Store (715/772-4221). This is a good place to buy cheese. The prices are probably the lowest around, and the walk-in cooler is a nice place to make your bulk selections. Water and toilet facilities available.

Decision Point: For the shortest and most scenic route to Spring Valley (Option B-1), go directly west for four miles on Elm Road and then join Wisc. 29 for an exhilarating coast into Spring Valley. This route, however, includes one mile of gravel road and one steep dip in and out of a scenic coulee. Total mileage to Spring Valley is 36 miles. The easier, and probably the fastest, way (Option B-2) is to go north one mile on Co. PP to Wisc. 29 and then west on Wisc. 29 to Spring Valley. This route passes one of the prettiest rural yards in the county -- a veritable flower garden of beauty. Total mileage is about 37 miles. Note that Wisc. 29 is busy.

OPTION B-1: *Straight to Spring Valley*

30.0   TURN LEFT (WEST) ON 890TH AVENUE (ELM). The first mile is gravel.

31.0   Begin downhill into coulee. Test brakes and look to your left as you start down for a preview of the valley you will be in. This portion of the road is mostly hard surfaced. The valley makes many people think of Switzerland. The top of the other side is reached at mile 32.9.

33.4   Cross Co. T and continue west past a Christmas tree farm on your right (north).

34.4   TURN LEFT (SOUTHWEST) ON WISC. HWYS. 29 and 128 and enjoy a fast ride down into Spring Valley.

35.4   At the Lutheran Church on your right, TURN RIGHT (WEST) on Wisc. 29 for the ride into Spring Valley.

36.1   Downtown Spring Valley.

OPTION B-2: *Circle North to Spring Valley*

30.0   CONTINUE NORTH ON CO. PP.

31.1   TURN LEFT (WEST) ON WISC. 29. This is a fairly wide, moderately traveled road with wide gravel shoulders.

33.4   Front yard on your right (north) is beautifully decorated with flowers from early summer until after the first frost of winter. It has become a community landmark.

34.1   Cross junction with Wisc. 128 and Co. T (marked by a stunning white Lutheran church on the north side) and continue southwest on Wisc. 29.

35.4   Pass Elm Road coming in from your left and start the long, fast glide down into the valley.

36.4	At the Lutheran Church, TURN RIGHT (WEST) for the ride into Spring Valley, staying on Wisc. 29.
37.0	Downtown Spring Valley.

OPTION C: *Lake Eau Galle and Valleys to the South*

14.5	TURN LEFT (NORTH) AND CROSS THE EAU GALLE RIVER AND THEN TURN RIGHT (EAST) ON BRIDGE ROAD and continue east to Co. D.
15.4	At T-intersection, TURN RIGHT (SOUTH) ON CO. D and go south for 0.5 mile.
15.9	TURN LEFT (EAST) ON CO. C. Co. C zigzags for 2.5 miles until junction with Co. Z is reached.
18.4	TURN RIGHT (SOUTH) ON CO. Z. Zigzag south and west toward Eau Galle. (Note: To go to Downsville, take either Co. Z north or Co. C east for about four miles.)
21.9	Pine Point Road comes in from your right and leads to Pine View Park along Lake Eau Galle, 0.5 mile away. Picnic area, swimming beach, bath house but no running water.
23.0	TURN RIGHT (WEST) ON CO. D and ride into the town of Eau Galle. Stay on Co. D. This is a pretty little town. You may wish to wander down by the lake to rest awhile or to picnic at the dam site park. (Bar and country store at west end of town.) To continue, just stay on Co. D going north of town.
26.2	TURN LEFT (WEST) ON CO. C.
26.5	Martin Van's Eau Galle Boat Shop is on one side of the road and his solar heated house is on the other. Martin will give a short tour of his canoe factory, time permitting. These are beautiful canoes. On one visit, we admired an 18-foot, 55-pound cedar strip canoe with near-zero rocker finished with clear fiberglass on both sides. Truly a work of art. Water and toilet facilities available.

26.8	CONTINUE STRAIGHT (WEST) ON 150TH AVENUE (HIGH ROAD), where Co. C turns north. Climb a hill, topping off at mile 27.0 and then descend a little for an easy roller-coaster ride into the bottom of a lush, well-farmed valley.
27.4	Pass 230th Street (Pleasant Valley Drive) coming in from your left. Pleasant View Farm is on your right. Continue west on 150th Avenue (which is now Pleasant View Drive, an appropriate name for a road with panoramic views of rolling farmland).
28.3	Pass 170th Avenue (Valley East Road) coming in from your right.
31.1	After a 0.5 mile climb, top of the world is reached. Ride along open farmland, as the road beings to roller coaster a little.
33.1	TURN RIGHT (NORTH) ON CO. P and soon head downhill into **Elmwood**.
34.5	Turn off to your left to Butternut Park. See narrative.
34.8	Cross Wisc. 72 and continue north on Co. P.
35.6	TURN LEFT (WEST) ON 690TH STREET (LINCOLN ROAD) and head up the hill. This is the last big climb on the route. For the remaining route back to Spring Valley, pick up route for Option A at mile 8.6 and continue. Total mileage is 44.5 miles.

TOUR 2: *Rural Church Route*

Trailhead: Park in Spring Valley at the shopping center (with the Super Valu store) at the south end of town. You can also start from the Golf and Ski Club if that is convenient. To standardize, the log will start from the junction of Co. B and 4th Street. This point is one block east of Main Street and one block north of the business area.

Distance: Main Route: 47 miles
Option A: 10 miles
Option B: 17 miles
Option C: 28 miles
Option D: 40 miles

Terrain: Fairly level for Wisconsin. Mostly rolling farmland with some historical towns located in valleys.

Highlights: The churches, memorial bells, and historical towns. The tour rides through scenic farm country with many panoramic views. Wisconsin's finest trout stream is near El Paso.

Route: Main Route: (0.0) West on 4th Street (also Co. B); (2.0) North on Co. B; (6.3) West on Co. N; (12.3) South on Co. Y; (20.3) South on U.S. 63; (23.2) East on 690th Avenue (Stonehammer Road); (25.0) South on 530th Street (Rush River Road); (26.0) East on Co. G; (29.0) **El Paso**; (33.8) North on Wisc. 183; (34.3) East on Co. G; (38.8) East on Wisc. 72; (39.2) North on Wisc. 128; (45.6) Southwest on Co. 29; (46.4) North on Co. B; (46.6) Spring Valley.

Option A: Take Main Route to mile 3.0, then go West on County Line Drive; (5.0) South on Co. BB: (6.0) East on Mines Drive back to Spring Valley at mile 10.0.

> **Option B:** Take main Route to Mile 8.4, then go South on Co. BB; (13.2) East on Mines Drive back to Spring Valley at mile 17.0.
>
> **Option C:** Take Main Route to mile 19.2, then go East on Co. 29 (which becomes Mines Drive after crossing U.S. 63) back to Spring Valley at mile 27.7.
>
> **Option D:** Take Main Route to mile 30.8, then go North on Co. BB: (36.3) East on Mines Drive back to Spring Valley at mile 40.3.

This pleasant ride is fairly level for Wisconsin. The trip starts in Spring Valley and goes through three town that have nearly dwindled away. The route passes as many as nine churches or their memorial bells. In 1985, the nine churches were still in place. Currently, five of the churches have services. The mileage ranges from 10 miles to as much as 47 miles depending on the choice of options.

Log

0.0 Junction of Co. B with 4th Street in Spring Valley. PROCEED WEST ON CO. B AND 4TH STREET, which becomes Miles Drive further west.

1.0 Junction with Van Buren Road. To the south 0.25 mile is the Golf and Ski Club. To the north is the Eau Galle Recreation Area (swimming, nice sand beach, picnic area, and nature trails). Continue west up a gentle hill along the creek.

2.0 TURN NORTH ON CO. B past the Madsons Sawmill and cross Mines Creek.

3.0 Junction with County Line Drive. Cross into St. Croix County and continue north on Co. B. **Note:** For Option A of 19 miles, turn west on County Line Drive for two miles and then turn south on Co. BB to Mines Drive. Finally, head east on Mines Drive back to Spring Valley.

3.8 Pass Boston Road coming in from your right (east). This road leads to one of the Eau Galle Recreation Areas (hiking and fishing).

6.3 TURN LEFT (WEST) ON ST. CROIX CO. N. Co. N is a most pleasant route for bicycling. You will be riding west through farmland and some woods. There are very good views to the north for the next five miles.

8.4 Junction with Co. BB. Continue west on Co. N. **Note:** For Option B of 17 miles, go south on Co. BB and turn left (east) on Mines Drive (4th Street) to Spring Valley. This is a fairly level ride through mixed farmland. The roads are lightly traveled. Keep in mind that you can return to Spring Valley by simply going south at any of the roads off Co. N to Mines Drive and then east on Mines Drive eventually to 4th Street.

11.3 Junction with Wisc. 63. The old school house and playgrounds here make a pleasant place to stop for a snack and rest. Toilets are available. Cross Wisc. 63 and stay on Co. N past the two Peace Lutheran Churches.

11.5 The Peace Lutheran Church. The two congregations are one again after 100 years of separate existence. The original Peace Lutheran Church congregation split. The group leaving went west 0.75 mile and built a pretty white church of wood for $8,000. Not to be outdone, the remaining group looked at their old church and decided they could do much better. They tore down the old building and for $16,000 built the elaborate brick structure you see here. This church is a favorite subject of many painters and photographers. The two congregations have recently reunited. They use the small wood church occasionally and the larger brick church for most services.

12.3 Peace Lutheran Church and town hall. TURN LEFT (SOUTH) ON CO. Y. More open farmland as Co. Y snakes southward through the Rush River drainage area. Stay on Co. Y.

15.2 18th Avenue comes in from your right and leads to a bridge just a block away. Nice spot for a snack break by the river.

16.7 Pass Co. YY coming in from your left. Continue south on Co. Y and turn right (west) across the Rush River.

17.1 New Centerville Methodist Church. Continue on Co. Y to Co. M. **TURN LEFT (SOUTH) ON CO. Y AND CO. M.**

18.9 Go past the Rush River Lutheran Church. Notice the pleasant pine woods planted by the congregation in the 1950s to break up what was a desolate landscape. It also prevents the wind from blowing across their parking lot.

19.2 Junction with Co. 29. Cross Co. 29 and continue south on Co. Y. **Note:** For Option C of 27.7 miles, go (east) on Co. 29 to junction with U.S. 63. Continue east on Mines Drive (4th Street) to Spring Valley. This provides you with a ride over gentle rolling farmland on a good road with very simple navigation (just continue east).

20.5 Junction with U.S. 63. Martell Methodist Church. This church was built in 1874 in New Centerville and moved to its present location in 1900. **Opportunity Time:** To go to the Red Barn Antique Store, which also houses a country cafe and ice cream store, head east on U.S. 63 about two miles past the abandoned Martell Lutheran Church, now a private home in Martell (the "Whitehouse"). Continue through Martell and up the hill to the State Wayside Park and the Red Barn. The yogurt is highly recommended. To return to the main route, retrace your path to the Martell Methodist Church. Or, if you don't mind a couple of miles of gravel, take an interesting shortcut back to the route by going south from the Red Barn on Wonderland Road, which becomes gravel after the first mile. Wonderland Road wanders through the woods then enters a picturesque valley and follows the Rush River until crossing the river and turning left (south) again on 530th Street (Rush River Road) (the first intersection after you are on gravel).

To continue from the Martell Methodist Church, HEAD SOUTH ON U.S. 63 for 2.7 miles to 690th Avenue (Stonehammer Road). (To avoid the busy traffic on U.S. 63, turn left (east) on Martell Road at mile 20.9, right (southeast) on Shady Road at mile 22.0 (which soon becomes gravel), and right (south) again on Wonderland Road (also gravel) at mile 23.3. Follow the route to Rush River Road described above.)

23.2 TURN LEFT (EAST) ON 690TH AVENUE (STONEHAMMER ROAD).

24.0 TURN RIGHT (SOUTH) ON 530TH STREET (RUSH RIVER ROAD) and continue south past the old Our Saviors Lutheran Memorial bell tower and cemetery. Many years ago, the Our Saviors Lutheran Church split. Local legend has it that the dividing issue was predestination. Some members actually shot at one another. The two congregations have successfully reunited and now host the regionally famous lutefisk dinner every year on the last Thursday in October.

25.0 Cross Pierce Co. N. Continue south on Rush River Road past the Our Saviors Lutheran Church.

26.0 TURN LEFT (EAST) ON CO. G. Sunny Side School. Co. G winds through some farmland and provides a spectacular view of the Rush River Valley just before a sweeping high speed coast down into El Paso. This ride is so pleasant it is hard to stop. However, half-way down is the St. Thomas Cemetery and Memorial Bell. A very pleasant place to stop and contemplate. Although it is now hard to imagine, El Paso was once one of the largest towns in Pierce County. Among other businesses were a hotel, shoemaker, clothing store, three grocery stores, blacksmiths, saw mills, and flour mills.

29.0 **El Paso** and the junction of Co. G with Co. N. TURN RIGHT (SOUTH) ON CO. G. Cross the river and go past the Log Cabin Bar. At the Log Cabin Bar, you might consider going south 0.5 mile to the end of Fisherman Road. There is a private campground on this road. Fishermen Note: Two of the Wisconsin record trout were caught in this area. Consider stopping in the Log Cabin Bar, built about 130 years ago.

Ernie Seifert has been operating the bar since 1937. It is a memorable spot for a cool drink. Continue east on Co. G up the long hill out of the valley.

30.8 Junction with Co. BB. **Note:** For Option D of about 38 miles, turn north on Co. BB for 5.5 miles to Mines Drive. Turn east on Mines Drive for four miles to Spring Valley. This route will take you on a gently rolling ride through pleasant farmland on good roads.

For main route, continue east on Co. G. Dip in and out of a rather steep valley and head for Wisc. 183 past some prosperous looking large farm operations.

33.8 TURN LEFT (NORTH) ON WISC. 183.

34.3 TURN RIGHT (EAST) ON CO. G through pleasant rolling farmland.

36.3 Junction with Co. S. (To go to Nugget Lake County Park, go south here for 5.5 miles on Co. S to Rock Elm. Turn sough on Poplar Hill Drive, cross Wisc. 72, and continue south on South Rock Elm Road to the park.) Continue east on Co. G.

37.7 Start a long, fast downhill run toward Elmwood.

38.8 TURN LEFT (EAST) ON WISC. 72 and ride toward Elmwood.

39.2 TURN LEFT (NORTH) ON WISC. 128 for the beautiful Eau Galle Valley ride to Spring Valley. See Tour 1: Eau Galle River Circle Tour for a detailed log. Simple instructions are: Ride north on Wisc. 128 to Spring Valley.

45.6 TURN LEFT (SOUTHWEST) ON CO. 29.

46.6 Back in Spring Valley.

TOUR 3: *Hatchville and Weston Circle Trip*

Trailhead:	Hatchville Creamery and Cheese Store. Junction of Co. Roads P and PP. To get to Hatchville: From I-94 go south on Wisc. 128 to Wisc. 29. Turn east on Wisc. 29 to Co. PP and then south on Co. PP for one mile to Co. P. Or from I-94, go south on Co. Q to Co. P and then west on Co. P for 1.75 mile to Co. PP.
Distance:	20 Miles
Terrain:	Varied-highlands to hills and valleys.
Highlights:	The Cheese Factory, pretty valley, and great top-of-hill views
Route:	(0.0) South on Co. P; (2.0) East on Co. X; (5.8) **Weston**; (6.2) North on 200th Street (Decker Road); (9.0) North on Co. D; (10.5) North on Co. K; (13.5) West on Co. P; (20.0) Hatchville Cheese Store. **Note:** In log some shortcuts are mentioned.

Starting at the Hatchville Creamery and Cheese Store (715/772-4221) (proprietor is Marie Howe) provides the advantage of good parking and a walk-in cooler you can visit afterward to make your bulk purchases. This store seems to have the lowest prices for cheese in the area. Water and toilet facilities are available.

The route starts in the highlands with great views and then gradually descends through a wooded coulee to Weston. You then circle back over hill and dale with more great views on the way.

Log

0.0	HEAD SOUTH ON CO. P from cheese factory.
0.5	On your right is an old log barn still in use.
1.7	Evangelical Lutheran Church.
2.0	TURN LEFT (EAST) ON CO. X.
3.0	On your left is a log building in a farm yard that looks good as new. Test your brakes; the next two-plus miles are an exhilaratingly fast descent through a narrow wooded coulee.
4.0	On your left for next mile is one of the longest farm fields in Dunn County.
5.6	Junction with 180th Street (Dunkard Road). CONTINUE EAST ON CO. X. (**Note:** For a shortcut of six miles, ride north on Dunkard Road for about 1/2 mile. At the Y-junction, turn left (northwest) on Dunkard and continue on Dunkard to Co. P. Turn left (west) on Co. P to Hatchville. Although part of this route is on a gravel road, it goes through a pleasant valley with fewer hills than the main route. Look for the wild flowers and berries in the ditches.
5.8	Pass **Weston** on your right. In town is a wayside tavern, a good place for a cool drink.
6.2	At T-intersection, TURN LEFT (NORTH) ON 200TH STREET (DECKER ROAD). There are some short, but very steep hills along this road. You may want to walk up if you don't have a third chainwheel.
6.6	Junction with 190th Street (Lemon Hill Road). Continue east on Co. X. (**Note:** For a shortcut of 13 miles, turn left (west) on Lemon Hill Road and then follow Lemon Hill Road northward to Co. P. Turn left (west) on Co. P and ride 3.6 miles to Hatchville. There is one mile of gravel road and one steep hill to climb on this route.)

9.0	At T-intersection, TURN LEFT (NORTH) ON CO. D and climb. Sweeping vistas in all directions.
9.5	Junction with 430th Avenue (Gypsy Hill Road). Continue north on Co. D. (**Note:** For a shortcut of 17 miles, turn left (north) on 430th Avenue (Gypsy Hill Road) and head north and west to 190th Street (Lemon Hill Road). Turn right (north) on Lemon Hill Road to Co. P. Turn left (west) on Co. P to Hatchville. This route offers a beautiful highland ride with good vistas, exposure to the breeze, and the only hard surface shortcut on this tour.)
10.5	TURN LEFT (NORTH) ON CO. K. Playground and toilet facilities. The next 1.5 miles follow steep rolling hills, mostly downhill.
11.9	330th Street (Rolling Road) straight ahead. TURN LEFT (WEST) ON CO. K. (Rolling Road goes straight north to Co. P but is steep and rolling.)
12.5	Irving Creek Cemetery is a good place to stop and contemplate.
13.5	At T-intersection, TURN LEFT (WEST) ON CO. P. This is a rolling route that initially traverses a valley and then climbs to the high farm country on top.
16.0	Pass 190th Street (Lemon Hill Road) coming in from your left as Co. P turns right.
18.0	Pass road leading to the Connell Apple Farm to the south. You may purchase apples and apple products in season. Open latter part of August to late October (715/772-4555).
18.5	Pass 110th Street (Dunkard Road) coming in from your left.
20.0	Co. P intersects Co. PP. Hatchville Cheese on southeast corner.

OSCEOLA, WISC. TOURS

The Osceola, Wisc. Tours begin either in or within the vicinity of Osceola, Wisc. They travel over glaciated terrain, distinguished by level countryside, pockets of lakes, rounded hills, and rocky moraines. Except in the level areas, the routes wind and roll to accommodate the ever changing contours of the land. In the open country, dairy farming predominates. In the more rugged tree-covered terrain, summer cabins and outdoor recreation hold sway. Each tour provides eye-filling scenery and lots of variety.

Tour 1: Osceola Circle Trip -- 19, 26, 35, or 41 miles
Tour 2: The Interstate Park Circle Trip -- 16, 19, 21, or 28 miles

About the Area

How to Get There: About 45 miles and 1 hour drive northeast from the Twin Cities. Head north either on Interstate 35W or 35E out of the Twin Cities and take the Forest Lake exit east on Mn. Hwy. 97 across Washington County to Mn. Hwy. 95 paralleling the St. Croix River. Head north on Mn. Hwy. 95 for about 7 miles and cross over the river to Osceola, Wisc., on Hwy. 243.

Perched above the St. Croix River next to Cascade Falls, Osceola provides a convenient assembling point for bicyclists. Initially named Leroy, after the first white man to die there, Osceola was founded in 1844 by William Kent and several other entrepreneurs from Maine. They built a sawmill here, drawing on the water power produced by Cascade Falls. Legend has it that Kent, in 1855, allowed James Livingston to change the name of what was then a flourishing logging town in exchange for two sheep. Livingston chose "Osceola" after Chief Osceola of the Sioux tribe.

Toward the end of the 19th century, Osceola became a watering hole in the purist sense. Fresh spring waters, laced with a felicitous mix of sulphate and chloride of sodium, were found flowing from springs just south of town. Resort hotels for people extolling the virtues of such water soon sprung up, and for a while, Osceola emerged as the Saratoga of the West. In 1893, Ole Larson opened the Bethania Mineral Springs Bottling Works. By the time the company closed in

1946, the production of Bethania mineral waters and beverages had become big business in Osceola. Today, as a rural residential retreat on the fringe of the metropolitan area, Osceola has mostly reverted to its character as a small river town with a diversified local service economy. There are, however, some special attractions for the venturesome visitor.

At the north end of town an 80 acre estate has been converted into an upscale environmental learning and wellness center - Aveda Spa Retreat (1-800/283-3202), with 10 guest rooms and an organic natural foods restaurant (meals by reservation only). Just south of town, at the historic Osceola Depot round trip excursion train rides can be taken to either Marine or Dresser on weekends and holidays (1-800/643-7412).

Downtown Osceola has a number of stores and eateries. For the browser, Old Mill Shops next to Cascade Falls has special appeal. This store is packed to the rafters with handmade artifacts sold on consignment by over 400 elderly artisans. Also check out Osceola Sports Station which carries the Bridgestone Bicycle line.

Visitors may obtain a brochure at Old Mill Shops that provides a short historical walking tour of Osceola. Included in that tour is the Osceola Inn Apartments constructed in 1917 and known for most of its years as the Hotel Osceola. The hotel was reputed to have operated a "blind pig" out of its basement during prohibition. Also in the tour is the St. Croix River Inn (715/294-4248), an elegant bed and breakfast overlooking the St. Croix River with seven luxurious suites, each with a Jacuzzi.

Schillberg's Brookside Campgrounds (715/294-4248), located just a little north of town provides wooded sites with many amenities including free showers and a swimming lake. A small picnic area in the Lower Mill Pond Park is located across the street from Cascade Falls. About 4 miles east of town is Pleasant Lake Inn (715/294-2545), a bed and breakfast (on Tour 2; Option A) overlooking a secluded lake.

The best of "Ice Age" camping is found at Interstate Park located 7.5 miles north of Osceola off Wisc. 35 just south of St. Croix Falls. The park is an alternative trailhead for Tour 2. Located at the terminus of the last glacial advance, this park provides magnificent camping, nature hikes, overlooks of the Dalles of the St. Croix, an inland swimming beach, a State Fish Hatchery, and, best of all, over walled, lava gorge" cut by the St. Croix River and giant potholes drilled by swirling, water-driven rocks provide dramatic evidence of the powerful glacial forces that shaped the park. Just north of the Park entrance is Amberwood Bed & Breakfast (715/483-9355.)

Two other special attractions outside of Osceola are the East Lake County Park (about seven miles east of town) and the State Fish Hatchery (about 2.5 miles north of town). Both of these places are included in each tour. The East Lake County Park is nestled at the north end of East Lake, a secluded tree-covered area ideal for picnicking (water pump, picnic tables, and toilet facilities). The State Fish Hatchery is located in a park-like setting. Visiting hours are 8:00 a.m. to 4:30 p.m. Monday through Friday and 8:00 a.m. to 3:00 p.m. Saturday and Sunday.

TOUR 1: *Osceola Circle Trip*

Trailhead:	Municipal parking lot in Osceola off Second Avenue behind stores on St. Croix River side.
	Alternative Trailhead: East Lake County Park, off 90th Street, one mile east of Co. MM reached by taking Co. M east out of Osceola for about 5 miles and then heading north on Co. MM for about 1.5 miles.
Distance:	Option A: 35 miles Option B: 41 miles Option C-1: 19 miles Option C-2: 26 miles
Terrain:	Varied with a number of climbs but no killer hills.
Highlights:	Open farm country, pocket lakes, West Emmanual Lutheran Church, East Lake Country Park, and State Fish Hatchery

Route: Option A: (0.0) South on Wisc. 35; (0.2) West on Ridge Street; (2.3) West on 60th Ave.; (5.6) East on 30th Ave.; (11.6) North on 220th Street; (12.0) East on Co. X; (13.6) South on Co. M; (13.9) East on Church Road; (16.9) North on 180th Street; (19.9) East on Co. K; (22.2) North on Co. M; (23.3) East on Co. Y; (23.6) North on Horse Lake Road; (24.2) North on 200th Street; (24.8) East on 90th Avenue; (27.1) South on Co. MM; (27.2) West on 90th Avenue; (29.1) West on Wisc. 35; (29.2) North on 240th Street; (29.9) West on 100th Avenue; (30.9) South on 248th Street; (33.5) West on Co. M; (35.1) North on Wisc. 35 into downtown Osceola.

Option B: Take Option A Route to mile 5.6, then South on 280th Street; (9.0) East on Polk-St. Croix Road; (16.6) North on 220th Street; (17.6) East on 10th Avenue; (18.8) North on Co. M and East on 200th Street; (20.4) East on Church Road; pick up Option A route at mile 14.6 on the Option A log.

Option C: (0.0) East on Second Avenue and South on Wisc. 35; (0.3) East on Co. M; (1.3) South on 240th Street; (2.1) East on 60th Avenue.

Option C-1: (6.2) North on Co. M and pick up Option A route at mile 22.2 on the Option A log; or

Option C-2: (6.2) South on Co. M; (7.1) East on 50th Avenue; (9.3) North on 180th Street and pick up Option A route at mile 18 on the Option A log.

This route makes a short climb out of the river valley on a narrow, remote country road. Upon reaching the top, take in the sweeping views of wide open farmland that dominates the scenery for the next 10 to 16 miles (depending on the option taken). Eventually all of the optional routes converge to twist and turn through somewhat hilly terrain pocketed with lakes and shrouded in trees. On the way, the picturesque white steepled church (West Emmanual Lutheran Church) just south of Pine Lake provides the perfect photo opportunity. The tour then reenters open land, eventually skirts the lapping shores of Horse Lake, and finally reaches East Lake County Park (the alternative trailhead). If not used as a starting point, stop at the park for at least a snack.

From the county park, the trail heads back over a hill to Osceola. On the way, visit the State Fish Hatchery. Note, however, the closing hours stated in the narrative.

Log

0.0	Trailhead: Depart Osceola from Old Mill Shops HEADING SOUTH ON WISC. 35. (Note that municipal parking lot trailhead is about 0.3 mile north of Old Mill Shops at west end of Second Avenue behind shops.)
0.1	Pass under bridge and head up hill.
0.2	TURN RIGHT (WEST) ON RIDGE STREET and continue climb.
0.4	Reach top and head south along ridge above St. Croix River to the west with few views of St. Croix but great views of open farmland to the east.
2.3	At T-intersection, TURN RIGHT (WEST) ON 60TH AVENUE.
2.6	Road makes 90 degree turn to the left and becomes 280th Street, which heads south away from the river into rolling farmland.
3.1	Pass 55th Avenue. Some roller coasting after a couple of miles.
5.6	30th Avenue comes in from your left (east). **Decision Point:** Either (1) turn left (east) for 35 mile Osceola Circle Tour (Option A), or (2) continue south for extended 5.8 mile circle tour (Option B). Option A will be described first.

OPTION A: *Medium Route*

5.6 Junction of 280th Street and 30th Avenue. TURN LEFT (EAST) ON 30TH AVENUE. Road climbs a little.

7.4 Junction with Wisc. 35. Friendly and clean bar, "My Sister's Place" (microwave food), on southwest corner in what is called East Farmington. Keep heading east on 30th Avenue into open farm country with some roller coasting.

11.6 At T-intersection, TURN LEFT (NORTH) ON 220TH STREET. More roller coasting.

12.0 Road merges with Co. X coming in from the north and turning east. TURN RIGHT (EAST) ON CO. X for slight climb and more gentle roller coasting.

13.3 Cross Horse Creek.

13.6 At T-intersection, TURN RIGHT (SOUTH) ON CO. M. At northwest corner is Horse Creek Store, a small Phillips 66 gasoline station/grocery store.

13.9 TURN LEFT (EAST) ON CHURCH ROAD (30TH AVENUE) and soon climb for 0.2 mile.

14.6 Cross 200th Street. More climbing and winding.

15.0 Pine Lake on your left with small sandy access point after 0.1 mile. Good place to wade. Road winds around south end of lake.

16.9 TURN LEFT (NORTH) ON 180TH STREET and climb for about 0.3 mile.

18.1 Road winds past small pond (Lee Lake) on left and merges with road coming from your right (east). BEAR LEFT ON 180TH and begin small climb 0.1 mile.

18.6 Picturesque white steepled church. West Emmanual Lutheran Church (founded in 1870) on your left. Nice place to pause. (Just north of church, a left turn leads to the south end of

	Pine Lake with small beach and swimming area 0.1 mile from turn and to Pine Lake Store, a small grocery store 0.5 mile from turn). Tour goes straight north on 180th with gradual climb. Road passes Pine Lake on your left for 0.5 mile and then climbs through trees.
19.9	Road T-intersects 60th Avenue/Co. K. Martin's Big Lake Store (small convenience store) is on southwest corner. TURN LEFT (EAST) ON CO. K. Proceed along south side of Big Lake and climb for 0.4 mile.
22.2	TURN RIGHT (NORTH) ON CO. M.
23.3	TURN RIGHT (EAST) ON CO. Y and cross at right angles tricky railroad tracks. Proceed along east side of Horse Lake. Road hugs shoreline with nice view of lake.
23.6	TURN LEFT (NORTH) ON HORSE LAKE ROAD and continue along east and north shore of lake.
24.2	At T-intersection, TURN RIGHT (NORTH) ON 200TH STREET.
24.8	At T-intersection, TURN LEFT (EAST) ON 90TH AVENUE and climb 0.4 mile followed by steep descent.
26.0	Road meets 210th Street from north. TURN LEFT (WEST) ON 90TH AVENUE (instead of heading north on 210th) and follow sign to East Lake County Park.
26.5	East Lake County Park on your left. Good place to stop. See narrative.
27.1	At T-intersection, TURN LEFT (SOUTH) ON CO. MM.
27.2	TURN RIGHT (WEST) ON 90TH AVENUE and soon climb 0.5 mile up wooded hill, followed by nice descent into flat farm country.
29.1	At T-intersection, TURN LEFT (WEST) ON WISC. 35.
29.2	TURN RIGHT (NORTH) ON 240TH STREET.

29.9	TURN LEFT (WEST) ON 100TH AVENUE.
30.9	TURN LEFT (SOUTH) ON 248TH STREET.
31.7	Junction with Wisc. 35. Just before intersection, 90th Avenue comes in from your right. An enjoyable diversion is the State Fish Hatchery just 0.5 mile east on 90th Avenue (see narrative). After visit to hatchery, return to 248th Street and HEAD SOUTH ACROSS WISC. 35 ON 248TH STREET.
33.5	TURN RIGHT (WEST) ON CO. M and follow Co. M 1.5 miles to downtown Osceola.
35.1	TURN RIGHT (NORTH) ON WISC. 35 and enter downtown Osceola.
35.3	TURN LEFT (WEST) ON SECOND STREET. (Municipal parking lot behind shops on left.)

OPTION B: *A 5.8-Mile Extension*

5.6	At mile 5.6 on log (junction of 280th Street and 30th Avenue), CONTINUE SOUTH ON 280TH STREET instead of turning east on 30th Avenue.
7.0	Zigzag around coulee and pass through more gentle farm country.
8.3	Ravine (old downhill ski tow) on your right. Nice place to snack. O'Brien State Park is just across river.
9.0	At T-intersection, TURN LEFT (EAST) ON POLK -- ST. CROIX ROAD. Continue east on this road for next 7.5 miles.
11.2	Crest of hill with great panoramic views to the east.
11.9	Cross Wisc. 35 and continue east through wide open farm country for next 4 miles.
16.6	At T-intersection, TURN LEFT (NORTH) ON 210TH STREET. Cedar Lake is 0.25 mile to the east.

17.6   At T-intersection, TURN RIGHT (EAST) ON 10TH AVENUE and descend about 0.5 mile to north shore of Cedar Lake.

18.8   At T-intersection, TURN LEFT (NORTH) ON CO. M AND, 1/2 BLOCK LATER, RIGHT (EAST) ON 200TH STREET. Begin gradual climb.

19.4   Lower Pine Lake on your right. Pass lake and resume climbing about 0.5 mile.

20.4   TURN RIGHT (EAST) ON CHURCH ROAD and pick up Option A tour at mile 14.6 on the Option A log.

OPTION C: *Short Route(s)*

0.0   Trailhead: Municipal parking lot in Osceola off Second Avenue behind stores on St. Croix River side. TURN RIGHT (EAST) ON SECOND AVENUE AND RIGHT (SOUTH) ON CASCADE STREET (WISC. 35).

0.2   Pass Wisc. 243 coming in from your right.

0.3   TURN LEFT (EAST) ON CO. M.

1.3   TURN RIGHT (SOUTH) ON 240TH STREET. Relative flat farm land.

2.1   TURN LEFT (EAST) ON 60TH AVENUE.

2.5   Begin gradual climb reaching top at mile 3.2 and then descend gradually with pretty vistas to the north. For next 3 miles, road roller coasters somewhat with many panoramic views.

4.1   Signs indicating FFA Vo.-Ag. Experimental Farm on both sides of the road.

6.2   Junction with Co. M. **Decision Point:** Either (a) turn left heading north on Co. M (Option C-1) and pick up Option A route at mile 22.2 on the Option A log (and thus save 16 miles); or (b) turn right on Co. M (Option C-2) and head south (and thus save 8.8 miles). The rest of this tour will assume that you took the Option C-2 route and have, therefore, TURNED RIGHT (SOUTH) ON CO. M.

7.1   TURN LEFT (EAST) ON 50TH AVENUE. (Emmanual Lutheran Church sign on southeast corner.)

8.0   Road curves south and begins to climb gradually, reaching top at mile 8.4 with more roller coasting as road again turns east.

9.0   Pine Lake Store (small country store) on your right. Nice views of Pine Lake to your left (north) with swimming area at mile 9.2.

9.3   Road T-intersects 180th Street. West Emmanuel Lutheran Church highlights southwest corner as route TURNS LEFT ON 180TH STREET and picks up the Option A route on the Option A log (thus saving 8.8 miles).

TOUR 2: *The Interstate Park Circle Trip*

Trailhead:	Same as Tour 1.
	Alternative Trailhead: Interstate State Park (just south of St. Croix Falls across from Taylors Falls). Take Wisc. 35 south from U.S. 8 about one mile before reaching park entrance.
Distance:	Option A: 28 miles (19-mile shortcut) Option B: 21 miles (or 16 miles back to Interstate Park entrance. Note that Interstate Park Spur adds maximum of 5 miles to each trip.)
Terrain:	Varied with no killer hills.

Highlights: Interstate State Park, glacial moraine, lake pockets, and East Lake County Park (and State Fish Hatchery for Option B only)

Route: Option A: (0.0) East on Second Avenue and North on Wisc. 35; (0.2) West on Third Avenue and North on River Street; (0.5) East on Seventh Avenue and North on Wisc. 35; (1.9) North on Co. S; (6.6) North on Wisc. 35; (7.4) East on Traprock Road; (9.4) South on 220th; (10.6) South on 210th Street; (12.8) West on 90th Avenue; (13.7) South on Co. MM, which becomes 218th Street after crossing Co. M; (16.4) West on 60th Avenue; (18.7) South on 240th Street; (20.3) West on 50th Avenue; (22.5) North on Wisc. 35; (23.0) West on 50th Avenue; (24.9) North on 280th Street; (25.6) North on Ridge Street; (27.8) North on Wisc. 35 and enter downtown Osceola.

Option B: Use Option A Route to mile 13.8, West on 90th Avenue; (15.7) West on Wisc. 35 and North on 240th Street; (16.5) West on 100th Avenue; (17.5) South on 248th Street; (19.2) West on Co. M; (20.0) Northwest on Third Street; (20.7) South on Wisc. 35 to trailhead.

This tour takes a back road to St. Croix Falls along a rock and boulder invested moraine which parallels the St. Croix River. A few steep short climbs are in route. Eventually you reach the entrance to Interstate State Park. After an appropriate stop at the state park (see narrative), the route then circles back through more rolling terrain (initially along a leg of the state's "Ice Age" trail that follows the edge of the last glacial advance). The route eventually reaches East Lake County Park, a nice place for a picnic. From the park, return over a hill to Osceola.

Log

0.0 Trailhead: Municipal parking lot in Osceola off Second Avenue behind stores on St. Croix River side. (Note that the Interstate Park trailhead entrance is found at mile 7.3.) TURN RIGHT (EAST) ON SECOND AVENUE AND LEFT (NORTH) ON CASCADE STREET (WISC. 35).

0.2 TURN LEFT (WEST) ON THIRD AVENUE (Osceola Inn Apartments on northwest corner) AND RIGHT (NORTH) ON RIVER STREET. St. Croix River Inn on your left.

0.4 On your left is statute of Chief Osceola carved out of a tree.

0.5 TURN RIGHT (EAST) ON SEVENTH AVENUE AND LEFT (NORTH) ON CASCADE STREET (WISC. 35).

0.9 Pass entrance to Aveda Spa Retreat on your left. (See narrative).

1.9 TURN LEFT (NORTH) ON CO. S.

2.3 90th Avenue comes in from your right. (About 0.3 mile east on 90th Avenue is the Osceola State Fish Hatchery, which is also accessible at mile 18.3 if Option B is taken. See narrative.) Continue north on Co. S. For next 4 miles, the road rolls along a glaciated, mostly wooded moraine. Note the protruding rocks and boulders.

5.0 Brace yourself for a couple of steep climbs ahead -- short but may be walkers for some cyclists.

6.6 At T-intersection, TURN LEFT (NORTH) ON WISC. 35. (2.5 foot paved shoulder). Gradual descent.

7.3 Entrance to St. Croix (Interstate State Park) on your left. (See narrative and description of Interstate Park Spur.)

7.4 TURN RIGHT (EAST) ON TRAPROCK ROAD which heads southeast. This is a narrow, wooded road. Amberwood B&B is to your left (West) on McKenney Street.

8.4	Cross railroad tracks at right angles and begin winding ascent.
8.6	Top is reached as road emerges from woods.
9.4	At T-intersection, TURN RIGHT (SOUTH) ON 220TH STREET.
9.6	Road turns east (becoming 120th Avenue).
9.9	Glimpse of Poplar Lake on your left.
10.6	Poplar Lake opens up. At T-intersection, TURN RIGHT (SOUTH) ON 210TH STREET. High farm country.
11.8	Gradual 1.5 mile descent on 210th Street begins.
12.1	Cross Co. F and continue south on 210th.
12.8	TURN RIGHT (WEST) ON 90TH AVENUE for final descent to East Lake County Park.
13.2	East Lake County Park on your left (see narrative).
13.7	At T-intersection, TURN LEFT (SOUTH) ON CO. MM/90TH AVENUE and enter wide valley.
13.8	90th Avenue turns right. **Decision time:** Either (1) continue south on Co. MM (Option A) for the full circle or (2) as a shortcut, turn right (west) on 90th and approach Osceola from the north (with opportunity to bypass Osceola altogether if Interstate Park trailhead was used). Option A will be described first.

OPTION A: *The Full Circle Trip -- Log*

13.8	CONTINUE SOUTH ON CO. MM.
14.9	Junction with Co. M. CONTINUE SOUTH ON 218TH STREET. (In the alternative, as a shortcut to Osceola, turn right (west) on Co. M, and head west to Osceola 4 miles away and save 9 miles.)

16.4	TURN RIGHT (WEST) ON 60TH AVENUE. Road roller coasters somewhat.
17.1	Pleasant Lake Inn (see narrative) down gravel road to your left (south).
18.7	At T-intersection, TURN LEFT (SOUTH) ON 240TH STREET.
19.2	Osceola Lake on your left. Small lake.
20.3	TURN RIGHT (WEST) ON 50TH AVENUE and climb a little topping off at mile 20.7.
21.7	Pass Cherry Road coming in from your right as road enters open flat farmland.
22.5	At T-intersection, TURN RIGHT (NORTH) ON WISC. 35. Narrow, paved shoulder.
23.0	TURN LEFT (WEST) ON 55TH AVENUE. More flat farmland.
24.9	At T-intersection, TURN RIGHT (NORTH) ON 280TH STREET.
25.4	Road doglegs to RIGHT (EAST) ONTO 60TH AVENUE.
25.6	TURN LEFT (NORTH) ON RIDGE STREET which follows the tree line along the ridge above the St. Croix River to the west.
27.6	Road descends with nice view of Osceola below to your left.
27.8	At T-intersection, TURN LEFT (NORTH) ON WISC. 35 and enter downtown Osceola.
28.0	TURN LEFT (WEST) ON SECOND STREET. Municipal parking lot behind shops on your left.

OPTION B: *Northerly Approach (and By-Pass) -- Log*

13.8 Junction of Co. MM and 90th Avenue. TURN RIGHT (WEST) ON 90TH AVENUE and soon climb 0.5 mile up wooded hill. Only the last 2/10th mile is steep.

15.0 Nice descent begins into open flat farmland.

15.7 At T-intersection, TURN LEFT (WEST) ON WISC. 35. AND RIGHT (NORTH) ON 240TH STREET.

16.5 TURN LEFT (WEST) ON 100TH AVENUE. Pass through cattle farm.

17.5 TURN LEFT (SOUTH) ON 248TH STREET.

18.3 Junction with Wisc. 35. Just before intersection 90th Avenue comes in from your right. An enjoyable diversion (if not taken earlier) is the State Fish Hatchery just 0.5 mile east on 90th Avenue. (See narrative.) After visit to hatchery, return to 248th Street and head south across Wisc. 35 on 248th. (**Note:** If bypass is taken, just continue east on 90th for additional 0.3 mile to where road T-intersects Co. 5 which is mile 2.3 on this log. Then turn right (north) on Co. S and head north back to Interstate Park.)

19.2 At T-intersection, TURN RIGHT (WEST) ON CO. M and follow Co. M for 1.5 miles to downtown Osceola.

20.0 TURN RIGHT (NORTHWEST) ON THIRD STREET, a back road into downtown Osceola.

20.7 TURN LEFT (SOUTH) ON WISC. 35. (Parking lot is 0.1 mile further south.)

Interstate Park Spur -- Log

0.0 Park entrance on west side of Wisc. 35.

0.2 Park office.

0.4	Ice Age Interpretive Center on your left.
0.5	Road begins to descend with views of Taylors Falls to the west as road winds downward.
0.9	Turn off to your right (north) to northern campgrounds (showers, flush toilets, etc.) and State Fish Hatchery beyond at 0.6 mile from turn-off. This will also take you to either U.S. 8 and Taylors Falls or St. Croix Falls.
1.1	Dramatic view of the St. Croix River and the sheer lava rock on your right as road levels off and proceeds through rock and boulder infested pine forest with glimpses of the river. Road dips a little.
1.5	Cross creek. Parking lot on your left. Picnic area and path to beach on Lake 'O' The Dalles.
2.0	Road forks to the left to group camp area but bears right for southern campgrounds. Stay right.
2.1	Turn off to southern campground. Turn left for campgrounds. (Bearing right leads to river and picnic area at about mile 2.6.)
2.5	Center of campgrounds. Pretty "primitive sites," some of which are along river. Watch for deer.

TAYLORS FALLS HISTORY TOURS

These two tours begin in historic and scenic Taylors Falls. They are easy biking with many interesting stops along the way. Tour 1 focuses on the rich heritage in Taylors Falls and explores the area's Swedish roots to the west of the city. Tour 2 follows some of the same route but circles back by way of Almelund, Wild River State Park and the St. Croix River.

Tour 1: Taylors Falls -- Center City -- Lindstrom -- 25 miles
Tour 2: Wild River State Park Circle Trip -- 26 miles

About the Area

How to Get There: Taylors Falls is about 45 miles and one hour northeast of the Twin Cities. Take Interstate 35E or 35W north to Mn. 97 exit. Go east on Mn. 97 to Mn. 95 and go north on Mn. 95 (picking up U.S. 8) to Taylors Falls.

While Taylors Falls shows its New England heritage, the surrounding countryside has its roots in the Swedish immigration of the 1850s. Bicycling in this area provides an opportunity to explore both the interesting architecture of the town and the historical Swedish settlements in Chisago County.

A one-day trip could begin in Taylors Falls with breakfast at The Chisago House Restaurant or Logjam Restaurant, lunch in Center City or Lindstrom, and a return to Taylors Falls in time to tour the Folsom House and the Angels Hill District. If you get back to Taylors Falls in time for lunch, the Border Bar is renowned for its great hamburgers.

A two-day stay could include exploration of Interstate Park or bicycling to Almelund and Wild River State Park.

Taylors Falls was founded in 1838 by men interested in logging the abundant pine forests of the area and was officially incorporated in 1858. Until 1856, the only "road" from Stillwater to Taylors Falls was the St. Croix River.

While biking or walking around town, look for the stone walls made without mortar by Swedish immigrants. Tour the Angels Hill district with its historical homes and 1861 Methodist Church. The Folsom House (612/465-3125) is open for tours from 1:00 p.m. to 4:00 p.m. daily, Memorial weekend through mid-October. Taylors Falls has a number of shops, restaurants, and lodgings available. There are five bed and breakfasts in the area: Country Bed and Breakfast (612/257-4773), and Old Franconia Hotel Bed and Breakfast (612/257-0779) both located in Shafer five miles west of Taylors Falls; McLane House Bed and Breakfast (612/465-4832) at the north end of Taylors Falls; the Cottage Bed & Breakfast (612/465-3595), a charming attached guest house (one couple only) on a bluff overlooking the St. Croix River; and The Old Jail Company (612/465-3112), a converted jail house, located at the foot of the Angels Hill District in Taylors Falls. Springs Inn Motel and Pines Motel are both located in town. For additional information on local tourist spots, services and area festivals contact the Chamber of Commerce (612/462-7550).

Center City is the center of early Swedish settlement and was originally an island before the railroad and highway started filling in some sections. The settlers founded the Evangelical Lutheran Church in 1854, and built the present church building in 1889 to replace one which burned. Some filming for the movie *Grumpy Old Men* was done in Center City. The row of historic houses along Summit Avenue were built between 1882 and 1910. It is easy to picture in your mind the stately life there at the turn of the century.

Lindstrom is a larger town with full services. Gustaf's, a gift and antique shop, carries imported gifts, many of them Swedish, and is worth a stop. The house was built in 1879 in the Italianate style but differs from others of this type in the area, being made of brick rather than of wood. At the other end of the main street is a statue of Karl Oskar and Kristina, fictional characters in Vilhelm Moberg's books, *The Immigrants, Unto a Good Land,* and *Last Letter Home*. The statue is modeled after one in the harbor park in Karlshamm, Sweden. The Lindstrom Tourist office is across the street one way and the library and city park the other way. Bus loads of Swedish visitors tour the Lindstrom-Center City area every year.

On U.S. 8 east of Center City is the Eichten's Cheese House, which sells the family's cheese made on the family farm just a few miles away.

Interstate Park is just south of Taylors Falls and has 148 camp sites and a primitive group camp. Canoe launching, boat trips, picnic facilities, nature walks, and interpretive services are available. The view of the river from the hill south of the park is spectacular. In 1988, new trails to the famous "pot holes" were opened, and research and restoration are continuing. These pot holes are among the deepest in the world, and together with the cliffs and other geological aspects make the park well worth a stop. Ranger information and self-guided walk brochures are available at park headquarters. Boat cruises on the St. Croix and recreational parks such as Wild Mountain are other local attractions. The Wisconsin section of Interstate Park has equally fine facilities.

Camping facilities are also found at Wild River State Park (612/583-2125) 14 miles north of Taylors Falls. Good hiking is available on 135 miles of trails, and naturalist programs are featured. Camp Waub-O-Jeeg (612/465-5721) two miles north of Taylors Falls has secluded sites overlooking the St. Croix. Both campgrounds are on Tour 2.

There is more bicycling available in the area but much of it includes portions on gravel which could be difficult. Information and Logger Bicycle Rental are at the Chamber of Commerce in Taylors Falls. Two nearby tours in Wisconsin are described in the Osceola Tours chapter.

Think of the early settlers with all of their worldly belongings making their way across these wooded lands on foot or with their ox carts. It makes bicycling seem like a speedy way of travel.

TOUR 1: *Taylors Falls -- Center City -- Lindstrom*

Trailhead:	Junction of Main and First Street in downtown Taylors Falls. Parking lots in the area.
Distance:	25 miles
Terrain:	Anyway you go out of Taylors Falls is uphill, but once up, the roads vary from level to slightly rolling.
Highlights:	Taylors Falls architecture, Angels Hill District, Folsom House, Karl Oskar and Kristina statutes, and Eichten's Cheese House.
Route:	(0.0) West on First Street, South on Government Road, West on Plateau Street, and West on First Street (Co. 20); (8.6) South on Co. 12; (10.8) South on Co. 9 and South on Summit Avenue -- **Center City:** (12.1) East on U.S. 8; (12.6) South on Co. 26; (17.7) North on Mn. 95; (21.5) East on U.S. 8; (25.0) Taylors Falls -- Trailhead.

This is a route on which you should take your time as there are so many things to see and explore. Imagine being an early Swedish settler or a New England lumberman as you bike.

Log

0.0 Beginning at the stop sign on Main and First Streets in Taylors Falls, TURN WEST ON FIRST STREET UP A HILL FOR ONE BLOCK AND THEN TURN LEFT ON GOVERNMENT ROAD. This takes you past the old jail, now a bed and breakfast, past the old depot, and past the oldest school house in Minnesota. Continue up the hill to the Folsom House and the 1861 Methodist Church. (See narrative). Ahead and to the right is the Angels Hill district of historic homes. Take time to bike around several of these blocks and look at the New England style architecture of these homes built before 1900. Cross Basil Street and TURN LEFT (WEST) ONTO PLATEAU STREET. At T-intersection, TURN LEFT (WEST) ON FIRST STREET (CO. 20).

1.0 At junction of Co. Roads 20 and 82 at First Street and Chestnut Street, TURN RIGHT (NORTH) ON CHESTNUT, staying on Co. 20. The road goes out of town through some wooded land and then heads west through farmland. Slightly rolling terrain and good road for the next 10 miles.

5.0 Pass Co. 21 coming in from your left. Stay on Co. 20. (For a short-cut, turn left (south) on Co. 21 to Shafer and return to Taylors Falls on U.S. 8 and Mn. 95 or continue south and join the main route at the junction with Co. 26.)

6.0 Shafer Town Hall on your left.

8.8 TURN LEFT (SOUTH) ON CO. 12. On your left is the old Furuby school house, an early center of Swedish life for settlers from Furuby Parish in Smaland, Sweden.

10.8 At T-intersection, TURN LEFT (SOUTH) ON CO. 9 which is soon joined by Co. 37/82 coming in from the left as Co. 9 turns right. Continue south and enter the village of Center City. North Center Lake is on your right. On your left is the Evangelical Lutheran Church and the row of historic houses. (See narrative.)

11.8 **Downtown Center City** is ahead and to your left. TURN LEFT (EAST) ON SUMMIT AVENUE. It leads through what there is of the downtown area to junction with U.S. 8 at east end of town. Country Squire Bar and County Seat Restaurant.

Lindstrom Spur: Mile 0 -- Continue south on Co. 9 to junction with U.S. 8. Turn right (west) on paved shoulder or on bike path on U.S. 8. Mile 1.2 -- **Lindstrom**. Gustaf Anderson's old house, gift and antique shop, and adjoining Christmas store are to your left. (See narrative.) Further on to your right is Shorty's Cycle & Hobby Shop. Toward the west end of the business district at mile 1.7 is the statue of

Karl Oskar and Kristina. (See narrative.) There is a park here but no public access to South Lindstrom Lake at this point. When entering or leaving Lindstrom, it is possible to avoid some of the downtown traffic by using St. Croix Avenue and Newell Avenue, south of the main street. Retrace pedals to Center City and junction of U.S. 8 and Summit Avenue for three and a half mile trip.

12. Junction of U.S. 8 and Summit Avenue. TURN LEFT (EAST) ON THE PAVED SHOULDER OF U.S. 8. Continue east on U.S. 8 until the junction with Co. 26.

12.6 TURN RIGHT (SOUTH) ON CO. 26. Pass Hazelden, world-famous drug addiction treatment center, on your right. Nice, easy rolling terrain with marshes, ponds, and farmland for next five miles.

Eichten's Cheese Shop Spur: Continue straight ahead (east) on U.S. 8 for 1.3 miles to the Cheese Shop on your left. Tour the cheese factory, buy an assortment of meats and cheeses, and look at one of the largest buffalo farms in Minnesota. Continue 1.2 miles further east on U.S. 8 and turn right (south) on Co. 21. Continue 2.3 miles to Co. 26, turn left (south) and rejoin main route, adding 1.7 miles to the trip.

15.6 Pleasant Valley Orchards on your left (northeast) just beyond intersection with Co. 21.

17.7 At T-intersection, TURN LEFT (NORTH) ON MN. 95. Wide paved shoulder.

21.5 At T-intersection, TURN RIGHT (EAST) ON U.S. 8. Wide paved shoulder. John Henry's Farm selling apples and farm produce on your left.

22.5 Beautiful views of the St. Croix. Long descent along the river valley.

23.9 Interstate Park (see narrative.)

25.0 Taylors Falls

TOUR 2: *Wild River State Park Circle Trip*

Trailhead:	Same as Tour 1
Distance:	26 miles
Terrain:	After the hill out of Taylors Falls, level to slightly rolling.
Highlights:	Almelund, Wild River State Park, Wild Mountain Recreation Area, and St. Croix River
Route:	(0.0) West on First Street, South on Government Road, West on Plateau Street, and West on First Street (Co. 20); (9.0) North on Co. 12; (14.0) **Almelund;** (14.5) East on Co. 16; (26.0) South on Mn. 95; (26.5) Taylors Falls -- Trailhead.

While this tour begins the same was as Tour 1, the finish is very different. More wilderness and more wooded areas highlight the second half of this trip. Following the St. Croix River, gives you an opportunity to watch for wildlife and the occasional bald eagle.

Log

0.0 From downtown Taylors Falls FOLLOW CO. 20 WEST. The road goes steeply uphill from town but then levels off and takes you through woods and farmland. See Log for Tour 1 for alternative route through Angels Hill District to Co. 20 and for notes on this part of the route. Stay on Co. 20 until junction with Co. 12.

8.8 TURN NORTH (RIGHT) ON CO. 12. More flat farmland.

13.5 Seasoned With Love Antiques on your right.

14.0 Cross St. Croix Trail (Mn. 95). Village of Almelund, settled by the Swedish. Talk to the locals about the history. Visit

Amador Heritage Center (open 1st and 3rd Sunday afternoons - June to September.) Another attraction is Emmanuel Lutheran Church (built in 1887). Rod's Country Corners has groceries, meats, and picnic supplies. (During October check out the popular Halloween display of hobgoblins in the front yard of the Halbert's house at the southwest corner of the intersection.)

14.5   Co. 12 goes straight ahead 2.5 miles to Wild River State Park. (See narrative.) If you are not stopping at the park, TURN RIGHT (EAST) ON CO. 16. Rolling hills, wooded areas. State park land on north side of road. Swedish immigrants settled along this road during the 1870s and 1880s.

17.0   Begin nice descent into St. Croix River Valley.

17.5   Road follows St. Croix River, with intermittent views of the river and bluffs on the Wisconsin side.

19.0   Wild Mountain Ski and recreation area on your right. Giant water slide, picnic and fast food facilities.

21.0   Road begins gentle climb topped with magnificent view of river valley. Note the modern wind machine rising above the treeline on your left.

23.0   Waub-O-Jeeg campgrounds on your right.

23.0   Wayside on river side with picnic facilities.

23.6   Taylors Falls Lions Park on your left - water, pavilion and restrooms. Road hugs the river for next mile.

24.5 Merrill's Landing set off by long flood wall. Launch for one way canoe-trips.

25.6 At T-intersection with Mn. 95, TURN SOUTH (LEFT) ON MN. 95. Antowine Trail begins here heading east onto the woods. This is an old pioneer trail used as a hiking path connecting with Bench Street in town.

26.0 Enter downtown Taylors Falls.

NOTES

MANTORVILLE -- DOUGLAS TRAIL TOURS

This tour is a circle trip which combines an easy ride along the Douglas Trail with a more challenging section on county roads. The tour could be started at any of several points. Pine Island is the closest to the Twin Cities, and if you start there, you can be in Mantorville for lunch. It would, however, be possible to begin the tour at Mantorville or at Oxbow County Park.

Tour 1: Pine Island -- Mantorville -- 35 miles (or 40 miles if entire Douglas Trail Route is taken)
Oxbow Spur: 6 miles

About the Area

How to Get There: To Pine Island: About 50 miles and 1¼ hours drive south of the Twin Cities on U.S. 52. Turn right (west) on Co. 11 into Pine Island.

The city of Pine Island has its heritage in cheese making and the annual Pine Island Cheese Festival in June commemorates this tradition. A clean, pleasant town, it offers all necessities to the traveler. It is also the northern trailhead for the Douglas Trail.

The Douglas Trail is a paved state trail constructed on an abandoned railroad right-of-way. It begins with a tree-lined section and winds its way through the farmlands and meadows that surround Pine Island.

The entire 12 blocks of downtown Mantorville are on the National Register of Historic Places, and the abundance of buildings dating from the late 1800s make the town a fascinating one to explore. The town was named after the Mantor brothers who arrived in 1853 and quarried the native limestone for use in their buildings and for shipping to other parts of the state. This limestone has survived and can be seen in the Dodge County Courthouse (the oldest working courthouse in Minnesota), the Hubbell House Restaurant, and a number of other buildings in town. The town's sidewalks are made from boards donated by people from around the country and world and are inscribed with the names of the donors. Tours of the historic landmarks are available. (Call the Chamber of Commerce at 507/635-3231.)

The Hubbell House (507/635-2331) was a stopping place on the Winona-St. Peter stagecoach line. Built as a log hotel in 1854, it was replaced by its present three-story structure in 1856. Now a world-famous restaurant, its decor of antiques and paintings are in keeping with its history. The food is good, the prices are reasonable, and bicyclists are welcome. While in Mantorville, don't miss the chocolate shoppe, a homemade candy and ice cream store next to the Hubbell House.

Other places of interest in Mantorville are the Restoration House (1856), the Post Office (1896), the First Congregational Church (1858), and the Mantorville Mercantile Co. (1856). A number of other old and not-so-old establishments add to the pleasure of exploring history or shopping in Mantorville. The Opera House (1918) has been restored and boasts melodramas on Friday and Saturday nights during the summer and early fall. Call 507/635-5132 for show and ticket information. The Dodge County Historical Museum is located in what was once the St. John's Episcopal Church. The first pastor's wife is buried under the altar. The museum and the one-room school next door are open daily except Mondays from May 1 to October 31.

The Grand Old Mansion, a Victorian home, is open for tours and also serves as a bed and breakfast (507/635-3231). Jacob's Inn, listed on the National Register of Places, is a restored 1905 mansion bed and breakfast located about three miles from Mantorville (507/634-4920). Eden Bed and Breakfast is a Victorian-styled country home located about seven miles from Mantorville (507/527-2311). There is camping in Oxbow County Park at the junction of Dodge Co. 16 and Olmsted Co. 5 or in the 10-site Stussy RV Park in Mantorville behind the bank. The city park in Mantorville overlooks the river and has nice picnic facilities. The Sag Wagon Bike Shop (507/635-5196), across the street from the Hubbell House, is a full service bicycle shop.

Oxbow Park covers 572 acres along the Zumbro River and includes picnic areas, playground, hiking trails, self-guided nature trails, camping, and a zoo and nature center. The zoo houses animals and birds native to Minnesota, most of which were injured and thus unable to live in the wild. The Nature Center offers programs for the public as well as special programs for school children during the school year.

The winding river and encircling hills enhance this attractive setting. For more information call 507/775-2451.

The little village of Douglas was named after the pioneer farmer Harrison Douglass (b. 1825--d. 1909), who owned the land where the town now stands. The story has it that the previous owner was losing the property and offered it to Douglass who had little money himself. Douglass didn't think he could arrange financing, but the owner took Douglass' jackknife as a downpayment. The Douglass family owned the property until 1944. The second "s" was dropped from the name by action of the post office, although descendants still keep two s's in their name. The original Douglass-family farm is west of the village on the south side of the road across from the cemetery. The railroad serving the town began operation on July 4, 1878. The railroad tracks have since been converted into the bicycle trail. The Douglas Trail Center building was once an elevator beside the tracks. It now houses a furniture store as well as a snack bar serving food and drinks to bikers.

The even smaller village of Genoa was settled in 1854 and at one time had three saw mills along the Zumbro River and a population of 800. Whiskey shops appeared in abundance in the early years, but later, due to the action of the Good Templars, the town was run strictly on temperance principles. Presently, Genoa is comprised of a collection of houses but no commercial establishments. The ride down into the valley surrounding the Genoa is worth the steep climb up.

TOUR 1: *Pine Island -- Mantorville*

Trailhead:	City park in Pine Island at junction of East Center Road and Northeast 1st Street one block east of Main Street.
Terrain:	Trail is level. Road through Genoa has several hills with one being quite steep. The rest of the route is gently rolling terrain.
Distance:	35 miles (or 40 miles if the entire Douglas Trail Route is taken)

> **Highlights:** Mantorville, Douglas Trail, and Oxbow Park
>
> **Route:** (0.0) South on Douglas Trail; (8.5) **Douglas** -- West on Co. 14; (10.0) **Genoa**; (13.5) South on Co. 5; (15.0) West on Co. 16; (19.0) South on Co. 11; (19.8) South on Mn. 57; (20.2) **Mantorville** -- turn around; (20.4) North on Co. 11; (23.0) East on Co. 18; (26.0) North on Co. 5; (32.0) North on Co. 3; (34.0) **Pine Island** -- East on East Center Street; (35.0) Trailhead.
>
> Oxbow Spur Option: (15.0) South on Co. 5; (17.0) East on Co. 4 and 101 and then North on Co. 105; (18.0) Oxbow County Park.

This tour can be a one-day tour with a stop at Mantorville or a two-day tour with an overnight at a bed and breakfast or at Oxbow County Park. The trailhead in Pine Island is one block off Main Street to the east and has toilets, parking, and shelters. You're on the trail for the first 8½ miles. After that gear up for pleasant country roads.

Log

0.0   City park in Pine Island at junction at East Center Road and Northeast 1st Avenue. Toilets, parking, shelters, and picnic facilities. Cool, tree-lined trail in the beginning with the Middle Fork of the Zumbro River as a companion for the first 0.5 mile. The trail soon opens up to pleasant pastoral views. HEAD SOUTH ON BIKE TRAIL.

3.9   Enter first of several more stretches of tree-lined trail.

5.3   Cross Co. 3 and south branch of the Zumbro River. (At north end of bridge, a narrow trail leads to river below.)

8.5   **Village of Douglas**. Parking and toilets. TURN RIGHT (WEST) ON CO. 14. This road is smooth with little traffic. Rolling hills, lovely views.

10.0	**Genoa.** Nice downhill into the valley. Steep hill leaving to the west. Might take a walk up this one.
13.5	TURN LEFT (SOUTH) ON OLMSTED CO. 5 (DODGE CO. 17). Mostly flat farmland ahead.
15.0	TURN RIGHT (WEST) ON DODGE CO. 16.
18.6	Mantorville water tower in view. Co. 11 comes in from the right.
19.0	TURN LEFT (SOUTH) ON CO. 11 at V in the road and head into town.
19.8	At T-intersection TURN LEFT (SOUTH) ON MN. 57 and continue downhill into town.
20.2	Mantorville City Park. Toilets, shelters, and picnic facilities. (See narrative.) When leaving, retrace the route to where Co. 11 heads north while Co. 16 continues east at mile 21.6. **Note:** If you want to return by way of the southern trailhead of the Douglas Trail, continue east on Co. 16 to the T-intersection. Turn right (south) on Co. 5, left (east) on Co. 4, and continue east past Co. 101 leading to Oxbow County Park and later past Co. 3 coming in from your left until the turnoff and parking area for the southern trailhead. The distance from the junction of Co. Roads 11 and 16 to the trailhead is 12.6 miles thus adding about 6 miles to the trip.
21.6	HEAD NORTH ON CO. 11. Pass stock farms with Morgan horses on one side and Belgian horses on the other.
23.0	TURN RIGHT (EAST) ON CO. 18.
26.0	At T-intersection TURN LEFT (NORTH) ON OLMSTED CO. 5 (DODGE CO. 17).
27.2	Pass CO. 14 coming in from your right.
31.0	Pass Island Rider Saddle Club on your left.

32.0	TURN LEFT (NORTH) ON CO. 3.
34.0	Pine Island. TURN RIGHT (EAST) ON CENTURY STREET just before Tipco Grocery Store to the park two blocks away.
35.0	Pine Island City Park.

SPUR TO OXBOW COUNTY PARK

0.0	At the junction of Dodge Co. 16 and Olmsted Co. 5 (mile 15 in above log), CONTINUE SOUTH ON CO. 5.
2.0	At the junction of Co. 5, Co. 4, and Co. 101, TURN LEFT (EAST) AT THE SIGN FOR OXBOW PARK AND THEN TURN LEFT (NORTH) IMMEDIATELY AGAIN ON CO. 105.
3.0	Oxbow County Park and Campground. (See narrative.)

ANNANDALE LAKES TOURS

Lakes, lakes, and more lakes are the highlight of the Annandale area bicycle tour. There are 26 lakes within a 10-mile radius of Annandale, and if both parts of this route are taken, you will pass at least 15 of them.

Tour 1: South Route -- 19 miles or 26 miles
Tour 2: North Route -- 6 miles, 21 miles, or 37 miles

About the Area

How to Get There: About 50 miles and 1¼ hour drive west of Minneapolis. Take Mn. 55 to Annandale.

Annandale was settled after 1850 and incorporated in 1888 by a mixture of nationalities relocating from New England. Soon the town became the resort and vacation center that it continues to be today. In the early years, many families spent the summer at their lake homes with the fathers commuting by train on weekends from Minneapolis. Today it is an easy one-hour drive from that city.

Main Street in Annandale has been fitted with wooden awnings over the sidewalks giving it the air of a western town. A mural, depicting early life in the area, has been painted on the sides of the grain elevator. The town provides all services to the traveler. Stanleys Family Restaurant on Main Street offers good small-town home cooking as does Butcher's Choice (Highway 55 east of town).

The old Thayer Hotel (612/274-3371) has been restored in its 1895 origins and offers bed and breakfast, dining rooms, and lounge. Rooms are decorated with period furnishings, and much of the original woodwork and pressed tin walls and ceilings have been restored. The dining rooms are open to the public for breakfast, lunch and dinner.

On the eastern edge of town is the Minnesota Pioneer Park. In this park is a frontier village, including barbershop, blacksmith's shop, post office, and other typical buildings from early days. There is a Soo Line Depot, an early Finnish Lutheran Church, and a one room school. A new Woman's World exhibit building has recently been opened as well as a log cabin and a sod hut. The nature trail passes the park's own maple syrup-making operation. Pioneer Park (612/274-8489) is open from 9:00 a.m. to 5:00 p.m., May 1 to September 15.

The City Park Beach is in town on the south side of Pleasant Lake, while Pleasant Lake-Clearwater Beach is on the north side of the lake. Both have picnic facilities, shelters, toilets and swimming beaches. Campsites are being planned for Pleasant Lake Park.

Camping facilities can be found at Schroeder County Park (toll-tree telephone number 800/362-3667) at the north end of Cedar Lake about 3.5 miles northeast of town (see mile post 31.1 on North Route Log) and at the St. Cloud/Clearwater KOA Campgrounds (612/558-2876) just outside of Clearwater (see mile 16.5 on the North Route log) about 20 miles north of the city.

South of town is an area of farms and lakes settled by the Finnish. French Lake (named for the fur trappers and traders who preceded the Finns) contains Lantto's Country Store and a Lutheran church. The South Route follows the Monticello-Forest City Road in part. Built in 1855, this was the first road built through the wilderness in this area. This route is nearly level and has very little traffic.

North of Annandale is resort country, and the roads are somewhat busier. The Annandale Chamber of Commerce (612/274-3395) has listings of the many resorts and their facilities. Camp Courage for the physically handicaped, Camp Friendship for the mentally handicapped, as well as veterans, scout, and Bible camps are located near Annandale.

Fair Haven is a historic settlement and the site of an old grist mill on the Clearwater River. This area is now a park with picnic and toilet facilities. The Mill building has been preserved but is not open to the public. This is a lovely little spot with shade trees overhanging the mill pond. Fairhaven Village has a store, Lutheran church, and city park.

Clearwater Lake is the largest lake in the area and is busy with fishermen and tourists all summer. Fishing is a major recreation for residents in the Annandale area, and the type of fish vary from lake to lake. Ask the locals for information. Mn. 24 down the east side of Clearwater Lake can be busy, although there are signs warning motorists of bicyclers and pedestrians.

Both routes provide a number of sites for picnics and/or swimming. Lakes passed are: Swartout (Swart Watts) Lake, Albion Lake, Edwards Lake, French Lake, Granite Lake, Skifstrom (Mud) Lake, Lake John, Pleasant Lake, Lake Augusta, Lake Caroline, Long Lake, Mill Pond, Otter Lake, Clearwater Lake, and Cedar Lake.

A one-day ride could include either the south or north route (or the shorter sections of both) and a return to Pioneer Park or to the Annandale City Park for a swim. A two-day ride could include going either south or north in the morning and relaxing in the afternoons.

TOUR 1: *South Route*

Trailhead:	City Park, Annandale; located four blocks north of Mn. 55 on Main Street.
Distance:	Option A: 26 miles Option B: 19 miles
Terrain:	Level to slightly rolling.
Highlights:	Pioneer Park, Mud Lake County Park, pleasant countryside, and lots of lakes.
Route:	(0.0) South on Main Street; (0.3) East on Mn. 55; (3.0) South on Co. 6; (5.5) West on Co. 37; (7.5) South on Co. 5; (11.5) West on Co. 35; (15.5) North on Co. 3; (18.5) French Lake; (21.5) Northeast on Co. 38; (26.5) Trailhead.

The South Route is a pleasant, easy ride through well-kept farmland (awash in alfalfa, soybeans and corn) and past small lakes. Mud Lake (Skifstrom is the other name for it on some maps) County Park would make a good stopping point for lunch or a snack. The proprietor of Lantto's Store in French Lake is knowledgeable about area history.

Log

0.0	Begin at Annandale City Park, four blocks north of Mn. 55 on Main Street. From the southeast corner of the park, HEAD SOUTH TO MN. 55 AND TURN LEFT (EAST) ON MN. 55 (paved shoulder).
1.0	Minnesota Pioneer Park Outdoor Museum on your right. (See narrative).
3.0	TURN RIGHT (SOUTH) ON CO. 6. Pass Swartout Lake and Albion Lake on your right.
5.5	TURN RIGHT (WEST) ON CO. 37. This is the Monticello-Forest City Road -- Big Woods Pioneer Trail. (See narrative). Pass Edwards Lake on your right and Slough Lake on your left.
7.5	TURN LEFT (SOUTH) ON CO. 5.

Option B: A shorter version is available here by continuing west on Co. 37 to French Lake, then turning north on Co. 3, and picking up the log again at mile 18.5. This route would be 19.5 miles long. The area between this spot and French Lake still has many residents of Finnish descent.

10.5	Pass Granite Lake. Public access and satellite toilet.
11.5	TURN RIGHT (WEST) ON CO. 35.
13.1	Pass Co. 4 coming in from your left. (1/4 mile south on Co. 4 is the turnoff to Mud Lake County Park with lake access, picnic tables, nice tree cover and toilet.) Pass Skifstrom Lake on your left.
14.3	Cross North Fork of Crow River and climb a little.
15.5	TURN RIGHT (NORTH) ON CO. 3.
18.5	Village of French Lake. Lantto's Store. Cross Co. 37.

21.5   TURN RIGHT (NORTHEAST) ON CO. 38. Pass Goose Lake.

24.5   Pass Lake John on your left. Many year-round homes.

26.5   Return to Annandale.

TOUR 2: *North Route*

Trailhead:	Same as Tour 1.
Distance:	Option A: 37 miles Option B: 6 miles Option C: 21 miles
Terrain:	Mostly level with a few dips.
Highlights:	Fairhaven Mill, Warner Lake County Park, lakes, and more lakes.
Route:	(0.0) Northwest on Co. 5; (2.0) West on Co. 101; (4.0) North on Co. 136; (6.0) North on Co. 2; (7.0) West on Birchdale Road for Fairhaven Mill Historic Site; (7.2) South on Bluffton Road to Mill Site 1/4 block away -- turn around and head north on Bluffton Road; (7.4) **Fairhaven** -- East on Co. 44; (7.5) North on Co. Roads 7 and 44; (8.5) Northeast on Co. 45; (16.5) North on Co. 44; (17.5) East on Co. 143; (19.3) Warner Lake County Park -- turn around and retrace route to junction of Co. Rds. 44 and 45 at mile 22.1 and continue south on Co. 44; (28.7) South on Co. 144; (30.5) South on Mn. 24; (36.7) Trailhead.

This ride is a little more challenging than the South Route, but there is only one small, steep hill at Fairhaven. Larger lakes on this side of Annandale mean more resorts and more traffic but these roads are still uncrowded. You might want to bring your swimming suit along on this ride and stop to cool off along the way.

Log

0.0 From the northwest corner of the Annandale City Park GO NORTHWEST ON CO. 5. (Paved bicycle shoulder).

2.0 Junction with Co. 101 and Co. 39. TURN LEFT (WEST) ON CO. 101. (**Option B:** A quick six-mile ride could be had by turning right, here on Co. 39 and going around Pleasant Lake, on separate bike path, to Co. 24 at mile 35.2 and back to Annandale on Co. 24.)

4.0 TURN RIGHT (NORTH) ON CO. 136.

6.0 At T-intersection, TURN RIGHT (NORTH) ON CO. 2.

7.0 On the left look for sign noting Fairhaven Mill Historic Site. TURN LEFT (WEST) ON BIRCHDALE ROAD FOR ONLY 0.2 MILE AND THEN LEFT (SOUTH) ON BLUFFTON ROAD to mill site 1/4 block away. Picnic facilities here. (See narrative). When leaving the mill site, TURN AROUND AND GO UPHILL ON BLUFFTON ROAD to Fairhaven.

7.4 **Fairhaven** is on top of hill. (See narrative). TAKE CO. 44 EAST ONE BLOCK where it joins with Stearns Co. 7. TURN LEFT (NORTH) ON CO. ROADS 7 and 44.

7.5 **Option C:** Co. 44 goes east here, and the route could be made 21 miles long by following Co. 44 to Co. 24 around Clearwater Lake and back to Annandale. The mileage log would begin again at junction with Co. 143 at mile 28.7. OTHERWISE CONTINUE NORTH ON CO. 7.

8.5 TURN RIGHT (NORTHEAST) ON CO. 45.

12.5 Co. 145 comes in from the right. TURN LEFT (NORTH) AND CONTINUE ON CO. 45. Slightly rolling road through fields and woods.

16.5 At T-intersection, TURN LEFT (NORTH) ON CO. 44 AND MILE LATER TURN RIGHT (EAST) ON CO. 143 TO

WARNER LAKE COUNTY PARK. Just before the freeway a 0.5 mile gravel road leads into the park picnic area reached at mile 19.3. (Across the freeway is the KOA Campground mentioned in the narrative.) There are toilets and a swimming beach in the park. No camping is allowed, and no motors are allowed on the lake. Turn around and retrace route to junction of Co. Rds. 44 and 45.

22.1　Return to the junction Co. Rds. 44 and 45. CONTINUE SOUTH ON CO. 44. Pass Long Lake on your right.

28.7　Co. 44 turns right (west). CONTINUE SOUTH ON CO. 143. Clearwater Lake is in sight.

29.1　Grass Lake meets Clearwater Lake and the road goes on a narrow bridge between the two. On the other side of the bridge, THE ROAD ENTERS WRIGHT COUNTY AND BECOMES CO. 128.

30.5　TURN RIGHT (SOUTH) ON MN. 24. This road can be busy so be careful for the next five miles.

30.0　Pass road to Clearwater Narrows and Camp Friendship on your right.

31.0　Pass road to Sugar Lake on your left.

33.1　Pass Co. 39 coming in from your left. Road leads east to Cedar Lake and to Shroeder County Park, one mile away, with camping, picnic, and swimming facilities. This is the road to Camp Courage. Clearwater Lake will be on the west side of the road. Pass Guptill's resort.

35.2　Co. 39 turns right (west) CONTINUE SOUTH ON CO. 24 along east end of Pleasant Lake. The new Pleasant Lake-Clearwater Beach Park is west on Co. 39.

36.0　Enter Annandale. Continue to Main Street and TURN RIGHT TO PARK.

36.7　Annandale City Park.

NOTES

MENOMONIE, WISC., TOURS

The Red Cedar river valley and environs in Wisconsin offer some of the best bicycling in the vicinity of the Twin Cities. Lush farmlands, rolling (but manageable) hills, striking views, and rustic communities abound. Located within 65 miles of the Twin Cities, this area provides an alluring escape for the weekend bicyclist. We have included five tours in this area. All begin in Menomonie. The first four tours explore the area to the south, using the Red Cedar River and adjacent state trail as the centerpiece. The last tour circles north of Menomonie through gently rolling farm and woodland.

Special notice for those persons who have the bad fortune to get lost while taking one of the southern tours. It is easy to do if you become mesmerized by the scenery, don't carry a map, and get away from the logged route. Just remember, the area you are in is bracketed by the Red Cedar River (which runs north and south) and Wisc. 29 (which runs east and west) to your north. *Do not panic, don't even worry*, just remember which side of the river you are on (ask someone if in doubt) and ride generally toward the river and north. If you reach Wisc. 29 first, ride toward the river (Menomonie) until you come to the trailhead. You can have as pleasant a ride as anyone in your group.

Tour 1: Red Cedar River Circle Trip -- 8, 16, or 40 miles
Tour 2: Red Cedar -- Eastern Farm Country Route -- 30 or 32 miles
Tour 3: Red Cedar -- Western Highlands Route -- 44 or 48 miles
Tour 4: Red Cedar -- Canoe to Durand and Bike Back -- 28 or 30 miles
Tour 5: Menomonie North -- 10 or 21 miles

About the Area

How to Get There: About 60 miles and 1¼ hours east of the Twin Cities just south of I-94 in Wisconsin at the 41A exit. Take Wisc. 25 into Menomonie.

During the 1800s Menomonie, Wisc., was a bustling lumber town. The Red Cedar State Park Trail begins where connecting railroad lines primarily served Knapp, Stout and Company. During the

1830s, this company grew from a small lumber camp to the largest lumber producing company in the world. Later, when the forests were cleared, the farm country of Caddie Woodlawn took hold, and James H. Stout, son of one of the lumber barons, founded Stout Manual Training School, the forerunner of the University of Wisconsin -- Stout, now attended by more than 7,000 students.

In 1973, the railroad right-of-way was abandoned and established as the Red Cedar State Park Trail. The trail is surfaced with compacted limestone. It extends 14.5 miles from the edge of Menomonie southward to the Chippewa River, along the Red Cedar River. (There are plans to extend the trail, as the Chippewa River Trail, to Eau Claire.) The trail is quiet and secluded and lets one drift along with the feel of the river. Many of us who live close to the trail like to ride it at least once a month to observe the changes in the wildlife and river. It's sheltered enough to be ridden comfortably right up until the ski season. The trail fees are:

- daily $2.00
- seasonal: $6.00

These fees are good for the entire Wisconsin trail system.

To learn more about the lumber baron days, visit the "Romanesque" Mabel Tainter Memorial Building (715/235-9725) in Menomonie. Catton Andrew Tainter, one of the founders of Knapp, Stout and Company, built this ornate fortress-like building in 1890 as a memorial to his daughter who had died four years earlier. Located within the building is a beautiful Victorian theatre restored to its original splendor and still actively used as a performing arts center.

Menomonie's Wilson Place Museum (715/235-2283) offers a similar glimpse of lumber baron life-styles. It has a stucco mediterranean exterior which conceals a Victorian era interior that coincided with Knapp, Stout and Company's period of greatest wealth. Also in town is the Heritage Center Museum operated by the Dunn County Historical Society. The museum contains a number of exhibits of rooms typifying Dunn County homes in the past. Regularly scheduled tours of this building are only available on Sundays and Thursdays from 1:30 p.m. to 4:00 p.m.

Ample lodging can be found in Menomonie, including the Katy May House (715/235-1792), a four room bed and breakfast accommodation (near the Tour 5 route), Anastasia's (715/235-6098), a bedroom-living room upstairs apartment about a mile from the Red Cedar State Park Trailhead, and the Bolo Country Inn (715-235-5596), a family run establishment named after Bolo, a champion black labrador retriever. Here a wake up call is a continental breakfast delivered in a basket, and steaks are the specialty of the house. The nearest campgrounds in the area are private. The Twin Springs Campground (715/235-9321) and Edgewater Acres Campground (715/235-3291) are both located on Cedar Falls Road next to Lake Menomin along Tour 5's Main Route. Further north are two public campgrounds, Myron Park on Co. I north of Sand Creek and Boyceville Airport Trailer Park on Wisc. 78 south of Wisc. 170. About 5 miles west of Cedar Falls is Clear View Hills (715/235-7180), a farm with bed and breakfast accommodations.

There are also plenty of other eating establishments in Menomonie. For breakfast, we enjoyed Main Street Bakery and Cafe for traditional down-home fare. At the Thunderbird Mall (the trailhead for Tour 5), fast food is served at Kentucky Fried Chicken, McDonald's, Dairy Queen, and Hardee's, while sit down restaurants include Country Kitchen, Hattie Maxwell, Pizza Hut, and Cheesy Pizza Factory. While at the mall, check out the small travel trailer parked in the corner of the parking lot. It is owned by the Menomonie Chamber of Commerce and has several useful handouts and maps.

The country roads used for optional trips take you through typical Wisconsin farmland and some patches of woods that were once home to a vast pine forest mostly cleared during the lumbering days. The famous children's book by Carol Ryrie Brink, *Caddie Woodlawn*, was set in this area. By going 0.5 mile north of Co. Y (just two miles west of Dunnville) on Wisc. 25, you can see the historic site with the original house in which the author was raised.

The Creamery (715/664-8354) is a restored creamery building 0.5 mile off the trail in Downsville on Co. C. The building houses a fine restaurant and lounge with a delightful outdoor patio overlooking the Red Cedar River valley and includes four rooms for lodging and a pottery showroom. It's an ideal spot for a lunch break as well as dinner and/or an overnight stay. It is closed on Mondays. At the same time, a visit to the Empire in Pine Lumber Museum also in Downsville shows life in the raw in the lumbering days, in stark contrast to the luxurious life of the wealthy lumber barons seen in the Wilson Place Museum and the Mable Tainter Memorial Building. Near Downsville, 0.4 mile south on Co. C, is the Cedar Trail Guesthouse (715/664-8828), a bed and breakfast at a working farm where the cookie jar is always full, and you will sleep under a wool comforter made from the proprietor's own sheep.

If you are planning an extended weekend, don't miss the outdoor summer band concerts and ice cream socials at Wilson Park in Menomonie every Tuesday at 8:00 p.m. The Ludington Guard Band has been performing these concerts since 1888.

A full-service bike shop, Red Cedar Outfitters, is located at the Red Cedar Trailhead (715/235-5431). Two other bicycle shops in the downtown area are Riverside Bike & Skate (715/235-9697) and Spoke House Cyclery (714/235-1990). The Chamber of Commerce can be reached at 715/235-9087.

Menomonie is an ideal town to explore on bicycle. It's too large to walk quickly and not easy to explore from a car. Ride around the town just for the fun of it. The following is a brief guide to Menomonie on bicycle.

Trailhead:	The Thunderbird Mall in the north part of town
Distance:	5 to 18 miles depending on your wanderings
Terrain:	Nearly level, unless you find the mountain bike trails
Highlights:	Parks, Evergreen Cemetery, outdoor bandshell, University of Wisconsin Stout Campus, river, and dam
Note:	The directions are general and no log will be given so that each person can wander and linger as he or she desires.

Look for the Chamber of Commerce trailer at the mall parking lot, where they have maps and information.

Start south from the mall on the alleys and back roads. This takes you to Sanna Park which overlooks Wilson Creek to the west yielding some exciting sheer drops to the water below. The Parkside Motel and Restaurant, which has a good buffet, is just across Wisc. 25.

Continue south. Plan to walk across the bridge over the dam on the sidewalk. Just to the south of the bridge is the Wilson Place Gift Shop. Turn right (west) on 1st Avenue. This road could lead you over the river and to the Red Cedar Trailhead. For uptown exploring, we will simply use it to by-pass Wisc. 25.

Turn left (south) on 2nd Street. After a few blocks turn left (east) on Main. This route will take you past the Mabel Tainter Memorial Building described earlier in the narration, and by Lake Menomin. Continue east and north as close to the lake as you can ride. Beyond the end of shoreline and 13th Street is Evergreen Cemetery. This has some very pretty riding on paved trails among the old memorials.

Continue east to 21st Street and then left (north) to Point Comfort Park, Beach, and Boat Landing.

To return to the town center, ride south on 17th or 13th to Wilson Avenue. Follow Wilson (west) past St. Joseph's Catholic Church, a modern soaring building, and past the Ludington Band Shell.

South of downtown is the Stout Campus. This area should be explored by bicycle at a leisurely pace.

When you decide to cross the bridge to return to north Menomonie be sure to note the Louis Smith Tainter House just south of the bridge that separates the town. After crossing the bridge northbound, stay close to the lake past the library on Whisky. At the end of Whisky (a short steep hill), go north on Wilson to Pine Avenue. Turn left (west) on Pine to the mall.

TOUR 1: *Red Cedar River Circle Trip*

Trailhead: The Red Cedar State Park Trailhead, located in Menomonie just south of Wisc. 29 and west of the Red Cedar River. From I-94, go south on Wisc. 25 into Menomonie, about 2-1/3 miles, to the junction with Wisc. 29. Turn right (west) on Wisc. 29 and head west about 0.5 mile across the Red Cedar River. Turn left (south) at the second driveway. Park next to the old railroad station. The office of the Wisconsin Department of Natural Resources is just across Wisc. 29. Toilets and water are available in the city park to the east. Red Cedar Outfitters, a full-service bike shop with rental of bikes, skis, canoes, and inner tubes is located just to the west.

Distance: Option A: 8, 16, or 30 miles (stay on trail)
Option B-1: 32 miles (follow the river)
Option B-2: 40 miles (hills and vistas)

Terrain: Option A -- Level
Options B-1 and B-2 -- level one way and moderate climbs, one long climb (or two if Option B-2 is taken), the other way

Highlights: Red Cedar River and valley; bald eagles, pileated woodpeckers, and osprey along trail; Chippewa River bridge; The Creamery; Empire of the Pines Museum; Devil's Punch Bow (Option B-1 only)

Route: Option A: Stick to the trail all the way.

Option B: (0.0) South on trail; (14.7) end of trail -- turn around; (16.4) East on Co. Y; (16.6) North on 510th Street (Hardscrabble Road); (21.8) West on Co. C; (22.6) **Downsville**; (22.8) Southwest on Wisc. 25 and one block later West on Wisc. 72; (23.1) North on 440th Street (River Road); (26.5) Decision Point:

> Option B-1: (26.5) East on 330th Avenue (River Road) and North on 420th Street (River Road); (28.7) East on Co. D and one block later, North on 410 Street (Paradise Valley Road); (32.0) Northeast on Co. P; (32.2) Southwest on Wisc. 29 to trailhead.
>
> Option B-2: (26.5) West on 330th Avenue (Daneville Road); (27.7) North on 350th Street (Calvary Road); (28.1) West on Co. D; (30.8) North on 430th Avenue (Gipsy Hill Road); (33.9) North on 470th Avenue (Wedan Road); (34.3) North on Co. K; (34.7) East on Co. P; (39.8) East on Wisc. 29 to trailhead.

This tour takes the Red Cedar State Park Trail going south. On the way back, you can choose between sticking to the trail (Option A) or taking country roads that generally stay close to the Trail (Option B). Although the country roads involve some climbing, the fabulous vistas on top are well worth the effort.

Log -- Mileage in parentheses is from south to north

0.0 (14.7)	The parking lot at the Red Cedar trailhead.
1.9 (12.8)	Riverside picnic table. Also note the sandstone cliffs along the west side of the trail.
3.0 (11.7)	Enter Irvington, named after George Irving who operated a sawmill here from 1854 to 1882. A bar, with bar food, picnic area in the back, and parking is just off the trail. Legend has it that just south of this area French soldiers cached equipment and gold when they were chased by Indians.
4.5 (10.2)	Road access on west side and good bass fishing.
4.9 (9.8)	Trail crosses Varney Creek where there was a lumber camp.

5.4 (9.3)   Riverside picnic table.

6.6 (8.1)   Riverside picnic table followed by nice shoreline for wading.

7.3 (7.4)   Riverside park bench.

7.9 (6.8)   **Downsville**, named after Burrage B. Downs who ran a sawmill here in the late 1800s. There is a bar with bar meals, a grocery store, and the Empire in the Pine Lumber Museum. Don't miss The Creamery 0.5 mile east on Co. C. (See narrative.) (A shortened version of this tour would be to visit The Pine Lumber Museum and The Creamery and then either call it quits or double back on the trail to Menomonie.)

8.3 (6.4)   Backwater on both sides with farm paths leading to river on the west and The Creamery on the east.

10.0 (4.7)   Several stone quarries once operated in this area. In the 1880s, high quality sandstone was taken for buildings and sculpture.

11.4 (3.3)   A small riverside rest area and picnic table is near Ulmer's Quarry.

13.0 (1.7)   Junction with Co. Y. The town of Dunnville was once located here. For the curious, old Indian mounds can be found by climbing the hill on the north side of Co. Y, east of the trail, and walking in a few hundred yards. Please remember to honor this ancient sacred ground.

14.7 (0.0)   The trail ends at the south end of the bridge which spans the Chippewa River. Suitable shoreline for picnic and sunbath on the north side of river just west of trail. With luck you will be able to pick a few berries by the trail. The trail will eventually be extended to Eau Claire and Durand on the abandoned railroad right-of-way. TURN AROUND and return to junction with Co. Y.

16.4 Junction with Co. Y again. **Decision Point:** Either (1) continue north on trail and return the way you came (Option A), or (2) turn right (east) and return by way of roads which generally follow the river (Option B).

OPTION A: Stay on the Trail

16.4 Junction of Co. Y and Red Cedar Trail. Continue north on the trail and return the way you came. The scenery is equally interesting going upstream.

OPTION B: Country Roads Return Route

16.4 Junction of Co. Y and the Red Cedar Trail. TURN RIGHT (EAST) ON CO. Y and start to climb.

16.6 TURN LEFT (NORTH) ON 510TH STREET (HARDSCRABBLE ROAD). Road is level for a while and then begins to climb.

17.5 Top of hill, great views east and west. Continue on this pleasant "top-of-the world" farm road for next 3.5 miles. The distant vistas and well-kept farms that abut the road make this leg of the trip a gem.

21.8 At T-intersection, TURN LEFT (WEST) ON CO. C.

22.1 Cedar Trail Guesthouse is on your right. (See narrative.) Ride down into Downsville.

22.4 The Creamery is on your left. A must stop. (See narrative.)

22.6 Enter Downsville. Note the Empire in the Pine Museum on your right (see narrative).

22.8 At T-intersection, TURN LEFT (SOUTHWEST) ON WISC. 25 AND CROSS THE RIVER, TURN RIGHT (WEST) ON WISC. 72 AND CO. ROADS C AND Z.

23.1 TURN RIGHT (NORTH) ON 440TH STREET (RIVER ROAD). This road offers glimpses of the river and some climbs to the highlands.

26.5 On your right a roll of golden corn bins mark this spot. At T-intersection with 330th Avenue (Daneville Road). **Decision Point:** Either (1) turn right (east) on River Road. Head towards river, and then proceed north along the river to Irvington for return trip along road that parallels river (Option B-1) or (2) turn left (west) and climb for a return trip that circles back high above the river (Option B-2). Option B-1 is described first.

OPTION B-1: Hug the River

26.5 T-intersection with 330th Avenue. TURN RIGHT (EAST) ON 330TH AVENUE (RIVER ROAD) AND NORTH ON 420TH STREET (RIVER ROAD).

27.4 Good views of river for next 0.3 mile.

28.7 Road T-intersects Co. D. TURN RIGHT (EAST) ON CO. D.

28.8 Just before the bridge, TURN LEFT (NORTH) ON 410TH STREET (PARADISE VALLEY ROAD) which parallels the river. In the alternative, take the trail north from this point. However, then you would miss Devil's Punch Bowl. The distance is about one mile longer by road.

30.0 Devil's Punch Bowl County Park on your right. This natural phenomenon is rather unusual in Wisconsin. A deep horseshoe gorge has been cut from the sandstone by ancient water flows. If you have time, climb down the stairs to the stream below and enjoy the sights. Imagine what it looked like 200 years ago. Representatives of the local Sierra Club, the Nature Conservation Society, and the Dunn County Park Board have worked together to keep this snug vest-pocket park free of debris.

31.3 Paradise Valley Farm on your left. Strawberries, blueberries and pumpkins for sale while in season.

32.0	At T-intersection, TURN RIGHT (NORTHEAST) ON CO. P.
32.2	At T-intersection, TURN RIGHT (SOUTHEAST) ON WISC. 29 and go toward the river one block to the Red Cedar trailhead. End of Option B-1.

OPTION B-2: Hills and Vistas

26.5	T-intersection with 330th Avenue. TURN LEFT (WEST) ON 330TH AVENUE (DANEVILLE ROAD) for a gently rolling climb beginning at mile 26.9. Nice farm country.
27.7	Top is reached. St. John's Cemetery on your left. TURN RIGHT (NORTH) ON 350TH STREET (CALVARY ROAD).
28.1	T-intersection with Co. D. TURN LEFT (WEST) ON CO. D. Spectacular views to north, east and south for next half mile. Pull over and soak in the scenery.
28.7	Horse farm on your right (north).
28.9	Cross Co. K.
30.8	TURN NORTH (RIGHT) ONTO 430TH AVENUE (GIPSY HILL ROAD) and climb steep hill, reaching top at mile 31.1.
31.6	Great views to the north.
32.5	Gipsy Hill turns left (east) while 430th Avenue (Wedan Road) continues north. GO STRAIGHT AHEAD ON 430TH AVENUE (WEDAN ROAD). More great views.
33.0	Steep descent to east with breathtaking views ahead. Test your brakes. Road levels off at mile 33.8.
34.3	At T-intersection, TURN LEFT (NORTH) ON CO. K.
34.7	At T-intersection TURN RIGHT (EAST) ON CO. P and begin steady climb.

35.4   Top of hill and follow ridge line. More great views for next two miles.

36.9   Descend into river valley leaving off at mile 37.2, then resuming descent at mile 37.5.

39.8   At T-intersection, TURN RIGHT (EAST) ON WISC. 29 and one block later turn right again to trailhead for Red Cedar River State Trail.

TOUR 2: *Red Cedar -- Eastern Farm Country Route*

Trailhead:	Same as Tour 1
Distance:	Option A: 30 miles Option B: 32 miles
Route:	(0.0) South on trail; (14.7) end of trail, turn around; (16.4) East on Co. Y; (16.6) Decision point: Option A: Continue East, North, and West on Co. Y; (28.1) **Menomonie**; (29.0) West on 13th Avenue; (29.5) North on Wisc. 25 and block later West on Wisc. 29; (30.1) Trailhead. Option B: North on Hardscrabble Road; (21.0) West on Co. C; (22.0) **Downsville** -- Turn around; (24.1) North on Co. Y; (30.0) **Menomonie**; (30.9) West on 13th Avenue; (31.4) North on Wisc. 25 and block later West on Wisc. 29; (32.0) Trailhead.

This tour follows the Red Cedar Trail south and circles back to Menomonie through rolling farmland east of the Red Cedar River.

0.0   Parking lot at Red Cedar Trailhead. Use log for Tour 1 south to end of trail and back to junction with Co. Y.

16.4	Junction of Co. Y and the Red Cedar Trail. TURN RIGHT (EAST) ON CO. Y and climb.
16.6	510th Street (Hardscrabble Road) comes in from your left. **Decision Point:** Either (1) continue east on Co. Y (Option A) or (2) turn left (north) on 510th Street, return to Downsville (using the Tour 1 log). Visit The Creamery and then double back to where 510th Street T-intersects Co. C. Head east on Co. C for 1.1 miles and pick up Option A at mile 22.2 at junction with Co. Y (Option B). The rest of the log assumes Option A is taken.
16.8	Top of hill. For next 3.5 miles, Co. Y winds through gently rolling countryside.
19.6	White steepled church and Pleasant Valley Cemetery on your right.
20.2	Zig-zag through marshy lowland.
21.4	TURN RIGHT (NORTH) ON CO. Y at the junction with 240th Avenue (Kyle Road).
22.2	Cross Co. C and continue north. (Co. C to the west (the Option B route) returns to Downsville.) For the next four miles, you travel along high farm country with some roller-coaster rides for the first 1.7 miles.
25.9	At T-intersection, TURN LEFT (WEST) ON EAST HILL TOP ROAD (AND CO. Y) AND RIGHT (NORTH) ON CO. Y. Pass old cemeteries.
28.1	Coming into Menomonie. Co. Y becomes 9th Street.
29.0	TURN LEFT (WEST) ON 13TH AVENUE.
29.5	TURN RIGHT (NORTH) ON WISC. 25 AND BLOCK LATER LEFT (WEST) ON WISC. 29 at JUNCTION WITH WISC. 25 and head west across the bridge to the trailhead.

30.1   Red Cedar Trailhead.

TOUR 3: *Red Cedar -- Western Highlands Route*

Trailhead:	Same as Tour 1
Distance:	Option A (Caddie Woodlawn and Eau Galle): 48 miles Option B (Downsville and Chimney Rock): 41 miles
Terrain:	Level one way and on the way back varied with mostly moderate but some challenging climbs.
Highlights:	Same as Tour 1 plus Caddie Woodlawn home and museum and Eau Galle Boat Shop (Option A only) or Chimney Rock (Option B only)
Route:	Option A: (0.0) South on Trail; (14.7) end of trail -- turn around; (16.4) West on Co. Y; (18.5) North on Wisc. 25 to Caddie Woodlawn and back to Co. Y; (19.3) West on 130th Avenue (Flick Road); (21.5) West on Co. Z; (25.0) **Eau Galle** -- Northwest on Co. Roads D and Z and North on Co. D; (28.2) Northwest on Co. C; (30.8) North across bridge and East on 210th Avenue (Bridge Road); (31.8) North on Co. D; (39.0) North on Co. K; (42.9) East on Co. P; (48.0) East on Wisc. 29; (48.1) Trailhead. Option B: (16.4) North on trail; (20.8) Southwest on Wisc. 25 across river and West on Co. Roads C and Z; (21.2) South and West on Co. C; (27.8) North on Co. D; (35.5) North on Co. K; (39.4) East on Co. P; (44.5) East on Wisc. 29; (44.6) Trailhead.

This route also follows the Red Cedar Trail south but explores a pleasant water drainage that parallels the Red Cedar River over the hills to the west before returning to Menomonie. The trip to and from this neighboring valley offers some sweeping highland scenery along the way.

Log

0.0	Parking lot at Red Cedar Trailhead. Use log for Tour 1 south to end of trail and back to junction with Co. Y.
16.4	Junction of Co. Y and Red Cedar Trail. **Decision Point:** Either (1) head west on Co. Y for Eau Galle (Option A) or (2) head north on trail to Downsville and head west on Co. C (Option B). Option A will be described first.

OPTION A: Caddie Woodlawn and Eau Galle Route

16.4	Junction of Co. Y and Red Cedar Trail. TURN LEFT (WEST) ON CO. Y and cross the river. Ride past the parking area and canoe launch spot and begin short zigzag climb out of woods westbound.
18.5	Junction with Wisc. 25. For a side trip to the Caddie Woodlawn Historical Park, TURN RIGHT (NORTH) ON WISC. 25 and go 0.75 mile to the historical marker. The house in this park was the setting for the books *Caddie Woodlawn* and *Magical Melons* by Brink. Also in the park are other pioneer buildings, toilets, a pump, shelters, and picnic tables. After this side trip, RETURN SOUTH ON WISC. 25 TO JUNCTION WITH CO. Y. TURN RIGHT (WEST) ON 130TH AVENUE (FLICK ROAD). (Co. Y goes south). 130th Avenue initially heads west, climbing a little, and then turns northwest for an easy zig-zag climb over wooded hill into the next water drainage.
21.5	Junction with Co. Z. BEAR LEFT (WEST) ON CO. Z.
24.0	Entrance to Pine View Park on the right (west) 0.5 mile further west on the shores of Lake Eau Galle. Picnic area, swimming beach, bath house, but no running water. Continue south on Co. Z.
24.6	Pass Co. Y coming in from your left.

25.0	At T-intersection, TURN RIGHT (NORTHWEST) ON CO. ROADS D AND Z and enter town of Eau Galle. Cross Eau Galle River, TURN RIGHT (NORTH) AND STAY ON CO. D through town (country store and bar at west end) and head north. A stop in town along Eau Galle Lake or at the picnic area by the dam on your right (north) may be in order.
28.2	TURN LEFT (NORTHWEST) ON CO. C.
28.6	Martin Van's Eau Galle Boat Shop is on one side of the road and his solar-heated house on the other. Martin will give a short tour of his canoe factory, time permitting. These are beautiful canoes. On one visit we admired an 18 foot, 55 pound cedar strip canoe with near zero rocker, finished with clear fiberglass on both sides. Truly a work of art. Water and toilet facilities available. Continue northwest on Co. C as it follows Eau Galle River.
30.8	Junction with road crossing river. BEAR RIGHT (NORTH) ACROSS THE RIVER AND THEN TURN RIGHT (EAST) ON 210TH AVENUE (BRIDGE ROAD).
31.8	At T-intersection, TURN LEFT (NORTH) ON CO. D.
33.3	At T-intersection, TURN LEFT (WEST) ON WISC. 72 AND CO. D, GO 0.25 MILE, THEN TURN RIGHT (NORTH) ON CO. D. Enter pretty valley drained by Knights Creek and continue north and east on Co. D for about 5.7 miles.
35.3	Pass Co. X coming in from your left (west).
36.7	Beautiful view of valley bending west as Co. D turns east and begins climb, reaching top at mile 37.3 with magnificent vistas to the south 0.5 mile further on.
39.0	TURN LEFT (NORTH) ON CO. K. Follow Co. K north to Rolling Road.
41.3	TURN LEFT (WEST) AND STAY ON CO. K. This route is a mile longer but has more gentle hills and takes you past a tree-shaded cemetery that makes a pleasant stopping place.

(For those in a hurry and up to the challenge, continue instead north on 430th Street (Rolling Road). You will find that this road is aptly named and that most people will walk up the hills.

41.9 Irving Creek Cemetery.

42.5 Pass 430th Avenue (Wedan Road) coming in from your left.

42.9 At T-intersection, TURN RIGHT (EAST) ON CO. P and climb the hill. At the top of this hill is a triple reward: (1) the scenic views are simply fabulous, (2) for next two miles it's mostly level and slightly rolling, and (3) it's all downhill after the ridge ride for a fast and exhilarating plunge into Menomonie.

48.0 TURN RIGHT (EAST) ON WISC. 29 and go one block to the Red Cedar Trailhead. End of Option A.

OPTION B: The Chimney Rock Route

16.4 Junction of Co. Y and Red Cedar Trail. HEAD NORTH ON TRAIL.

20.8 Trail intersects Wisc. 25 at Downsville. TURN LEFT (SOUTHWEST) ON WISC. 25, CROSS RIVER AND TURN RIGHT (WEST) ON CO. ROADS C, Z and WISC. 72.

21.0 Co. Roads C and Z turn left while Wisc. 72 goes straight. TURN LEFT (SOUTHWEST) ON CO. ROADS C AND Z.

21.2 Co. Z turns right (west) while Co. C goes straight. CONTINUE SOUTH ON CO. C.

21.7 Begin long climb out of river valley.

22.6 Pull over on left with magnificent view to south. (Trail to Chimney Rock is 0.1 mile further up hill on right. Nice five minute scramble/hike and great views on top.) Road soon levels off with spectacular view to the west and then climbs again reaching top at mile 23.

23.5	Road begins 4.5 mile roller-coaster ride into western valley drained in part by the Eau Galle River and Knights Creek.
25.7	Cross Co. Z.
26.8	At T-intersection, TURN RIGHT (NORTH) ON CO. C AND 290TH STREET (HAY CREEK DRIVE) as road begins to zigzag.
27.8	At T-intersection, TURN RIGHT (NORTH) ON CO. D.
28.3	210th Avenue (Bridge Road) comes in from your left (west). (At this point the route picks up the Option A route via Eau Galle at mile 31.8.)

TOUR 4: *Red Cedar -- Canoe to Durand and Bike Back*

Trailhead:	Same as Tour 1 in adjacent park
Distance:	Option A: 30 miles Option B: 28 miles
Terrain:	Option A: Mostly moderate, some challenging climbs Option B: Nearly level
Highlights:	Option A: Same as Tour 3, Option A, except for Eau Galle Boat Shop Option B: Broad valley and high vistas

This is a fun Red Cedar River trip for those who like to combine canoeing and biking. Put your canoe in the river at the park located adjacent to the trailhead. This can work well solo by placing your bike and some ballast in the front of the canoe. Two bikes must be placed quite carefully in the canoe. The river is very pleasant to canoe, with many spots to stop and rest, eat, or take a dip. Downsville, Dunnville (Co. Y bridge), and Durand have fair take out points and

> **Route:** Option A: (0.0) Durand -- West on U.S. 10; (3.0) North on Co. D; (8.2) Northwest on Co. C; (12.8) North across bridge and East on 210th Avenue (Bridge Road); (13.8) North on Co. D; (21.0) North on Co. K; (24.9) East on Co. P; (30.0) East on Wisc. 29; (30.1) Trailhead.
>
> Option B: (0.0) Durand -- West on U.S. 10; (3.0) North on Co. D; (7.0) North on Co. Z; (10.5) East on 130th Avenue (Flick Road); (12.5) North on Wisc. 25 to Caddie Woodlawn and back to Flick Road; (13.3) East on Co. Y; (15.4) North on Red Cedar Trail; (28.4) Trailhead

good road access.

Warning: If you leave your canoe near the river, be sure to tie it securely. The river flow is controlled by a dam at Menomonie. Depth changes of 18 inches in four hours have occurred. We recommend staying overnight in Durand. Motels in Durand include the Blue Roof (715/672-8241) and the Motel Durand (715/672-8149).

Durand to Menomonie Route

0.0 Start at your motel, ride downtown to the U.S. 10 bridge over the Chippewa River.

1.0 CROSS THE RIVER ON U.S. 10 AND HEAD WEST. This highway is quite busy but has good paved shoulders for most of the two-mile segment.

3.0 TURN RIGHT (NORTH) ON CO. D.

7.0 Junction with Co. Z at the outskirts of Eau Galle. **Decision Point:** Either (1) follow the Tour 3 -- Option A route at mile 25 on the log by heading northwest on Co. D (for a total of 28 miles of biking) or (2) follow the Tour 3 -- Option A route at mile 25 in reverse by heading north on Co. Z and return by way of Dunnville (for a total of 32 miles of near-level biking).

TOUR 5: *Menomonie North*

Trailhead: The parking lot at the north end of Menomonie in the Thunderbird Mall at the junction of U.S. 12 and Wisc. 25.

Distance: Option A: 21 miles
Option B: 10 miles

Terrain: Fairly level with many gently rolling hills.

Highlights: The mix of farm and woodland, the hills to the north, power dam at Cedar Falls, Lake Menomin, and Tainter Lake.

Route: Option A: (0.0) West on U.S. 12; (1.4) North on 429th Street (Railroad Lane); (1.8) East on Co. BB and one block later North on 430th Street (Elaine Road); (2.6) East on 700th Avenue (North Line Road); (3.7) North on Co. F; (8.7) East on 865th Avenue (Woods Road); (11.7) South on Wisc. 25 and one block later East on 850th Avenue (Suckow Road); (12.7) South on Co. Roads G and D; (14.0) Cross river on Co. G; (15.6) West on Co. BB; (16.3) **Cedar Falls**; (16.8) south on 530th Street (Cedar Falls Road); (20.1) South on Wilson Road; (20.8) West on Pine Street; (21.3) Trailhead.

Option B: (0.0) Same as Option A to mile 3.7; (3.7) Continue East across Wisc. 25 and onto Co. BB; (5.2) South on 530th Street (Cedar Falls Road); (8.5) South on Wilson Road; (9.2) West on Pine Street; (9.7) Trailhead.

This ride is a pleasant, varied ride over lightly traveled roads in a circle route north of Menomonie. Once you get out of town, you travel north first through rolling farmland, next some wetlands, then east on a wooded roller coaster ride, followed by flat open fields. As the road dips towards the Red Cedar River, pine trees close in, providing most of the cover for the rest of the trip. This mix of farm and woodland with the rough hills visible to the north, gives a pleasant impression of country living. (See narrative about Thunderbird Mall.)

Log

0.0	Trailhead: Parking lot in Thunderbird Mall at junction of U.S. 12 and Wisc. 25. At north end of Mall, HEAD WEST ON U.S. 12. This route soon heads north of town and passes under I-94.
1.4	GO STRAIGHT (NORTH) ON 429TH STREET (RAILROAD LANE) while Co. 12 bears left.
1.8	AT T-intersection, TURN RIGHT (EAST) ON CO. BB FOR 100 YARDS, THEN LEFT (NORTH) ON 430TH STREET (ELAINE ROAD). Two short steep hills lie ahead.
2.6	TURN RIGHT (EAST) ON 700TH AVENUE (NORTH LINE ROAD).
3.7	Junction with Co. Roads F and J. **Decision Point:** Either (1) turn left (north) on Co. Roads F and J and take the full 21 mile tour (Option A) or (2) continue east on 700th Avenue (North Line Road), which becomes Co. BB, and take a ten-mile shortened version of the tour (Option B). Option A will be described first.

OPTION A: The Main Route

3.7	TURN LEFT (NORTH) ON CO. ROADS F AND J.
4.1	Co. J turns left. Continue north on Co. F for long climb.
4.6	You've reached the top. Enjoy the view and then coast down.
5.1	BEAR LEFT (WEST) ON CO. F (instead of taking 480th Street (Rodey Road) heading north). Soak in the wide valley with the rolling hills on both sides and working farms that line the road.
6.0	Begin long, gradual climb to a sheep farm on top.
7.0	Look around to see the view behind as well as in front at the crest of the hill. Coast for 0.5 mile.

7.9	Cemetery on your left and Sherman Town Hall on your right. Continue north on Co. F through marshland.
8.7	TURN RIGHT (EAST) ONTO 865TH AVENUE (WOODS ROAD) (paved back road, but a little rough in spots.) The road roller coasters for first mile, giving a nice view of the farmlands to the south.
9.9	For next 2 miles, the route winds through patches of woods.
11.7	TURN RIGHT (SOUTH) ON WISC. 25 AND LEFT (EAST) ON 850TH AVENUE (SUCKOW ROAD) 0.1 MILE LATER and peddle through flat open terrain.
12.7	Junction with Co. Roads G and D. TURN RIGHT (SOUTH) ON CO. ROADS G AND D as pine trees start to appear.
13.9	The Red Cedar River. Jake's Restaurant, on the west side of the river, serves lunch specials, as well as evening meals.
14.0	CROSS THE RIVER ON CO. G (instead of turning right on Co. D). This brings you to Lands Creek Bridge Park, a good place for a picnic.
14.6	CO. BB joins from the left. CONTINUE SOUTH ON CO. ROADS G AND BB through flat farmland.
15.6	At T-intersection, TURN RIGHT (WEST) ON CO. BB.
16.0	TURN LEFT (SOUTH) ON CO. BB.
16.3	**Cedar Falls.** On your left is the Cedar Falls Country Store (groceries, pop, and pump).
16.5	Cross bridge. Note the power dam on your right (worth a visit).
16.8	TURN LEFT (SOUTH) ON 530TH STREET (CEDAR FALLS ROAD).

17.6	Pass Edgewater Acres Campground on your left. (See narrative). Slight climb ahead.
18.0	Pass Twin Springs Campground on your left. (See narrative.) While wandering along this curving road, consider a stop under one of the shade trees to contemplate the meadows and peaceful surroundings.
19.8	Dotseth Trucking on your right. The logo on their trucks makes them great community boosters.
20.1	TURN LEFT (SOUTH) ON WILSON ROAD.
20.4	Cross bridge over I-94.
20.5	Katy May Bed and Breakfast on your right. (See narrative)
20.8	TURN RIGHT (WEST) ON PINE STREET to return five blocks to The Thunderbird Mall parking lot.
21.3	Thunderbird Mall.

OPTION B: The Short Tour

3.7	Cross Wisc. 25 and continue east on Co. BB. Climb a fairly gentle hill, with a good view of the north hills on top.
5.2	TURN RIGHT (SOUTH) ON 530TH STREET (CEDAR FALLS ROAD) and pick up main route at mile 16.8.

NOTES

LAKE PEPIN EAST TOURS

For the hearty bicyclist, some of the most rewarding bicycle tours in the area are found along the Wisconsin side of the Mississippi River between Maiden Rock and Pepin. Each tour originates out of either Maiden Rock, Stockholm, or Pepin and climbs out of the river valley to converge in Plum City before returning by a different route to Lake Pepin. The high ground in this area has been deeply dissected by several water drainages (Rush River, Plum Creek, Arkansas Creek, and the Chippewa River) to provide stunning scenery in bold relief.

In shimmering contrast is Lake Pepin below, a classic "river lake" created where the Chippewa River joins the Mississippi. The sediment from the swifter moving Chippewa has settled to form a sand bar which has backed up the sluggish Mississippi. Both Maiden Rock and Stockholm have carved out niches next to the high bluffs, which rise just above the upper end of the lake, with each town providing its own native charm. At the other end is Pepin, spread out on the ancient bottom lands of the Chippewa.

Tour 1: Maiden Rock/Plum City/Pepin Tour -- 42 miles
Tour 2: Pepin to Plum City Circle Trip -- 51, 16, or 35 miles
Tour 3: Maiden Rock to Plum City Circle Trip -- 33 miles
Tour 4: The Stockholm Spur -- 52, 43, 52, 17, or 36 miles

About the Area

How to Get There: Southwest of the Twin Cities, about 65 miles and 1-½ hours drive to Maiden Rock; 71 miles and 1-½ hours drive to Stockholm; and 77 miles and 1-3/4 hours drive to Pepin. Take either U.S. 61 or U.S. 52 (crossing over to U.S. 61 on Mn. 50) south to Red Wing. Cross over on U.S. 63 to Wisc. 35 in Wisconsin and follow Wisc. 35 southeast to Maiden Rock, Stockholm, and Pepin.

Maiden Rock had its beginnings in the early 1850s as a steam boat landing for local trade on Lake Pepin. The city was named after the famed rock just a few miles south where Winona, daughter of Sioux Chief Red Wing, made her legendary leap for love of the brave she could not marry. Hemmed in by wooded hills and bluffs to the east and Lake Pepin to the west, Maiden Rock has always been a small river town heavily dependent on tourist trade. In addition to the Water

Front Cafe, drinks and snacks on the small porch next to the Lakeside Bar provides restful conclusion to an all day bike ride.

Initially settled by Swedish immigrants, over the last two decades both Maiden Rock and Stockholm have been recolonized by a mix of liberated urbanites and aspiring artists and crafts people. In Maiden Rock, the Maiden Rock Arts Center (open Thursday and Friday from 1:00 p.m. to 5:00 p.m. and Saturday and Sunday from 10:00 a.m. to 5:00 p.m.) has original paintings, caricatures, sketches, collages, candle sculptures, and pottery on display. Also in town, the historic Mercantile Building offers antiques for sale, and a hardware store exhibits a collection of 400 dolls.

Stockholm provides a number of browsing opportunities within a one block area, including an arts and crafts gallery, a pottery shop, and a jewelry store specializing in hand-crafted jewelry designed around native Mississippi freshwater pearls. Another shop features assorted Amish handiworks. Also in town, the Stockholm Institute maintains a museum and archive to preserve the history of Stockholm and a record of its Swedish heritage.

Camping facilities are available at the Maiden Rock Campground (where a packet boat once brought supplies from Frontenac) or Stockholm's well-developed Village Campground ($5.00 primitive camping fee). For a bit of 19th century living, stay at the Harrisburg Inn (715/448-4500), a four room bed and breakfast on a hill overlooking Lake Pepin at the north end of Maiden Rock. Four miles further north of town is Eagle Cove (800/467-0279), a ridge top bed and breakfast, with four rooms and outdoor spa. About two miles south of town is Pine Creek Lodge (715/448-3203), a two room bed and breakfast located on 80 acres.

Built in 1864, the Merchant's Hotel (715/442-2118) in downtown Stockholm offers three bedrooms with double beds and kitchen facilities. At the south end of town is the Great River Farm (715/442-5656), a 1869 farmhouse with two bed and breakfast guest rooms. For a tasty in-town dinner, we recommend Jenny Lind on Co. J, a cozy basement restaurant open during the day until 6 p.m.

The route along Wisc. 35 from Maiden Rock to Pepin offers some magnificent views of the bluffs and Lake Pepin but unfortunately attracts heavy traffic. The road has recently been upgraded to provide a paved shoulder for most of the way.

Pepin is situated on the bottom lands where the Chippewa flows into the Mississippi. The city is proud of its ties to Laura Ingalls Wilder, the famed children's book author. In the center of town is the Laura Ingalls Wilder Park. In addition, the Laura Ingalls Wilder Society maintains the Pepin Historical Museum, which displays historical artifacts, tools, and Wilder memorabilia. Seven miles northwest of Pepin (along the route for Tour 2) is the Little House Wayside, the author's birth place (1867), where a replica log cabin has been built.

Pepin also has a number of stores, a municipal beach (toilets and showers in adjacent marina service building), antique shops, and campgrounds. A favorite spot for tourists is the Harbor View Cafe, well-known for its excellent cuisine and quaint setting on the harbor front. In the center of town, the Pepin Depot Museum (no fee) takes one back in time when rail and water were the only real links with the outside world. Located in town near the river is Pepin Prairie Winds (715/442-2149), a bed and breakfast Victorian house and Riv-Way Motel and Campground (715/442-2592).

TOUR 1: *Maiden Rock/Plum City/Pepin Trip*

Trailhead:	Downtown Maiden Rock: Junction of Co. 3 and Wisc. 35 (parking west across railroad tracks in Maiden Rock Campground)
Distance:	42 miles (trip ends in Pepin -- drop car at Pepin Railroad Depot Museum on Wisc. 35)
Terrain:	Varied with three significant climbs

> **Highlights:** High farm country, thrilling downhill plunges, and fertile valleys with pleasant river towns at both ends
>
> **Route:** (0.0) East on Co. S; (8.9) **Plum City** -- East on Pine Street and North on Co. S; (13.1) East on co. Z, which becomes Co. X at mile 20.5; (21.5) east on U.S. 10; (21.8) South on Co. N; (22.4) **Arkansas**; (23.0) West on Co. Y; (24.0) South on Lamphere Road, which becomes Plummer Road at mile 25.0; (26.5) East on Co. SS; (27.0) South on Co. N; (41.7) **Pepin** -- North on Wisc. 35 to Pepin Depot Museum at mile 42.1.

This tour starts in Maiden Rock with a climb out of the river valley up a manageable coulee leading to a pleasant romp through wide open farm land followed by a two mile descent into Plum City. The second leg of the trip trails the Plum Creek water drainage through a wide valley before turning east and ascending to the heights again for more wide open farm country. The route then dives into another valley of rich farm land drained by the Arkansas Creek and heads south for Pepin. On the final leg, you pass through Arkansas, thread your way between the Chippewa River to the east and wooded slopes to the west, and then make one more ascent before dropping into Hicks Valley just north of Pepin.

Log

0.0 Trailhead: Junction of Co. S and Wisc. 35 in Maiden Rock. (Parking west across railroad tracks in Maiden Rock Campground.) HEAD NORTHEAST ON CO. S (a steady but gradual climb out of river valley that levels off at mile 1.7).

2.0 Pass Co. H coming in from right. Nice panoramic views of slightly rolling farmland.

4.0 At T-intersection, TURN LEFT (NORTH) ON WISC. 183 AND CO.S.

5.0	Co. S turns right while Wisc. 183 goes straight. TURN RIGHT (EAST) ON CO. S.
6.9	Road begins 1.3 mile descent into Plum City.
8.9	T-intersection in center of Plum City with Co. S turning left and Co. U coming in from your right. TURN LEFT (NORTH) ON CO. S. Hardware store and Grandma's Place on your right.
9.1	Small vest pocket park on your left with pond and ducks. Ingli's Korner Cafe on your right. TURN RIGHT (EAST) ON PINE STREET.
9.2	TURN LEFT (NORTH) ON CO. S.
9.5	Cross U.S. 10. Pastoral cemetery soon appears on your right with cows grazing on the edges. Scenic open valley with tree-covered hills on all sides.
10.7	Road cuts through pretty farm house on your left and barn and outhouses on your right. Look for a jolly pumpkin display on the lawn during October.
11.1	Road begins gradual ascent and levels off on high plateau farmland at mile 11.9.
13.1	TURN RIGHT (EAST) ON CO. Z.
14.1	Pass Co. ZZ coming in from your right.
16.6	Glorious descent along side of hill into another farmed valley drained by Arkansas Creek. Bottom out at mile 17.2.
17.9	Cross creek and pass between two farms. Nice place to pause and behold.
19.5	Pass Co. C coming in from your right.
20.5	Co. X comes in from your left and replaces Co. Z. Small brick church on your right. GO STRAIGHT (EAST) ON WHAT IS NOW CO. X.

21.5	At T-intersection, TURN LEFT (EAST) ON U.S. 10.
21.8	Cross Arkansas Creek and TURN RIGHT (SOUTH) ON CO. N.
22.1	On your left is Arkansas Creek Park - a snug vest pocket park abutting Arkansas Creek with exposed limestone bluffs on the opposite side. Toilet facilities and covered picnic area but no running water.
22.4	Parking lot at beginning of Arkansas Creek Park as road enters small town of Arkansas.
22.5	Archie's Bar on your left. Good place for hamburgers, homemade chili, and some friendly chit chat. Continue south on Co. N.
23.0	TURN RIGHT (WEST) ON CO. Y. The Columbia Heights uplift looms to the west.
24.0	TURN LEFT (SOUTH) ON LAMPHERE ROAD.
25.0	Cross Co. D and CONTINUE STRAIGHT ON ROAD RENAMED PLUMMER ROAD.
26.0	Road becomes gravel for next 0.5 mile.
26.5	At T-intersection, TURN LEFT (EAST) ON CO. SS.
27.0	At T-intersection, TURN RIGHT (SOUTH) ON CO. N. Frankford Town Hall on northeast corner.
27.5	Road begins to roller coaster a little with Chippewa River soon appearing on your left and the sloping hills of Columbia Heights closing in on your right.
30.3	Small picnic area on bank of river.
30.4	Gasoline station on your left with pop inside (if open). (This is the town of Ella).

31.8	Pass Co. D coming in from your right. (Tour 2 joins the route at this point.)
32.0	Cross Plum Creek and begin slight climb reaching top at mile 32.3 as road enters broad farm valley fed by Little Plum Creek.
33.	Picturesque Little Plum Lutheran Church and abandoned church on your left.
34.5	After turning south, begin a gradual climb out of valley, which becomes more steep at mile 35.1.
35.7	Pass Co. I coming in from your right. (A shortened version of Tour 2 joins the route at this point.) Top is soon reached.
35.9	Pepin Hill Evangelical Free Church on your left. Nice shaded trees for well-deserved rest. Steep downhill soon begins, bottoming out at mile 36.9 as route enters more narrow farm valley (Hicks Valley) and heads south for Pepin.
40.4	Wagon Wheels Antiques on your right.
41.3	Enter outskirts of Pepin.
41.7	TURN RIGHT (NORTH) ON WISC. 35.
42.1	Railway Express Agency/Pepin Depot Museum on your right. Good Place to park. Coffee shop across the street.

TOUR 2: *Pepin to Plum City Circle Trip*

Trailhead: Center of Pepin at Pepin Depot Museum on east side of Wisc. 35

Distance: Option A: 51 miles
Option B: 16 miles
Option C: 35 miles

Terrain:	Varied with three significant climbs (one climb if Option B is taken)
Highlights:	Fertile valleys, thrilling downhill plunges, and Little House Wayside (also top-of-the-world views for Option C).
Route:	Option A: (0.0) West on Wisc. 35; (0.4) North on Wisc. 183; (8.4) East on Co. SS; (12.2) Northwest on Co. UU; (14.1) Northeast on Co. U; (17.8) **Plum City** -- North on Co. S, East on Pine Street, and North on Co. S; (22.0) East on Co. Z, which becomes Co. X at mile 29.4; (30.4) East on U.S. 10; (30.7) South on Co. N; (31.3) **Arkansas**; (31.9) West on Co. Y; (32.9) South on Lamphere Road, which becomes Plummer Road at mile 33.9; (36.4) East on Co. SS; (36.9) South on Co. N; (50.6) **Pepin** -- North on Wisc. 35 to Pepin Depot Museum at mile 51.

Option B: Take Option A Route to mile 5.5, then East on Co. I; (9.8) South on Co. N; (15.8) **Pepin** -- North on Wisc. 35 to Pepin Depot Museum at mile 16.4.

Option C: Take Option A Route to mile 12.2, then continue Northeast on Co. S; (15.6) East on Co. D; (16.1) South on Co. D; (21.3) Left fork on gravel road; (23.9) West on Co. N; (33.8) **Pepin** -- North on Wisc. 35 to Pepin Depot Museum at mile 34.6. |

From Plum City, this tour follows the same route as Tour 1. The tour originates, however, in Pepin and reaches Plum City by an entirely different route. This leg of the trip follows a river that provides a gentler, longer, and more scenic climb out of the Mississippi river valley than the ascent out of Maiden Rock. The route eventually passes the Little House Wayside and then after a short wander through high farm country, drops into the Plum Creek river valley. At that point, the tour follows Plum Creek upstream through a lovely valley and eventually reaches Plum City.

A much shorter version of Tour 2 (Option B) doubles back to Pepin just before the Little House Wayside is reached. After making the climb out of the river valley, this route keeps to the high ground just east of Pepin and returns by way of Hicks Valley.

Another variation of Tour 2 (Option C) also by-passes Plum City by first following Plum Creek downstream and then heading northeast along Porcupine Creek through a broad, winding valley. Before circling back to Pepin, the route ascends to the high ridges of Columbia Heights with glorious view both to the east overlooking the Chippewa River and to the west. Unfortunately, the descent off the ridge is on a gravel road which links up with Option A's return route to Pepin just south of Ella.

Log

0.0   Trailhead: Pepin Depot Museum located on east side of Wisc. 35 next to Laura Ingalls Wilder Park in center of Pepin. HEAD WEST ON WISC. 35. Paved shoulder.

0.4   TURN RIGHT (NORTH) ON WISC. 183.

1.3   Cemetery on your right (Oakwood Cemetery).

1.9   Cross small creek. Road gradually climbs out of Mississippi River bottom initially through a broad, well-farmed valley.

5.2   Valley narrows as road continues gradual climb through tree cover and gets steeper at mile 5.4.

5.5   Co. I comes in from right. **Decision Point:** Either (1) stay on Wisc. 183 (Option A) or (2) turn right on Co. I (Option B). Option A is described first.

OPTION A: Plum City Circle Trip -- Log

5.5   Continue climbing on Wisc. 183 finally reaching top at mile 5.7. Nice views to the east.

7.3   Little House Wayside on your right. Covered picnic areas, water pump, public rest rooms, and replica log cabin.

8.1   Round barn tucked behind trees to your right.

8.4   T-intersection with Wisc. 183 turning left and Co. SS turning right. TURN RIGHT (EAST) ON CO. SS and climb a little.

8.9   On top of the world. Rolling farmland in all directions.

11.0   Road plummets 0.5 mile and then levels off somewhat as it enters valley drained by Plum Creek and rimmed by wooded hills.

12.2   Co. UU comes in from your left. **Decision Point:** Either (1) turn left on Co. UU for Plum City (Option A) or (2) stay on Co. SS (Option C). This part of the log assumes Option A is taken. (See below for Option C.) TURN LEFT ON CO. UU and climb a little topping off at mile 12.3 as road traces picturesque river valley.

14.1   At T-intersection, TURN RIGHT (NORTHEAST) ON CO. U and cross small creek.

15.1   Pass North Maple Road coming in from your right.

17.8   Co. S comes in from left as Co. U enters middle of Plum City and merges with Co. S. At this point, use the log for Tour 1 starting at mile 8.9.

OPTION B: Mini-Route

5.5   At junction of Co. I and Wisc. 183, TURN RIGHT (EAST) ON CO. I instead of continuing north on Hwy. 183. Road dips a little as it traverses broad open ridge for next 4.3 miles. (Note: Before heading east on Co. I, you may want to make a side trip to the Little House Wayside 1.8 miles further north on Wisc. 183.)

9.8 At T-intersection, TURN RIGHT (SOUTH) ON CO. N and rejoin main route (Option A) of Tour 2. At this point, use the log for Tour 1 starting at mile 35.7.

OPTION C: *Columbia Heights Assault*

[Note: This route, though spectacular, contains 2.7 miles of gravel road.]

12.2 At point where Co. UU comes in from your left, instead of turning left on Co. UU for Plum City, CONTINUE STRAIGHT (NORTHEAST) ON CO. SS.

13.1 Cross Plum Creek. Road dips a little and starts gentle climb at mile 13.8 topping off at mile 14.2 with lovely panoramic view down the valley to the right (south) and also ahead to the east.

15.6 Co. D comes in from your left and merges with Co. SS. KEEP STRAIGHT (EAST) ON CO. ROAD SS/D.

16.1 Long, steep climb begins.

16.9 Climb ends where Co. D turns right and SS bears left. TURN RIGHT (SOUTH) ON CO. D and ride the crest of Columbia Heights for next 4.5 miles.

18.0 Beautiful view of the Chippewa River to the south. Nice place for a snack break.

20.0 Road becomes gravel for next 2.7 miles.

20.6 Steep descent begins.

21.3 Fork in road. TAKE LEFT FORK as road levels off and winds through a rugged, marshy vale drained by Plum Creek.

22.7 Road becomes paved as valley opens up a little.

23.9   At T-intersection, TURN RIGHT (WEST) ON CO. N and rejoin main route of Tour 2. At this point use the log for Tour 1 starting at mile 31.8.

TOUR 3: *Maiden Rock to Plum City Circle Trip*

Trailhead:	Same as Tour 1
Distance:	33 miles
Terrain:	Varied with two significant hills
Highlights:	High farm country, thrilling downhill plunges, pleasant river valley, and Nugget Lake County Park
Route:	(0.0) East on Co. S; (8.9) **Plum City,** North on Co. S, East on Pine Street, and North on Co. S; (11.1) North on road to Nugget Lake County Park; (11.5) Northwest on Park Hill Drive; (14.1) East on Johnson Road (430th Avenue); (14.9) North on Adams; (15.4) West on Washington Drive (450th Avenue), which becomes Co. HH at mile 16.7;(18.4) South on Wisc. 183; (20.0) West on Halverson Hill Road (390th Avenue); (22.5) South on Oskey Road; (24.2) West on U.S. 10; (24.5) South on Co. A; (27.9) East on East Rush River Road (385th Street); (32.6) Northeast on Wisc. 35 to trailhead in Maiden Rock at mile 33.3.

This tour takes the same route to Plum City and beyond followed by Tour 1. At mile 11.1, however, it climbs north out of the Plum Creek watershed rather than east so that you may circle back to Maiden Rock. The climb runs into some gravel but is well worth the effort and leads to a picnic spot at the north end of Nugget Lake at Nugget Lake County Park. (The park also has 6 miles of hiking rails and camping facilities.) After the park, the route wanders through high farm country before descending down a winding defile into the broad

Rush River valley below for a leisurely trip south back to Maiden Rock.

Log

0.0 Trailhead: Junction of Co. S and Wisc. 35 in Maiden Rock. (Parking west across railroad tracks in Maiden Rock Campground.) HEAD EAST ON CO. S (a steady but gradual climb out of river valley). At this point use the log for Tour 1 until mile 11.1.

11.1 Paved road leading to Nugget Lake County Park comes in from your left. TURN LEFT OFF CO. S ONTO PAVED ROAD AND HEAD NORTH.

11.5 Road forks. TAKE LEFT FORK ONTO PARK HILL DRIVE (right fork is gravel). Cross creek and start gradual, one mile climb. Road is paved but a little rough.

12.3 Road turns to gravel (for next 1.7 miles) finally topping off at mile 12.5. Magnificent panoramic views.

13.3 Road begins to roller coaster a little.

14.1 Road T-intersects Johnson Drive. **Decision Point:** Either (1) turn left (west) onto Johnson Drive and follow gravel road (0.7 mile) for shortcut to Nugget Lake County Park 0.9 miles away or (2) if you hate gravel and want to reach the park by paved roads or if you intend to by-pass the park altogether, turn right (east) onto Johnson Drive. (The gravel shortcut descends through a pretty valley with rolling hills, rising at mile 14.5 and finally becoming paved at mile 14.8. At mile 15, turn left onto Park Drive, pass through park entrance (pop machine) and descend reaching bottom at mile 15.1 ending at parking lot at mile 15.7. A pretty well-kept picnic area is located here at the north end of Nugget Lake fed by Plum Creek. To get back on main route, turn around and return to road on top. Turn left on Co. HH and pick up main route at mile 16.7 by turning left (west) where road T-intersects Washington Drive.) The rest of the log assumes that, instead of taking the shortcut, you

TURNED RIGHT (EAST) ON PAVED PORTION OF JOHNSON ROAD (430TH AVENUE).

14.9 At T-intersection, TURN LEFT (NORTH) ON ADAMS.

15.4 TURN LEFT (WEST) ON WASHINGTON DRIVE (450TH AVENUE).

15.8 Gigantic junk yard on your right.,

16.7 Pass Co. HH coming in from your left (the turn off to Nugget Lake County Park 0.5 mile away).

17.0 Cross Plum Creek. Road dips and climbs a little.

18.4 At intersection, TURN LEFT (SOUTH) ON WISC. 183. More gentle climbing.

20.0 TURN RIGHT (WEST) ON HALVERSON HILL ROAD (390TH AVENUE). For next 2.5 miles, road dips a little through mostly open farm land interspersed with some trees.

22.5 TURN LEFT (SOUTH) ON OSKEY ROAD.

22.8 Descend in stages dropping through a narrow defile and levelling off at mile 23.7 along the Rush River.

24.0 Picnic area on right (with outhouse) next to Rush River.

24.2 At T-intersection, TURN RIGHT (WEST) ON U.S. 10, CROSS RUSH RIVER, AND AT MILE 24.5, TURN LEFT (SOUTH) ONTO CO. A. For next 8 miles, follow river valley south with intermittent views of Rush River during the first half.

27.9 TURN LEFT (EAST) ONTO EAST RIVER ROAD (385TH STREET), cross Rush River, and head over to the east side of valley where route resumes its southerly course on pleasant back country road.

32.6   At T-intersection, TURN LEFT (NORTHEAST) ON WISC. 35. Road climbs slightly as it enters Maiden Rock topping off at mile 32.8 and then descends into center of town.

33.3   Junction with Co. S. End of tour.

TOUR 4: *The Stockholm Spur*

Trailhead:	Downtown Stockholm where Co. J T-intersects Wisc. 35
Distance:	The spur is 6.3 miles and lengthens Tours 1 and 3 by 9.7 miles and Tour 2 by 0.8 mile
Terrain:	Varied with climb out of river valley replacing alternative climb out of valley from either Maiden Rock or Pepin
Highlights:	Same as other tours joined
Route:	(0.0) East on Co. J; (5.8) East on Wisc. 183; (6.3) Lots of choices described in log.

Most of the Lake Pepin East Tours could start in Stockholm. In each case, the tour begins with a climb out of the river valley, which is slightly steeper than the climb from Maiden Rock. At the top, the road winds through high farm country and eventually connects with the route out of Pepin just east of Lund. At that point, you must decide which tour to join.

Log

0.0   Trailhead: Center of Stockholm at junction of Co. J and Wisc. 35. Merchant's Hotel on northeast corner. HEAD EAST ON CO. J and begin climb (gradual initially, then much steeper).

0.7   Pass Co. E coming in from left. BEAR RIGHT ON CO. J and begin steeper climb.

1.4 Top is reached.

1.8 At T-intersection, TURN LEFT (NORTH) ON CO. J.

2.3 At T-intersection, TURN RIGHT (EAST) ON CO. J. Road winds through high farm country.

5.4 Sabylund Lutheran Church on your right. Pretty red brick church with stately steeple.

5.8 In tiny town of Lund, road T-intersects Wisc. 183. TURN RIGHT (EAST) ON WISC. 183 and pass Little House Store on right, a small boutique. No place to eat.

6.1 One Mission Covenant Church on your right.

6.3 Wisc. 183 turns right while Co. SS goes straight. Tour 2 is joined. **Lots of choices:** (1) Go straight on Co. SS and head for Plum City for either (a) continuing Tour 2 which returns to Pepin or (b) joining Tour 3 which returns to Maiden Rock; (2) Go straight on Co. SS and take Option C version of Tour 2; or (3) Turn right on Wisc. 183 and head for Co. I, which is 1.9 miles away to take Option B of Tour 2.

LAKE PEPIN WEST TOURS

The road on the Minnesota side of Lake Pepin, with its wide paved shoulder, offers the bicyclist unsurpassed views of the lake along most of its shoreline. Anchored in the north by Red Wing and the south by Wabasha, two of the Lake Pepin West Tours work their way inland and then proceed along the shoreline to provide an enjoyable mix of steep gorges, serpentine valleys and ridges, and shimmering lake views. Both tours are planned so that you can enjoy the majestic sweep of Lake Pepin in the afternoon as the sun begins to cast sharply focused shadows off the high bluffs in the west. At the days end, each tour concludes in Lake City, midway between Red Wing and Wabasha, providing a fitting finale to a full day of bicycling. A third tour takes portions of the two other tours for a pleasant romp along the lake shore.

Tour 1: Lake City to Wabasha Circle Trip - 26 or 33 miles
Tour 2: Red Wing to Lake City Trip - 20 or 23 miles
Tour 3: Lake Pepin Ramble -- 18 or 24 miles

About the Area

How to Get There: About 70 miles and 1.5 hours drive southeast of the Twin Cities. Take either U.S. 61 or U.S. 52 (crossing over to U.S. 61 on Mn. 50) to Red Wing. Continue on U.S. 61 to Lake City -- 17 miles south of Red Wing.

As the last glaciers to cover Minnesota receded, they left behind a varied imprint in Minnesota and Wisconsin. Perhaps the most dramatic outcome is the broad Hiawatha Valley -- an area of rugged beauty along the shoreline of the Mississippi River extending from Hastings to Winona. This great gorge is the product of torrential meltwater which gradually eroded through alternating layers of durable limestone and crumbling sandstone. Though surrounded time and again by glacial advances, the land through which the Mississippi cut remained unglaciated by the grinding ice flows. Thus, instead of gentle rolling terrain and boulder infested moraines, the great Mississippi River gorge just cut deeper. Today layered bluffs of sandstone and dolomite rim both sides of the river, soaring almost straight up from the valley floor 500 feet below.

On the Wisconsin side of the Hiawatha Valley, southeast of Pepin, the churning Chippewa River emptied its sediment into the sluggish Mississippi to form Lake Pepin -- the widest and longest river lake along the river. In Minnesota at the midway point along the lake shore is Lake City -- a haven for boaters and other outdoor enthusiasts. Lake City is officially recognized as the "birthplace of water skiing," started by Rolf Samuelson on Lake Pepin in 1922.

Lake City's centerpiece is the Lake City Marina where more than 600 boats can be moored at one time. In addition to a municipal swimming pool, Lake City offers three lake front parks: Ohuta near the swimming beach, McCahill Hill Play Park just south of the marina, and Roschen Park (sheltered picnic tables, grills, and rest rooms) at the south end of town. Maps are provided for an historic walking tour with numerous examples of architecture dating from 1856 to 1923.

In addition to numerous motels in the area, Lake City now has three bed and breakfast establishments within the city and another one in the farm country eight miles out of town.

- The Red Gables Inn (612/345-2605), a charming mixture of Italianate and Greek revival, was built in 1865 by a wealthy wheat merchant from Wisconsin. It has four guest rooms furnished in Victorian elegance (gourmet supper and picnic lunches upon request).

- The Victorian Bed and Breakfast (612/345-2167), each room has a view of Lake Pepin (shared bath only and continental breakfast).

- The Pepin House (612/345-4454) includes a queen size canopy bed, fireplace, and air conditioning in each room.

- The out-of-town establishment is Evergreen Knoll Acres (612/345-2257), a 1920s farmhouse on a dairy farm with rooms decorated in antique and country furnishings. (Owners will pick up bikes and bicyclists in Lake City.)

Also in Lake City is the Lake City Country Inn (612/345-5351), with 23 renovated rooms (some suites and jacuzzies) and a continental breakfast to boot. For a list of other lodgings, call the Lake City Chamber of Commerce (612/345-4123).

For a unique dining experience in the English manner, stop at the Chickadee Cottage Tea Room & Restaurant for breakfast, lunch or high tea. If you're a boat watcher, wonder down to Marina Main Deck & Pub for a cool drink on the deck.

Just north of Lake City is Hok-Si-La Municipal Park (612/345-3855), the former state boy scout campground with ideal primitive campsites along the lake for bicyclists. (Tent camping was $8.00 per tent in 1993.) Nice swimming beach. Pop machine but no concession stand. Further north is Frontenac State Park (612/345-3401), offering campers 2,773 acres, campsites (showers), picnic grounds, 13 miles of nature trails, rolling woodlands, and superb bluff views of Lake Pepin, providing front row seats during the annual bird migration. This park is located 1.5 miles east of Frontenac just off U.S. 61.

Wabasha, once the sight of an Indian settlement known as Wa-Pa-Sha's Village, was named in honor of a Sioux chief, Chief Wa-Pa-Sha. Wabasha claims to be Minnesota's oldest city. The red brick buildings that line the downtown business district have changed little since they were first erected at the end of the last century.

Wabasha also features Minnesota's oldest operating country inn, The Anderson House. This establishment has excellent dining facilities (renowned dutch kitchen cuisine) and an atmospheric basement bar-lounge called the Lost Dutchman. Forty "old fashioned" rooms (with a cuddly cat supplied on request as a bed warmer) are available at bed and breakfast rates. The Minnesota toll free number is 800/862-9702. A little apple brandy pie a la mode and hot tea in the afternoon in Grandma's Parlor are special treats for the weary cyclist. For information on other lodgings in the area, call the Wabasha Chamber of Commerce (612/565-4158).

The Kruger Recreation Area (612/345-3216) is 0.5 mile south, off Co. 81 about 5 miles west of Wabasha and only 0.5 mile off the route for Tour 1. It provides 18 primitive campsites tucked in the hardwood forests, 5 miles of hiking trails, and access to the Zumbro River. Also in Wabasha is the Wapashaw Resort (612/565-3341) which has 11 campsites, a swimming beach on the Mississippi, and a restaurant/bar, and the Cottonwood Inn (612/565-2466), a 5-room bed & breakfast in a restored Italianate home built in 1872.

Old Frontenac, established in 1839 as a trading post known as Waconia, was renamed Frontenac in 1859 in honor of Count Frontenac, who had been governor of the North American Territories in 1671. Soon afterwards, Frontenac became known as the "Newport of the Northwest," a fashionable, summer retreat where Minnesota's first resort hotel, the Lakeside Hotel, once stood.

For those who lived year-round in the community, Frontenac was a haven for its distinguished, old-line families led by General Israel Garrard. Many of the elegant homes built by the founders of Frontenac remain in Old Frontenac along Lake Pepin. This small community is truly steeped in a blissful history, eloquently captured in Ivan Kubista's *This Quiet Dust*. When the railroad came, General Garrard reputedly gave the Chicago, Milwaukee and St. Paul Railroad some land two miles west of Frontenac to assure that his secluded hamlet would remain untouched by both the railroad and speculators alike. The new Frontenac thus sprang up around a railroad depot along what is today U.S. 61. It has a gas station, a small cafe (Whistle Stop Cafe), and a country store.

Old Frontenac provides lodging at Chateau Frontenac (612/345-3146), a restored riverside Methodist church camp, with a lodge, private cottages, and family style meals on request. Just south of Old Frontenac on the way to Lake City is Villa Maria, a chateau-like building which was once a convent. The villa remains open as a retreat and workshop center and is still operated by the Ursulin Sisters who arrived in "New France" (the North American Territories) in 1727.

TOUR 1: *Lake City to Wabasha Circle Trip*

Trailhead:	Wild Wings Gallery parking lot south of downtown Lake City on river side of U.S. 61.
Distance:	Option A (Ridge Route): 26 miles Option B (Inland Route): 33 miles
Terrain:	Varied with one significant hill on the Ridge Route and two significant hills on the Inland Route
Highlights:	Ridge Route: scenic crest ride, Anderson House, and Lake Pepin shoreline Inland Route: high farm country, broad valley, spectacular hillside view of Mississippi River valley, Anderson House, and Lake Pepin shoreline
Route:	Option A: (0.0) Southeast on U.S. 61; (0.4) West on Co. 4; (2.5) Southeast on Co. 10; (12.4) Southeast on U.S. 61; (13.0) **Wabasha** - Northeast on Co. 30 (10th Street); (13.4) East on Hiawatha Avenue; (14.0) North on Pembroke Avenue (Mn. 60); (14.4) Northwest on Main Street; (14.8) Southwest on Bridge Avenue; (15.1) Northwest on Grant Blvd. West; (16.6) Northwest on U.S. 61; (16.8) North on side road; (17.6) **Reads Landing** -- Southwest on Ninth Street and Northwest on U.S. 61; (26.4) Trailhead. Option B: Take Option A Route to mile 2.5 and continue South on Co. 4; (7.2) East on Mn. 60, which becomes Pembroke Avenue in Wabasha at mile 20.5; (21.4) Northwest on Main Street and resume Option A route at mile 13.4.

This trip begins with a long climb out of the river valley up through a wooded gorge. At the top, you must choose between the Ridge Route (Option A), which winds along the crest of the bluffs parallel with the river, or the Inland Route (Option B), which heads further inland before wheeling south for Wabasha.

On the Ridge Route, you follow a winding road with many textured vistas of rolling terrain, cornfields, pastures, wooded areas, and inviting vales. The route then descends to the Mississippi and Wabasha further south.

The Inland Route initially proceeds through rolling farm country and then enters a broad valley drained by the Zumbro River and its tributaries. The final assault for this route is a somewhat arduous climb up Greenfield Hill followed by a plummeting descent down Wabasha Hill (with a pull over and a magnificent vista half way down).

Both routes meet at the Anderson House in Wabasha. The return trip works it way back to U.S. 61 and, after taking a side road to Read's Landing, follows the Lake Pepin shoreline back to Lake City for 8-2/3 miles.

NOTE: If you start at municipal parking lot next to marina, use the North leg of Tour 3 to get to Co. 4 and add 5 miles to trip.

OPTION A: Ridge Route -- Log

0.0   Trailhead: Just south of Lake City at Wild Wings Gallery parking lot on east side of U.S. 61. HEAD SOUTHEAST ON U.S. 61.

0.4   TURN RIGHT (WEST) ON CO. 4. Cross bridge and begin long, steady 1.8 mile climb out of Mississippi River valley up through wooded ravine.

2.5   TURN LEFT (SOUTHEAST) ON CO. 10. Rolling farmland.

2.7   Picture postcard view of Lake Pepin looking east through tree-covered valley.

7.2   Pass Co. 77 coming in from your left and at mile 8.2 begin the winding descent into a narrow wooded valley. The road eases

	off at mile 10.1 but still gradually descends as the valley opens up with a view of the bluffs across the river.
12.4	At T-intersection, TURN RIGHT (SOUTHEAST) ON U.S. 61 (paved shoulder).
13.0	TURN LEFT (NORTHEAST) ON CO. 30 and follow Co. 30 (10th Street) towards downtown Wabasha.
13.4	TURN LEFT (EAST) ON HIAWATHA AVENUE.
13.8	Pass Bridge Street coming in from your left.
14.0	TURN LEFT (NORTH) ON PEMBROKE AVENUE (MN. 60).
14.2	Imposing brick St. Phelix Catholic Church on your left.
14.4	TURN LEFT (NORTHWEST) ON MAIN STREET. Ahead at mile 14.8 is the Anderson House on the southwest corner of Main Street and Bridge Avenue.

OPTION B: Inland Route -- Log

0.0	Trailhead: Just south of Lake City at Wildwings Gallery parking lot on east side of U.S. 61. HEAD SOUTH ON U.S. 61.
0.4	TURN RIGHT (WEST) ON CO. 4. Cross bridge and begin long, steady 1.8 mile climb out of Mississippi River valley up through ravine.
2.5	Pass Co. 10 coming in from your left. For next 4.5 miles Co. 4 roller coasters through wide open farm country.
7.2	TURN LEFT (EAST) ON MN. 60. Begin gradual climb.
8.8	Top reached. Begin winding descent through wooded defile that bottoms at mile 10.5. Broad, level valley, drained by Zumbro River and its tributaries, unfolds for next 6 miles.

14.0	Dumphrey's Restaurant on your right. Clean, attractive restaurant. Good place for a break.
16.9	Pass Co. 81 coming in from your right. Kruger Campground and Recreation Area next to Co. 81, 0.5 mile away. Begin tough climb, reaching the top at mile 17.7.
18.7	Pass Skyline Drive coming in from your left. (A left turn onto Skyline Drive and 0.5 mile ride along ridge leads to Coffee Mill Golf and Country Club-Bar and Lounge.) Begin 1.5 mile descent.
18.8	Pass gravel road coming in from your right and leading to Arrowhead Bluffs Exhibits 0.8 mile south. Local native displays. There is a $3.25 charge per adult to see the exhibit.
19.2	Magnificent scenic overlook on your right showing Mississippi River bottom and rising bluffs on east side of river. Winding descent continues.
20.2	Long downhill descent ends.
20.5	CROSS U.S. 61 AND STAY ON MN. 60 (PEMBROKE AVENUE).
21.4	TURN LEFT (NORTHEAST) ON MAIN STREET. Anderson House is ahead on left side of Main at mile 21.6.

OPTIONS A AND B: Return Trip from Anderson House in Wabasha

0.0	Junction of Main Street and Bridge Avenue with Anderson House on southwest corner. Clustered next door on both side of Main are two trim houses with tempting craft shops ("Just for You" on east side and "Country Bouquet" on west side). For trip back to Lake City, TURN LEFT (SOUTHWEST) ON BRIDGE AVENUE.
0.3	TURN RIGHT (NORTHWEST) ON CO. 59 (GRANT BOULEVARD WEST).

0.6	Cross tracks. Stay on Grant.
0.9	St. Elizabeth Hospital and Nursing Home on your right.
1.6	Cross dangerous railroad tracks at right angle.
1.8	At T-intersection, TURN RIGHT (NORTHWEST) ON U.S. 61 which has paved shoulder.
2.0	TURN RIGHT (NORTH) ON CO. 77 that comes in at angle from north.
2.6	Nice views of river as road leads into Read's Landing.
2.8	**Reads Landing.** Way station for migrating eagles in November. TURN LEFT (SOUTHWEST) ON NINTH AVENUE.
2.9	Road intersects U.S. 61. Just across road on Co. 77 is the Wabasha County Historical Society Museum (open Saturday and Sunday from 1:0 p.m. to 5:00 p.m.). The building that houses the museum was built in 1870 as Read's Landing School. TURN RIGHT (NORTHWEST) ON U.S. 61. Countless views of Lake Pepin on east side of U.S. 61 for next 8.5 miles.
4.4	Turn off for scenic overlook of lake.
5.4	Another scenic overlook.
11.2	Pass Co. 4 coming in from your left (west).
11.6	Wildwings Gallery on your right -- Trailhead.

TOUR 2: *Red Wing to Lake City Trip*

Trailhead:	Either Red Wing trailhead for Cannon River Trail (north end of downtown 0.1 mile east of U.S. 61 at Bench Street turnoff) or St. James Hotel at intersection of Main and Bush Streets.
Distance:	23 miles (or 20 miles if St. James Hotel shortcut is taken). One-way route.
Terrain:	Varied with two significant hills.
Highlights:	High farm country, broad river valley, Frontenac State Park, Old Frontenac, and Lake City Marina.
Route:	(0.0) South on Bench Street and East on U.S. 61; (0.2) South on Co. 1 (Bench Street); (0.6) East on Pioneer Road (Co. 66); (3.9) South on Mn. 58; (5.3) Southeast on Co. 5; (10.1) Northeast on Co. 2; (14.8) **Frontenac;** (16.3) **Old Frontenac;** (18.1) Southwest on U.S. 61; (22.7) **Lake City** -- East on North Park Street; (23.3) to parking lot next to marina.

This tour ends 17 miles south of Red Wing in Lake City. A car should, therefore, be dropped at the municipal parking lot next to the Lake City Marina. The tour first heads inland by climbing out of the river valley into the high farm country above Red Wing, turns south, and then works its way back to the Mississippi through a broad river valley drained by Wells Creek. After passing through Frontenac and then Old Frontenac on the river, the route heads south and eventually reaches Lake Pepin for a shoreline ride into Lake City.

Log

0.0 Trailhead: Cannon River Trail (north end of downtown Red Wing 0.1 mile east of U.S. 61 at Bench Street turnoff). (Note: there is parking at the trailhead.) (Alternative Trailhead: St. James Hotel at junction of Bush and Main Streets. Head south on Bush which merges with Mn. 58 and picks up trip where Pioneer Road T-intersects Mn. 58 at mile 3.9. Saves about 3 miles.) HEAD SOUTH ON BENCH AND TURN LEFT (EAST) ON U.S. 61.

0.2 TURN RIGHT (SOUTH) ON CO. 1 (BENCH STREET).

0.6 TURN LEFT (EAST) ON PIONEER ROAD (CO. 66).

1.3 Cross bridge and begin easy climb reaching top at mile 1.7.

2.5 Cross Twin Bluff Road.

2.8 Begin gradual ascent which gets steeper at mile 3.3 and tops off at mile 3.7.

3.9 At T-intersection, TURN RIGHT (SOUTH) ON MN. 58. Busy road. Casey's General Store and Gasoline Station on southwest corner.

4.9 Hay Creek Valley Saddle Club on your right.

5.3 Mn. 58 bears right while Co. 5 turns left. TURN LEFT (SOUTHEAST) ON CO. 5. Large AT&T radio tower dead ahead (for landmark). Road climbs a little, reaching top at mile 5.6. Rolling countryside ahead. Great pastoral scenes.

6.8 Steep winding descent through wooded valley begins.

8.2 Bottom is reached. Co. 5 merges with Co. 45.

8.8 Co. 45 turns left. STAY ON CO. 5 through a pretty open valley.

10.1 TURN LEFT (NORTHEAST) ON CO. 2 and traverse another broad valley drained by Wells Creek.

12.8	1912 stone barn on your left.
14.8	Railroad crossing followed by junction with U.S. 61. (Red Wing is 10.4 miles north on 61.) CROSS U.S. 61 and enter **Frontenac**. (Note: Country Store and Whistle Stop Cafe are 0.25 mile south on U.S. 61.)
14.9	Trailer court on your left. TURN RIGHT (EAST) ON PAVED ROAD.
15.0	TURN LEFT (NORTH) BACK ONTO CO. 2. St. John's Church on southwest corner.
15.2	Cross small bridge that spans stream with slough on the right. Gradual climb soon begins.
15.9	Entrance to Frontenac State Park (camping, rest room facilities, and 6.1 miles of hiking trails).
16.3	Top reached. Christ Episcopal Church (built in 1868) on your right. Enter **Old Frontenac**. See narrative.
16.7	Road reaches Lake Pepin and turns right along lake. Nice views of lake on your left and elegant houses on your right. (Note: A left turn takes you past some more stately homes to Chateau Frontenac, a historic resort -- see narrative.)
17.6	Pass turn-off to Villa Marie on your right. See narrative.
18.1	At T-intersection, TURN LEFT ON FRONTAGE ROAD which connects to U.S. 61. Indian mounds are a short walk across U.S. 61. TURN LEFT (SOUTHWEST) ON U.S. 61. Nice paved shoulder.
19.0	Lake Pepin comes into view on your left as you enter outskirts of Lake City.
19.4	Entrance to wayside rest area on your left next to Lake Pepin. Rest room facilities, running water, picnic tables, etc.

21.2	Entrance to Hor-Si-La Municipal Park on your left 1/3 mile away. (See narrative).
22.0	Road returns to lake for more shoreline cycling. Great views of the lake.
22.7	TURN LEFT (EAST) ONTO NORTH PARK STREET and continue to follow the lake.
23.0	Lakeside picnic tables followed by beach on your left.
23.3 *	Lake City Marina on your left. Public parking on your right.

TOUR 3: *Lake Pepin Ramble*

Trailhead:	Municipal parking lot next to Marina Cafe off Marion Street in Lake City.
Distance:	Option A (North Leg): 18 miles Option B (South Leg): 21 miles
Terrain:	Flat
Highlights:	North Leg: Lake Pepin, Villa Marie, Old Frontenac, and Frontenac State Park. South Leg: Lake Pepin and Wabasha County Historical Society Museum.
Route:	Option A: (0.0) Northwest on Franklin Street; (0.6) Northeast, then Northwest on North Park Street; (1.6) Northwest on U.S. 61; (6.2) North on Co. 2; (7.6) **Old Frontenac;** (9.1) Entrance to Frontenac State Park -- turn around and return on the same route to trailhead at mile 18.2.

> Option B: (0.0) Southeast on Franklin Street and Southwest on Marion Street; (0.1) Southeast on U.S. 61; (0.8) Northeast on Illinois just beyond Roschen Park and Southeast on South Oak Street; (2.3) Southeast on U.S. 61 to **Reads Landing** at mile 10.7, then turn around and return on same route to trailhead at mile 21.4.

This tour is divided into two trips: one (Option A) heading north along the lake to Frontenac State Park and back and the other (Option B) heading south along the lake to Read's Landing and back. You can, of course, shorten the trip by simply turning around at any point on the way. The North Leg keeps Lake Pepin in view for most of the first 5.5 miles before turning on Co. 2, which leads to Old Frontenac through mostly tree-covered level terrain.

Once the route gets out of town, the South Leg follows the Lake Pepin shoreline for the rest of the trip providing countless views of the lake as the road crowds the continuous hillside to the west. In the shadows of the afternoon, the bluffs, silhouetted against the lake, create dramatic vistas to be absorbed and enjoyed. There are no stores at Read's Landing so pack a lunch (unless the trip is extended an additional 3 miles into downtown Wabasha).

NORTH LEG -- Log

0.0   Trailhead: Municipal parking lot next to Marina Cafe off Marion Street in Lake City. NORTHWEST ALONG FRANKLIN STREET with Lake Pepin on your right.

0.1   Lake City Marina on your right.

0.7   TURN RIGHT THEN LEFT ON NORTH PARK STREET.

1.6   At T-intersection, TURN RIGHT (NORTHWEST) ON U.S. 61. Nice shoulder. Great views of lake.

3.1   Hor-Si-La Municipal Park on your right 1/3 mile off road.

5.0	Wayside on your right (rest room facilities, running water, picnic tables, etc.).
6.2	TURN RIGHT ONTO FRONTAGE ROAD LEADING TO CO. 2. TURN RIGHT (NORTH) ON CO. 2 and head for Old Frontenac beyond. (See narrative.)
6.8	Pass turn off to Villa Marie on your left. (See narrative.)
7.8	Road turns left away from lake. (Straight ahead leads to Chateau Frontenac.) TURN LEFT (WEST) ON CO. 2.
8.3	Christ Episcopal Church (built in 1868) on your left. Begin gradual descent.
8.7	Entrance to Frontenac State Park on your right (picnic area, rest room facilities, and 6.1 miles of hiking trails). Visit the park and then return on same route.

SOUTH LEG - Log

0.0	Trailhead: Same as north leg. HEAD SOUTHEAST ON FRANKLIN STREET, THEN SOUTHWEST ON MARION STREET.
0.1	TURN LEFT (SOUTHEAST) ON U.S. 61.
0.3	Overlook and marina on your left.
0.8	Roschen Park on your left. Illinois Road comes in from your left next to park. TURN LEFT (NORTHEAST) ONTO ILLINOIS.
0.9	At T-intersection, TURN LEFT (SOUTHEAST) ON SOUTH OAK STREET.
2.0	Gravel road comes in from your right leading to Wild Wings Gallery 0.1 mile away. Definitely worth a visit.
2.3	At T-intersection, TURN LEFT (SOUTHEAST) ON U.S. 61. Lake soon comes into view after which there are countless

	views of the lake as road follows the shoreline for the next 9 miles to Reads Landing.
2.4	Pass Co. 4 coming in from your right.
8.2	Scenic overlook of lake.
9.2	Another scenic overlook.
10.7	**Reads Landing** -- Junction with Co. 77 coming in from your right and paved road from river coming in from your left. Turn right to Wabasha County Historical Society Museum on your left (open Saturday and Sunday from 1:00 p.m. to 5:00 p.m.). Downtown Wabasha is 3 miles away. See Tour 1. Return the way you came.

WATERVILLE--SAKATAH TOURS

Surprise! There are lakes in southern Minnesota and there is good fishing, and recreation in those lakes. The communities of Madison Lake, Elysian, Waterville, and Morristown are all located on the "Trail of Lakes." Making use of the Sakatah Singing Hills State Trail and a number of county roads, our bike routes go in and around these communities and lakes.

Tour 1: Waterville--Faribault via Trail and Co. 12--34 miles (or an 8.5-mile shortcut)
Tour 2: Waterville--Faribault via Trail and Co. Roads 13 and 99--34 miles
Tour 3: West from Waterville--21, 35, or 46 miles

About the Area

How to Get There: About 1-1/2 hours and 70 miles south of the Twin Cities. Take I-35 south to Faribault and then Mn. 60 west to Waterville.

This is an area that lies in the transition zone between what once was known as the "Big Woods", and the vast prairie. It has lakes, woods, farms, prairie, and a variety of recreational opportunities. Hiking trails, resorts, campgrounds, and historic sites are in the area as well as good bicycling.

The Sakatah Trail follows an abandoned railroad right-of-way from Mankato to Faribault. It's limestone surface is expected to be paved in the next couple of years. We begin our routes in Waterville where access to the trails and county roads is convenient. Waterville calls itself "The Bullhead Capital of the World," but the fish hatchery two miles west of town hatches walleyes, muskies, bass, and catfish for lakes in the nearby seven counties. The locals claim, however, that there is nothing as tasty as bullhead when it is properly cooked. The Chamber of Commerce in Waterville (RFD 2, Box 92a, Waterville, MN 56096) (507/362-4609) has information on the area and on their celebration of Bullhead Days.

The Sakatah Bay Motel (507/362-8980) is on the eastern edge of Waterville on Lake Sakatah near the park. There are so many other resorts and campgrounds in the area that the Chamber of Commerce is the best resource. In town is Wallace's Family Inn Restaurant with great buffet-style meals. Their hot buffet is available every day except Saturday. Livingood's Bakery and Diner has an "all-you-can-eat" Sunday brunch. It also has serve-yourself coffee and fresh baked goods along with regular restaurant fare.

West of Waterville are the towns of Elysian and Madison Lake. Elysian lies between Lake Frances and Elysian Lake and boasts the LeSueur County Historical Museum. Located in an 1895 school house, the museum has a variety of pioneer artifacts as well as two authentically reproduced rooms of a 1900 country store and church. An art display includes pictures by local and world famous wildlife artist Roger Preuss. It is open June, July, and August from 1:30 p.m. to 5:30 p.m. Wednesday through Sunday and May and September from 1:30 p.m. to 5:30 p.m. Saturday and Sunday. Madison Lake, the town, is located on Madison Lake, the lake, which is noted for its huge black crappies. On Main Street are Memory Manor Country Store (featuring crafts) and Town Pump, the local bar.

Sakatah State Park (507/362-4438) is only two miles east of Waterville. Consisting of 842 acres with 3.5 miles of shoreline on Sakatah Lake, the park has hiking trails, an interpretive program, and a 60-site campground. The bicycle trail goes through the park. A bicycling touring camp is also located in the park.

Further east is Morristown, which has a convenience store, and Canon Lake and Wells Lake. Ahlman's Gun Shop, workshop, and museum is two miles north of Morristown.

At the eastern end of the trail is Faribault. It began as a fur trading site in 1826 but was a settled town by the mid 1800s. Alexander Faribault built a home there in 1852. That house and a number of other historical buildings remain and are open to the public. The Chamber of Commerce at 228 Central Avenue (507/334-4381) has a wide variety of information on the area. The historical downtown area includes two art galleries, a wood carving studio, the Minnesota State Academy for the Blind and Deaf, and the nationally famous Faribo Woolen Mills. Also in town is the luxurious Cherub Hill Victorian Bed and Breakfast (507/332-2024).

Faribault is considerably larger than the other towns in the area, providing a nice contrast for visiting and shopping. The eastern end of the bicycle trail stops just west of Faribault. To reach the downtown area, continue east on the shoulder of Mn. 60 (the trail parallels Mn. 60). Cross under the freeway overpass and continue straight into town on 4th Street until reaching Central Avenue. Downtown Faribault is about two miles from the end of the bicycle trail.

TOUR 1: Waterville--Faribault--via Trail and Co. 12

Trailhead:	Casey's General Store at the junction of Mn. 13 and Main Street on the east edge of Waterville. Park to one side of Vern's Bait and Tackle, where information on the Waterville area is available.
Terrain:	Trail is level; roads are level to slightly rolling.
Distance:	34 miles (or an 8.5-mile shortcut)
Highlights:	Lakes, fishing, Faribault for shopping and historic buildings, and Sakatah State Park.
Route:	(0.0) East on Sakatah Trail; (14.0) West on Co. 12; (23.0) South on Co. 16; (26.0) West on Co. 14 which becomes Co. 10; (32.0) South on Mn. 13; (34.0) Waterville--Trailhead.

This tour passes through the typical topography of the area with some lakes, farmlands, and woods. The bicycling is easy, and the variety of terrain makes it interesting.

Log

0.0   Begin at Casey's General Store on Mn. 13 on the east edge of Waterville. To reach the trail, head south for one block on Mn. 13. TURN LEFT (EAST) FOR ONE BLOCK ON

PAQUIN STREET AND THEN RIGHT (SOUTH) ONE BLOCK ON HAMILTON STREET TO THE TRAIL. HEAD EAST ON TRAIL. The trail soon passes through a wooded area with trees almost meeting overhead.

2.0   Sakatah Lake State Park (See narrative). Access road to park and campground on your right, and on the lake side, access to beach and picnic grounds.

3.5   On your left is a sign for Eggers Prairie, a registered Minnesota Nature Area of the Nature Conservancy.

3.7   A gravel cross road. (For an 8.5-mile shortcut back to Waterville, turn left (North) here for 0.3 mile, then left (West) again on LeRoy Trail (Rice Co. 99; LeSueur Co. 131) along the scenic shoreline of Upper Sakatah Lake, and finally left (South) on Mn. 13. (Only 0.3 mile is gravel.)

6.5   Cross Cannon River. Morristown, population 639, south of the trail (see narrative).

12.5 Shager Park. Public access to Cannon Lake, shelters, toilets, and picnic facilities. The trail follows the east side of Cannon Lake.

14.0 TURN LEFT (WEST) ON CO. 12. Road follows lake with homes and cabins. (Continue straight ahead on trail for three miles to visit Faribault. Return and pick up route at this point.)

15.0 Ackman Park. Public access to Cannon Lake. The road crosses between Cannon and Wells Lakes.

15.5 Stay on Co. 12 (also Douglas Avenue) as it turns right then left. Rolling farmland, wooded areas.

19.5 Cedar Lake on your right.

23.0 TURN LEFT (SOUTH) ON CO. 16 (ALSO KANABEC AVENUE).

26.0 TURN RIGHT (WEST) ON CO. 14 (230TH STREET).

29.0 Camp Omega, Lutheran Church Camp, and Horseshoe Lake. Cross from Rice County into LeSueur County. YOU ARE NOW ON LESUEUR CO. 10.

32.0 At T-intersection, TURN LEFT (SOUTH) ON MN. 13. Good shoulder on road. Lake Tetonka, Lake Sakatah.

34.0 TURN RIGHT (WEST) ON MAIN STREET TO GO TO DOWNTOWN WATERVILLE or stop back at parking area at Casey's General Store (see narrative).

TOUR 2: Waterville--Faribault--via Trail and Co. Roads 13 and 99

Trailhead:	Same as Tour 1
Terrain:	Trail is level, roads are rolling.
Distance:	34 miles
Highlights:	Lakes, Faribault, pleasant countryside, and Sakatah State Park.
Route:	(0.0) East on Sakatah State Trail; (14.0) West on Co. 12; (16.0) Southwest on Co. 13; (20.0) West on state trail; (26.0) North on Co. 99; (29.0) North on Leroy Trail; (33.0) South on Co. 13; (33.5) Waterville--Trailhead.

This tour is very similar to Tour 1 but is slightly more challenging and would provide a different route if one were spending several days in the area.

Log

0.0 Casey's General Store--see Tour 1. Follow the state trail east through Sakatah State Park, Morristown, and Warsaw to junction with Co. 12. See Tour 1 for log.

14.0	TURN LEFT (WEST) ON CO. 12.
15.0	Ackman Park on the left. Public access to Cannon Lake.
16.0	TURN LEFT (SOUTHWEST) ON RICE CO. 13 (CANNON LAKE TRAIL). This follows along the west side of Cannon Lake. Nice views of lake.
19.5	At T-intersection, TURN LEFT (SOUTH) STAYING ON CO. 13. Warsaw Antiques at this intersection.
20.0	Pass Willing Campground on the river. Public camping. TURN RIGHT (WEST) BACK ONTO THE STATE TRAIL.
25.0	Cross Co. 16. Continue on trail. Pass Camp Maidenrock. Cross Cannon River.
26.0	TURN RIGHT (NORTH) ON RICE CO. 99 (ALSO JACKSON AVENUE). Rolling hills, farmland, wooded areas. Lower Sakatah Lake eventually appears to your right.
29.0	At T-intersection, TURN RIGHT (NORTH) ON LEROY TRAIL (STILL CO. 99). Rolling hills for next three miles. Pass between Upper and Lower Sakatah Lakes. The road then follows the north side of Upper Sakatah Lake--a scenic shoreline ride.
30.0	Cross from Rice to LeSueur County on what is now Co. 131.
32.5	Camp Dels. Large campground with docks on lake, recreation area, pool, and cabins.
33.0	McWhirter's Hillside Resort on your right. Cabins. At T-intersection, TURN LEFT (SOUTH) ON MN. 13 to Waterville.
33.5	Junction of Mn. 13 and Main Street of Waterville. Casey's General Store.

TOUR 3: West from Waterville

Trailhead:	Same as above
Distance:	Main Route: 46 miles Option A: 21 miles Option B: 35 miles
Terrain:	Rolling hills, nothing steep
Highlights:	LeSueur County Historical Museum, lakes, state trail, and towns of Elysian and Madison Lake.
Route:	Main Route: (0.0) West on Sakatah State Trail; (6.0) Elysian; (13.0) Madison Lake; (16.5) North on Co. 27; (20.8) West on unmarked road; (21.3) North on Co. 19; (25.0) East on Co. 18; (33.7) South on Co. 13; (34.4) East on Co. 12; (44.5) South on Mn. 13; (46.5) Waterville--Trailhead. Optional A: (0.0) West on Sakatah State Trail; (6.0) North on Co. 11; (10.0) East on Co. 12; (18.8) South on Mn. 13; (20.8) Waterville--Trailhead. Option B: (0.0) West on Sakatah State Trail; (13.0) North on Co. 26 which becomes Co. 15; (18.5) East on Co. 18; (21.7) South on Co. 13; (27.2) East on Co. 12; (32.5) South on Mn. 13; (34.5) Waterville--Trailhead.

After passing through several small towns along the trail, this tour travels along pleasant country roads and past a number of lakes. The roads are very lightly traveled, and the options allow for a variety of distances.

Log--Main Route

0.0 From Casey's General Store, the trail zig-zags through the streets of Waterville following bicycle signs to Reed Street on the western edge of town. A simpler route is to cross Mn. 13 HEADING WEST ON PAQUIN STREET for five blocks to Reed Street. TURN LEFT (SOUTH) ON REED STREET for approximately five blocks to the trail. TURN RIGHT AND PROCEED WEST ON THE STATE TRAIL.

1.0 Rest area with toilets and shelter appears soon after beginning the trail on the western edge of town.

6.0 Elysian (see narrative). The LeSueur County Historical Society Museum (see narrative) is on top of hill in the old school house. Lake Elysian, Lake Frances, Rays Lake, and Perch Lake are all in this area. (For the 21-mile tour, turn right (north) on Co. 11 and follow directions for Option A).

6.1 Wayside rest with shelter and toilets.

8.8 Entrance to Greenland Supper Club.

10.9 Cross into Blue Earth County.

13.0 Madison Lake with the lake itself on your left. Junction with Co. 26. (For the 35-mile tour, turn right (north) on Co. 26 and follow directions for Option B.)

16.5 TURN RIGHT (NORTH) ON CO. 27 where the trail comes to a power transformer. This is difficult to spot because the trail is not marked here. Watch for the big power transformer station right next to the trail. Co. 27 is marked when you cross Co. 26 one mile north. Continue north on Co. 27. Rolling hills and farmland.

19.3 Lake George County Park straight ahead. Boat launching, very small lake, picnic, and toilet facilities. The road veers left. Nice view of Wita Lake to your left (west).

20.8 At T-intersection, TURN LEFT (WEST) ON CO. 2 (not marked).

21.3	TURN RIGHT (NORTH) ON LESUEUR CO. 19. Nice views.
22.4	Cross Co. 101. Continue on Co. 19.
23.6	Entrance to Lake Washington County Park on your right.
25.0	TURN RIGHT (EAST) ON CO. 18. Farmlands and rolling hills.
28.0	Dog Lake on your right.
29.5	At T-intersection, Co. 15 comes in from your left and joins Co. 18. TURN RIGHT (SOUTH) ON CO. 18. Pass Lake Henry on your left and Lake Jefferson on your right.
30.5	Road comes to a Y. Co. 15 goes right and Co. 18 goes left. BEAR LEFT (NORTHEAST) ON CO. 18. Lake Jefferson again.
33.7	At T-intersection, TURN RIGHT (SOUTH) ON CO. 13. Pass Hi Lo Terrace Resort and Casta-Line Resort.
34.4	TURN LEFT (EAST) ON CO. 12. (Just a little further south on Co. 13 is the Geldner Sawmill, which was built in 1876. It is the last remaining early sawmill in LeSueur County.)
35.0	German Lake to your right. Public access. Nice views of lake.
35.7	Co. 11 joins Co. 12 from your left. Stay on Co. 12.
38.8	St. Peter's Lutheran Church on your right.
39.2	Co. 11 turns right (south) to Elysian. BEAR LEFT (EAST) STAYING ON CO. 12.
40.2	Emmanuel United Methodist Church.
44.5	At T-intersection, TURN RIGHT (SOUTH) ON MN. 13. Lake Tetonka on your right.

46.5	Casey's General Store. Pirate's Galley Drive Inn across the street.

OPTION A: Waterville--Elysian--Waterville

0.0	Head west on the trail from Casey's General store as in Tour 3 following log.
6.0	Elysian. TURN RIGHT (NORTH) ON CO. 11. (See narrative and Tour 3 for specific information about the area.) Stay on Co. 11, passing Co. 14 coming in from your right at mile 6.8 and Co. 13 coming in from your left at mile 7.9.
10.0	TURN RIGHT (EAST) ON CO. 12. Follow log for Tour 3 beginning at mile 35.7 back to Waterville.
20.8	Back at Casey's General Store in Waterville.

OPTION B: Waterville--Madison Lake--Waterville

0.0	Head west on the trail from Casey's General Store as in Tour 3 following log.
6.0	Elysian.
13.0	Madison Lake. (See narrative and log for Tour 3 for specific information about the area.) TURN RIGHT (NORTH) ON CO. 26. Plainsmen Restaurant .2 mile south of trail. Pass road leading to downtown Madison Lake at mile 13.2 and Duck Lake at mile 13.8, both on your left.
15.0	Cross at intersection to LeSueur County. Road changes from Blue Earth Co. 26 to LeSueur Co. 15. Continue north on Co. 15 past wildlife area on your left.
18.5	Pass between Lake Jefferson and Lake Henry. TURN RIGHT (EAST) ON CO. 18. Continue following log for Tour 3 beginning at mile 30.5.
34.6	Back at Casey's General Store in Waterville.

HINCKLEY/MOOSE LAKE FIRE TRAIL TOURS

Barren, scrubby, and flat. Those words conjure up an image shared by many who pass through, but don't visit, the Hinckley/Moose Lake area of Minnesota. Leveled by mighty glaciers and desolated by fires, this place offers ample intrigue to the trained eye and attuned ear.

At the bottom of a mid-continental sea, the accumulation of silica and sand settled and fused over geologic time to create a bedrock of sandstone. Then the glaciers came, and as the last glacier receded 10,000 years ago, its meltwater overflowed the basin where Lake Superior now lies to lay bare the sandstone in a myriad of runoff streams that gave shape to the area. The stingy soil though gave birth not to flowing fields and lush vegetation but to an interminable forest of giant pine.

A succession of settlers worked this rugged environment -- first as hunters; then as fur traders and voyagers; later as foresters and quarrymen; and finally as farmers, merchants, and tradesmen. Through this land, a railroad line was built in 1870 to connect Duluth with St. Paul. In 1894, the railroad line provided a desperate escape route from the inferno that engulfed the area. Nearly a hundred years later the line now serves as a paved bicycle trail connecting Hinckley with Moose Lake and Barnum beyond. For the imaginative cyclist, the story of the age-old struggle to tame and survive the forces of nature can be relived along the Hinckley-Moose Lake Fire Trail Tours offered in this chapter.

Tour 1: Hinckley/Moose Lake Fire Trail -- 20 to 66 miles round trip
Tour 2: Hinckley to Grindstone Lake Circle Trip -- 31 miles
Tour 3: Finlayson to Banning State Park Circle Trip -- 20, 33, or 56 miles
Tour 4: Moose Lake to Willow River to Sturgeon Lake Circle Trip -- 25 miles
Tour 5: Moose Lake to Kettle River Loop - 25 miles
Tour 6: Moose Lake to Barnum Circle Trip -- 13 or 15 miles

About the Area

How to Get There: About 1½ to 2 hours and 75 to 105 miles north of the Twin Cities, depending on the tour taken.

To Hinckley: Take I-35 north about 75 miles, turn off at exit 183, and go west on Mn. 48 into town.

To Finlayson: Take I-35 north about 87 miles, turn off at exit 195, and go west on Mn. 23. At T-intersection, head north and follow Mn. 18 into town.

To Moose Lake: Take I-35 north about 105 miles, turn off at exit 214, and go west on Mn. 73 into town.

The people in this area take pride in their heritage. From the Mission Creek 1894 Theme Park (1-800/228-1894) and the Hinckley Fire Museum in Hinckley to the Banning Quarry Self-Guided Trail in Banning State Park, the interpretive programs at St. Croix State park, the Pine County Museum in Askov, the "pioneer" town of Finlayson, and the Fire Trail itself, the past is brought into the present. And now the most popular and, in some ways, most fitting attraction of all - the Grand Casino Hinckley (1-800/GRAND21), owned by the Ojibwe Indian tribe that had settled in the area long before any white settlers had arrived.

In Hinckley, just 1/2 mile south of Tobie's on the west side of I-35 is Mission Creek 1894, a theme park which features a turn-of-the-century village, an animal park, a voyager camp, an Indian village, a settlers fort (with craft demonstrations), village shops, an amphitheater (with homespun plays about the area), and many other attractions. At the other end of town near the trailhead for the Hinckley/Moose Lake Fire Trail is the Hinckley Fire Museum (open daily from 10:00 a.m. to 5:00 p.m.). This restored depot tells the fascinating story of the forest fires that erupted on September 1, 1894, and completely destroyed Hinckley, Brook Park, Mission Creek, Sandstone, Askov, and Miller, killing more than 400 people.

In addition to the popular Tobie's Restaurant and Cassidy's just off I-35 if you can resist the allure of the Grand Casino Hinckley, try Marge's Cafe in the center of town for a less fancy, down-home place to eat or LaPaysanne (The Peasant) for a wide variety of sandwiches, 0.8 mile east of I-35 on Co. 48. Jeffrey's is also a good place for pastry and yogurt. There are a number of motels in the area. Call the Hinckley Chamber of Commerce (612/384-7837) for a current listing.

If you are looking for bed and breakfast accomodations, try either The Dakota Lodge (612/384-6052) located on Co. 48 just 10 miles east of Hinckley and six miles west of the turnoff for St. Croix State Park, or Victorian Rose (612/233-7531) in Finlayson adjacent to the Fire Trail (3 rooms). Camping facilities found on the way to the state park include Grand Casino RV Resort (1-800-468-3517), Pathfinder Village (612/384-7726), Fleming Campground (612/384-7255), and Lake Our's Campground (612/384-6037). In Hinckley, primitive camping is available on a first come, first served basis at the American Legion Park, a municipal park located next to the Grindstone River near the trailhead.

Three magnificent state parks and one state forest are within reach of the bike tours. The furthest from the bike routes, St. Croix State Park, is Minnesota's largest state park. It is located on the banks of the St. Croix and Kettle Rivers 16 miles east of Hinckley among forests of pine, birch, and oak, with plenty of semi-modern, primitive, and group campsites (612/384-6591), endless hiking trails, and six miles of biking trails.

Right off one of the bike routes about four miles north of Sandstone is Banning State Park (612/245-2668). The park is situated along a 10-mile stretch of the Kettle River's most spectacular rapids. It was once the town site for a flourishing village of 300. The little town burst upon the scene during the heyday of quarrying when the pink Hinckley sandstone was in great demand as a building material. In a little over 20 years, the town all but disappeared as fire laid waste to a dying community. It could not survive the replacement of structural steel and concrete for building blocks. A 1.8-mile Banning Quarry Self-Guided Trail takes the inquisitive hiker along the river's edge and "through rock formations, woodlands and ruins that silently recount the town's short life" between 1892 and 1912. The park has 31 rustic campsites and 14 miles of hiking trails.

Just north of Willow River, the Fire Trail passes along the edge of the General C.C. Andrews State Forest, a forest nursery named after the man who spearheaded the reforesting of 15,000 acres in Pine County after World War II. In this preserve, tall mature pine provide a glimpse back into time when in the early 19th century the red and white pine dominated the landscape. Forty-one campsites are located under this pine cover in the Willow River Campgrounds (1-800/652-6699) next to Stanton Lake.

Moose Lake Recreation Area (612/465-4059), the last of the three state parks in the area, is located on a gently sloping hill next to Echo Lake 2.5 miles east of the Moose Lake end of the Fire Trail. The park has a sandy swimming beach, wooded hiking trails, and 18 rustic campsites.

Other camping and lodging facilities in the area as you head north are:

- Banning Junction Campground (612/245-5273), I-35 and Mn. 23 near Finlayson;
- Wolfstar Lodge (612/233-7100) near Finlayson.
- Waldheim Resort and Campground (612/233-7405), Big Pine Lake near Finlayson;
- D.A.R. Memorial State Forest (218/485-4474), Mn. 23 near Askov;
- Obie's Chengwatana Trail Campground (612/233-7678), Rutledge;
- Wilderness Campgrounds (218/372-3993), Long Lake, Willow River;
- Wishing Well Motel (216/372-3951), Willow River;
- Timberline Campground (218/372-3272), Sturgeon Lake;
- Edelweiss Campground (218/372-3363), Sturgeon Lake;
- Sturgeon Lake Motel (218/372-3194) just off I-35;
- Sand Lake Resort (218/485-8164), Sturgeon Lake;
- Sun-Bay Camping (218/485-4869), Moose Lake;
- Wicklund's Campground (218/485-4837), Little Moose Lake;
- Moose Lake Municipal Campground (218/485-4010);
- Moose Lake Motel (218/485-8003), Moose Lake;
- Hart's Motel and Cabins (218/485-4300), south shore of Moosehead Lake, Moose Lake;
- Northwoods Motel (218/389-6951), Barnum; and

- Big Hanging Horn Lake, Bear Lake Park (218/384-4281), and the city park, three public campgrounds (218/485-9906) found in the Barnum area.
- Hanging Horn Village (1-800/450-5676) lodging.

A must stop along the Fire Trail is Finlayson, a small town constructed before the turn of the century that somehow escaped the great forest fires. We particularly enjoyed The Old Fashioned Inn for a hearty dish of apple pie a la mode. You should also visit the town's "combination" railroad depot museum restored to its original appearance. The depot, designed to handle both freight and passengers, sums up the history typical of Pine County's railroad villages. Depots placed at various points along the land-grant railroad fixed the locations for intense logging and sawmills. After the lumberjacks cleared the area near the depot, the railroad platted the town (1895 for Finlayson) and promoted agricultural settlement. Eventually, as farming in the cut-over hinterland expanded, the town became a flourishing agricultural trade center. The Finlayson depot was enlarged to its present size in 1909.

Not far from Finlayson is Giese Bed & Breakfast Inn (612/223-6429), a 4-room inn on 160 acres of woodland with a shop and gallery of collectibles located in one wing of the house.

Another recommended diversion further north along the trail is Willow River Mercantile, a general store established in 1901. This store has remained true to its motto as "The store that has everything." Also in Willow River is T & M Athletics which provides bike repair and accessories.

At the north end of the Fire Trail is Moose Lake. This city is nestled next to Moosehead Lake near the headwaters of Portage River (Mud Creek) and Moose Horn River. It has a thriving business district and a charming residential area near the lake. Initially settled by Scandinavians, Moose Lake has become a summer retreat for persons from afar who, with the year-round residents, enjoy its surrounding lakes and rugged terrain. Because of the abundance of agates found in the area, the city celebrates Agate Days each summer, when agates mixed with sand are spread down Elm Street and snatched up by frenzied rockhounds.

Moose Lake was spared the ravages of the Hinckley Fire. In 1918, however, equally devastating forest fires swept through Moose Lake, Kettle River, and other parts of Carlton County. Again the railroad line between Duluth and St. Paul provided aid and succor, this time in the form of relief supplies trained in from the Twin Cities and Duluth. That and other lore about the city is woven into a "Walking History of Moose Lake," which is available at the city's information center. The Chamber of Commerce telephone number is 218/485-4145.

TOUR 1: *Hinckley/Moose Lake Fire Trail*

Trailhead:	Hinckley: parking lot at north end of downtown Hinckley just west of Co. 61 on north side of Co. 18. (To get to Hinckley Fire Museum from trailhead, turn east on Co. 18, cross railroad tracks, and go south 0.2 miles on Old Mn. 61.)
	Moose Lake: Parking lot at south end of town 1/4 mile south off Mn. 73 on west side of South Arrowhead Lane. (Alternative Trailhead: Moose Lake Municipal Park. See trailhead description and log for tour 4.)

Distance:	From Hinckley:
	    to Finlayson and back: 26 miles
	    to Willow River and back: 46 miles
	    to Moose Lake and back: 66 miles
	
	From Moose Lake:
	    to Willow River and back: 20 miles
	    to Finlayson and back: 40 miles
	    to Hinckley and back: 66 miles

Terrain:	Level

> **Highlights:** Varied tree cover, marshland, farms, historic Skunk Lake, and railroad towns
>
> **Route:** Stay on trail whether going north or south

This tour sticks to the "Fire Trail" segment of the Willard Munger State Trail, a paved bicycle trail that follows an abandoned railroad right-of-way from Hinckley to Moose Lake. (The trail has been extended to Barnum and will eventually go on to Carlton.) The name of the trail commemorates the key role this railroad line played as an escape route during the great Hinckley fire of 1894 and as a supply route when Moose Lake was mostly destroyed by a similar raging forest fire in 1918.

At the Hinckley Fire Museum, just 1/4 mile from the Hinckley trailhead, one can get a copy of Lee Guptill's moving account of the 1894 fire. Guptill describes how man and nature set the stage for the holocaust. Lumber companies moved into the virgin forests to harvest the giant pine. Poorer growths were left standing, "choked with the limbs and stumps of the giants which the loggers had felled and hauled away." The slashings lay where they fell, getting dryer each year. Then in the summer of 1894 no rain fell for three months. The resin and pitch of the pine slashings oozed as never before. Small fires, some caused by sparks from the railroad engines, were periodically ignited and put out. The air seemed always hazy from the smoke. On September 1, 1894, a number of small fires were fanned by a breeze, which later became a wind and then a gale. Soon the fires joined forces to become one gigantic wall of flames. Guptill then recounts the escape:

> Many of the townspeople, especially on the west side, sought the refuge of the afternoon 'Limited' from Duluth on the Duluth-St. Paul line which was due in Hinckley at four o'clock. However the fire beat the train to Hinckley so these people ran northward up the tracks to meet it, or, perhaps, to try to escape the fire itself. This was Jim Root's train and he brought it to a halt about a mile north of town, took on the fleeing people and then, putting the engine in reverse,

raced the fire back to Skunk Lake, about four miles, where he stopped the train and people flung themselves into the muddy and swampy water of the pond. The train itself burned up on the tracks.

Few pine are seen now along the southern two-thirds of the trail. In their place poplar and birch line the way, interspersed with bogs, swamps, and farm sites. Beautiful bog rosemary, swamp laurel, and Labrador tea can be seen in the bogs which are populated with spongy hummocks. Deer can be spotted in the farm fields. The scars of the great fires disappeared long ago as new growth emerged to create more diverse vegetation and a richer habitat. Along the northern third of the trail, a new growth of pine appear -- thanks to the restoration efforts led by General C.C. Andrews (see narrative).

Log -- Mileage from north to south is in parentheses

0.0 (33.1)		Hinckley Trailhead. Satellite toilet.
0.2 (32.9)		Cross Grindstone River. Picturesque manmade falls on west side.
0.3 (32.8)		Pretty pond on west side.
2.0 (31.1)		Beaver dam on east side.
4.9 (28.2)		Cross Co. 26 (Friesland road sign -- no stores).
5.9 (27.2)		Skunk Lake on east side. During the fire of 1894, desperate residents from Hinckley rushed by train to this swamp and plunged into its muddy waters to escape the fire. See narrative.
7.1 (26.0)		Cross Co. 27. (Return point from Grindstone Lake for Tour 2 and departure point to Banning State Park for Tour 3.)
9.4 (23.7)		Park bench overlooking small lake on west side amidst flowing open fields.
10.0 (23.1)		Cross Co. 28 (Groningen -- no stores).

12.9 (20.2)	Cross Mn. 18. Satellite toilet just south of road on west side. Downtown **Finlayson** is 0.2 miles west. See narrative. Turn south off Mn. 18 onto Front Street and a block later west on Finland Avenue. Turn-of-the-century caboose and railroad depot on west side of Front Street. The Old Fashioned Inn is a block and a half west on Finland Avenue. The Hinckley fire stopped just short of this lumber town.
14.1 (19.0)	Cross Co. 34.
15.7 (17.4)	Bogs. Look for bog rosemary and swamp laurel.
15.9 (17.2)	Begin (or end if heading south) a pleasant swing east along farm site boundaries as trail dips a little. Look for deer.
16.7 (16.4)	End (or begin if heading south) of eastern loop described above.
17.6 (15.5)	Cross Pine River (park bench).
18.1 (15.0)	Cross Co. 39 (Rutledge -- the Flamingo Inn has a bar and restaurant on Co. 61 to the east).
18.4 (14.7)	Prairie grass.
18.6 (14.5)	Cross road. Polly's Crafts on road north on trail. Little Bluestem is abundant in this area.
19.1 (14.0)	Cross Kettle River. A windbreak of tall pine begins to line the trail on the east side.
22.9 (10.2)	**Willow River.** Small city park on the east side. Cross Main Street, Visit Willow River Mercantile on west side. Squirrel Cage, bar and restaurant, on the east side. See narrative.
23.1 (10.0)	Cross Willow River.

23.2 (9.9)	Stately pine to the east in General C. C. Andrews State Forest. See narrative.
23.4 (9.7)	Cross Co. 41. (For a lakeside view and dip, go east on Co. 41, south on Co. 61, and east on gravel public access road to lake next to dam only 0.2 mile from trail.) A second growth of pine begins to line much of the route all the way north to Moose Lake, as the trail initially cuts through a portion of General C.C. Andrews State Forest. See narrative.
23.9 (9.2)	Slough and open water east across Co. 61.
24.9 (8.2)	Pasture and barn break up the woodland to the west.
25.5 (7.6)	Entrance to General C.C. Andrews State Forest Nursery east across Co. 61. Self-Guided Forest Management Tour is available at the office.
26.4 (6.7)	Cross Co. 52.
27.3 (5.8)	Marshland on both sides with slough and open water to the east.
27.4 (5.7)	Cross Co. 46. (Departure point to Sturgeon Lake for Tour 4.)
27.5 (5.6)	Lumber yard on west side.
29.1 (4.0)	Nice views of Coffee Lake to the east across Co. 61.
33.1 (0.0)	Turn off to South Arrowhead Lane on east side of trail (satellite toilet) and parking lot 0.1 mile north. Trail actually ends 0.2 miles north at edge of Moose Horn River. (You must bike on roads through Moose Lake before the trail resumes at the north end of town.)

TOUR 2: *Hinckley to Grindstone Lake Circle Trip*

Trailhead:	Same as Hinckley trailhead for Tour 1
Distance:	30 miles
Terrain:	Level to slightly rolling
Highlights:	Open country, Grindstone Lake, and trail scenery (including Skunk Lake)
Route:	(0.0) West on Co. 18; (8.2) North on Co. 20; (15.1) East on Co. 21 which becomes Co. 27; (18.3) Grindstone Lake; (23.1) South on Fire Trail; (30.2) Trailhead.

This route takes a back country road through a mix of open farmland and pine and deciduous tree cover. The tour skirts the south shore of Grindstone Lake and returns to the trailhead by way of the Fire Trail.

Log

0.0   Hinckley trailhead. Satellite toilet. HEAD WEST ON CO. 18 and enter relatively flat farmland interspersed with clumps of trees. For the first 8.2 miles, this route has a fair amount of traffic.

2.6   Cross Co. 17.

6.1   Freshly paved road (in 1989) as area becomes more wooded.

8.2   TURN RIGHT (NORTH) ON CO. 20. Little traffic with more open farmland.

12.3   Pretty white church on your left (west).

14.1   Road begins to dip a little.

15.1 TURN RIGHT (EAST) ON CO. 21.

16.4 Road becomes Co. 27.

17.1 Road begins to rise and dip a little more as it passes through a wooded area.

18.3 **Grindstone Lake** on your left (north). Public beach at the north end though swimming at south end is permitted.

20.7 Tiny Lutheran church on your right (south).

23.1 Intersect Fire Trail. TURN RIGHT (SOUTH) ON TRAIL. Use Tour 1 log (north to south mileages) for return trip of 7.1 miles (mile 26.0 to 33.1 on log).

TOUR 3: *Finlayson to Banning State Park Circle Trip*

Trailhead:	Downtown Finlayson next to The Old Fashioned Inn
Distance:	Option A: 21 miles Option B: 36 miles Option C: 56 miles
Terrain:	Level with one significant hill on 56-mile route
Highlights:	Fire Trail scenery (with Skunk Lake included only in Option B), Banning State Park, Sandstone, Hinckley (Option B only), Kettle River Valley, Askov, and back country roads (Option C only)
Route:	Option A: (0.0) Pick up Fire Trail 0.2 miles east of town and go south; (5.6) East on Co. 27 and North then East on Co. 61 which also becomes Mn. 23 after crossing I-35; (9.1) Downtown **Sandstone**:

> (12.3) East on Mn. 18 which again becomes Mn. 23 after crossing I-35; (13.3) **Banning State Park** on right; (14.7) picnic grounds in park -- turn around; (16.9) West on Mn. 23 which becomes Mn. 18 after crossing I-35; (17.9) North on Mn. 18 and Co. 61; (19.4) West on Mn. 18; (21.4) Finlayson
>
> Option B: Add 15 miles to trip by continuing south on Fire Trail to Hinckley and returning to mile 5.6 in Option A (now making it mile 21.4 instead)
>
> Option C: Same as Option A up to mile 16.9; East on Mn. 23; (20.5) **Askov** -- East on Co. 32; (26.5) North on Flemming Road; (32.8) **Bruno** -- West on Co. 44 which becomes Co. 43 after crossing Mn. 23; (44.3) **Willow River** -- South on Fire Trail; (55.6) Finlayson.

This trip combines a segment of the Fire Trail with a visit to Banning State Park and a hike along its 1.8-mile Banning Quarry Self-Guided Trail. (See narrative). On the way, you can check out downtown Sandstone and pass through a second growth of red and white pine.

The extended versions of this trip allow for more bicycling on the Fire Trail and a visit to the Hinckley Fire Museum (Option B) or the Pine County Museum in Askov and Willow River Mercantile and General C. C. Andrews State Forest in or near Willow River (Option C).

On the 56-mile trip (Option C), a steep descent into and a long climb out of the Kettle River valley east of Banning State Park provides a breathtaking change of pace. Afterwards, the route resumes its level course along lightly travelled country roads that cut through a patchwork of pine, deciduous trees, and scrubby pastures. You may wish to split this trip into two days, tack on the Option B segment to

Hinckley, and camp out at Banning State Park at the end of the first day.

Note that all options include some manageable gravel roads in Banning State Park and, in the case of Option C, a three-mile stretch of gravel east of Askov.

Log

OPTION A: Banning State Park

0.0   Finlayson Trailhead. GO EAST ON FINLAND AVENUE. TURN LEFT (NORTH) AT DEPOT ON FRONT STREET. TURN RIGHT (EAST) ON MN. 18 AND RIGHT AGAIN (SOUTH) ON FIRE TRAIL. Use the log for Tour 1 (north to south mileages) from mile 20.2.

5.6   TURN LEFT (EAST) ON CO. 27 and, at T-intersection, TURN LEFT AGAIN (NORTH) ON CO. 61.

7.8   CROSS I-35, PICK UP MN. 23 and paved shoulder, and enter outskirts of Sandstone. This small town, like Banning, got its start with quarrying, a fact that is celebrated every year in August during "Quarry Days." As a sideline, bottled Sandstone water from the artisan wells in the Sandstone Quarry became a hot item in Chicago and other midwestern cities. Now, Sandstone Federal Prison and Banning State Park help breathe economic life into this small farm community.

8.2   Mn. 23 and Co. 61 bear left (north) while a spur into downtown Sandstone goes straight. FOLLOW SPUR INTO SANDSTONE.

9.1   Center of town. City park with picnic tables and gazebo on your left (west) and Stacy's Pastry Shop and Eat'n Place on your right (east). CONTINUE NORTH OUT OF TOWN BEARING LEFT AT SPLIT IN ROAD AND TURN RIGHT (NORTH) BACK ONTO MN. 23 AND CO. 61 AT MILE 9.3.

11.8   Cross I-35 again at which point only Co. 61 remains.

12.3   TURN RIGHT (EAST) ON MN. 18.

12.8   Cross I-35 again at which point Mn. 23 resumes.

13.3   Entrance to Banning State Park. TURN RIGHT (SOUTH) INTO PARK and follow road 1.4 miles to picnic grounds. The Banning Self-Guided Trail begins here. Nice views of river on return hike. Turn around and retrace your route.

16.9   From the park entrance, TURN LEFT (WEST) BACK ONTO MN. 23 and return one mile to intersection with Co. 61 and Mn. 18.

17.9   At T-intersection, TURN RIGHT (NORTH) ON MN. 18 AND CO. 61 and pick up paved shoulder.

19.4   TURN LEFT (WEST) ON MN. 18. Slightly rolling terrain with open farmland to the north.

21.2   Cross Fire Trail and return to trailhead in Finlayson at mile 21.4.

OPTION B: *Hinckley Extension*

0.0   Follow Option A route to turnoff for Sandstone at mile 5.6.

5.6   Instead of turning left, CONTINUE SOUTH ON FIRE TRAIL to Hinckley. Visit the Hinckley Fire Museum and return on Fire Trail back to turnoff for Sandstone. Use the Fire Trail log for Tour 1, mile 26.0 to 33.1 (going north to south) and 0.0 to 7.1 (return trip).

OPTION C: *Askov, Bruno, and Willow River Extension*

0.0   Follow Option A route to Banning State Park where route rejoins Mn. 23 at mile 16.9.

16.9   TURN RIGHT (EAST) ON MN. 23.

17.4   Begin steep descent into forested Kettle River valley, leveling off and crossing river at mile 17.7. Climb out of valley for long ascent reaching top at mile 19.2.

19.5   Pass Co. 123 coming in from your right.

20.3	Mn. 23 bears left (northeast) while Co. 32 heads straight into **Askov.** Go STRAIGHT ON CO. 32 INTO ASKOV. Formerly named Partridge, this town was renamed Askov (meaning "ash grove") soon after the influx of Danish immigrants who resettled the area following the fire of 1894.
20.5	Co. 32 turns right (southeast) while Co. 66 goes straight into downtown Askov. Take side trip into town center. The Pine County Historical Museum (open daily from 1:00 p.m. to 4:00 p.m.), a restored railroad depot, is on your right at mile 20.6. Picnic grounds, water, and toilet facilities are across the street. For a home-cooked meal or cup of coffee, stop at the Partridge Cafe a little further up the road. After exploring the town, return to Co. 32 and HEAD SOUTHEAST ON CO. 32 across railroad tracks and through a small residential area. Road soon begins to dip a little as it proceeds east through a patchwork a pine, deciduous trees, brush, and pasture.
25.5	Road becomes gravel.
26.5	TURN LEFT (NORTH) ON FLEMING ROAD (gravel for next two miles). Open farmland eventually replaces initially scrubby terrain.
27.5	Co. 22 comes in from your right to replace Fleming Road. CONTINUE NORTH ON CO. 22.
32.8	TURN LEFT (WEST) ON CO. 44 and enter **Bruno** (no stores except a tavern at junction with Mn. 23).
33.0	Cross Mn. 23 and CONTINUE WEST ON CO. 43. Road winds a little before heading west for a seven-mile straight shot through a mostly wooded area.
42.0	At intersection with Co. 152, stay on Co. 43 which heads north for awhile, then west again.
43.1	TURN RIGHT (NORTH) ON CO. 43.
43.4	TURN LEFT (WEST), cross I-35 (Phillips 66 gas station and cafe on northwest corner), and enter outskirts of **Willow River**.

44.1 At T-intersection, TURN RIGHT (NORTH) ON CO. 61 AND TWO BLOCKS LATER LEFT (WEST) ON CO. 41 AND LEFT AGAIN (SOUTH) ON FIRE TRAIL. See narrative for places to visit in Willow River.

44.3 Head south on Fire Trail using log for Tour 1 (from mile 10.1 to mile 20.2 going north to south).

55.4 TURN RIGHT (WEST) OFF FIRE TRAIL ON MN. 18 and return to Finlayson trailhead at mile 55.6.

TOUR 4: *Moose Lake to Sturgeon Lake Circle Trip*

Trailhead:	Moose Lake Municipal Park located next to Moosehead Lake east of the center of town at the end of Third Street four blocks from intersection with Mn. 73.
Distance:	21 miles
Terrain:	Level to slightly rolling
Highlights:	Moosehead Lake, Fire Trail, tall pine, and Sturgeon Lake
Route:	(0.0) South on Birch Ave; (0.2) West on First Street; (0.4) South on Elm Avenue which becomes Lakeshore Drive; (0.9) South on Mn. 73; (1.0) Southwest on South Arrowhead Lane; (1.5) Enter Fire Trail -- Head South; (6.5) East on Co. 46; (8.9) **Sturgeon Lake**; (11.5) Turn around -- West on Co. 46; (14.3) North on Co. 51; (18.0) West on Co. 10 over I-35 and then North; (19.5) Northwest on Mn. 72; (20.5) East and North on Lakeshore Drive back to trailhead; (21.4) Trailhead.

This circle route combines a segment of the Fire Trail with pretty shoreline rides and a sampling of the tall pine cover that once dominated the landscape. You could extend the tour by heading further south on the Fire Trail and then doubling back to the turn off for Sturgeon Lake. It could also be shortened by covering only a portion of the south shore of Sturgeon Lake before returning to the intersection with Co. 51. The ride back to Moose Lake takes in slightly more rolling terrain that eventually opens up to nice views of Island Lake and gentle sloping hills.

Log

0.0   From Moose Lake Municipal Park trailhead, TURN LEFT (SOUTH) ON BIRCH AVENUE WHICH BECOMES FIRST STREET when, two blocks later, it turns right (west).

0.4   TURN RIGHT (SOUTH) ON ELM AVENUE which soon becomes Lakeshore Drive as you ride along the shoreline of Moosehead Lake. Lovely views of the lake on your left.

0.9   TURN RIGHT, THEN LEFT (SOUTH) ONTO BIKE PATH NEXT TO MN. 73, CROSS MOOSEHORN RIVER, AND ONE BLOCK LATER TURN RIGHT, THEN LEFT (SOUTHWEST) ONTO SOUTH ARROWHEAD LANE.

1.5   Entrance to Fire Trail. Satellite toilet. HEAD SOUTH ON FIRE TRAIL. For the next five miles, the trail parallels Co. 61 as it passes through a mix of open fields to the west and pine and deciduous trees to the east.

6.5   TURN LEFT (EAST) ON CO. 46, THEN LEFT AGAIN (NORTH) ON CO. 61, AND A BLOCK LATER RIGHT (EAST) ON CO. 46 marked by a pretty white church on the northeast corner. Tall pine line most of the route for the next two miles.

8.3   Cross I-35.

8.7   Co. 51 comes in from your left (north) with the Red Oak Inn on the northwest corner and Lake Sturgeon dead ahead. For the next two miles, Co. 46 skirts the south shore of Sturgeon Lake with unobstructed views of the lake most of the way. Summer cottages line the south side of the road. Continue east until pavement ends at mile 11.4. Then turn around and return to the Red Oak Inn, a friendly bar/restaurant that provides a welcome break. If you're hot and sticky, stop for a swim at the beach on the southeast side of the lake about two blocks from the Inn.

14.1 From Red Oak Inn, HEAD NORTH ON CO. 51, which initially cuts through more pine and then generally parallels I-35 over slightly rolling terrain with glimpses of Island Lake to the east.

17.8 At T-intersection, TURN LEFT (WEST) ON CO. 10, CROSS I-35, AND THEN TURN RIGHT (NORTH) ON CO. 10 for slight downhill ride into Moose Lake.

19.3 At T-intersection, TURN LEFT (NORTHWEST) ON MN. 73. Nice paved shoulder. (Moose Lake State Park is just a mile away in the opposite direction.)

19.7 Pass Hwy. 295 coming in from your right. (An optional route would follow Hwy. 295 for a short circle ride around the Moose Lake Regional Treatment Center and ramble along Lakeshore Drive which rejoins Mn. 73 at the Moosehead River crossing.)

20.4 Cross Moosehead River and return to trailhead along Lakeshore Drive. (Another tempting side trip would be to turn onto Lakeshore Drive just before the crossing and ride over to Hart's Old Tyme Coffee House just a block away for a dinner. See narrative.)

TOUR 5: *Moose Lake to Kettle River Loop*

Trailhead:	Moose Lake City Park located four blocks east of Mn. 73 at the end of Third Street
Distance:	25 miles
Terrain:	Mostly flat except for slight hill in and out of Moose Lake
Highlights:	A patchwork quilt of trees and fields, punctuated in season by rolls of hay
Route:	(0.0) West on Third Street; (0.3) North on Mn. 73; (0.4) West on Mn. Hwys. 27 and 73; (5.3) Southwest on Mn. 37; (10.9) North on Mn. 12; (17.5) **Kettle River**; (23.7) East on Mn. Hwys. 27 and 73 -- retrace route back to trailhead at mile 25.

This trip introduces you to the desolate beauty of the isolated farm sites that lie west of Moose Lake. After a slight climb out of the city, the tour cuts through a great flat expanse characterized by cleared fields in the midst of an encroaching forest of pine, poplar, and birch. These woodlands are said to be teeming with wildlife. In the fields, hay is grown, and after a cutting, rolls of hay lie in place giving added texture to the landscape.

The area is sparsely populated. On the way back to Moose Lake, the route passes through Kettle River, the only community on the trip. This small rural settlement was named after the Kettle River that skirts the town on its winding journey south to the Mississippi River.

Log

0.0 From trailhead at Moose Lake City Park, GO EAST ON THIRD STREET through residential district into town center.

0.3 TURN RIGHT (NORTH) ON MN. 73.

0.4 TURN LEFT (WEST) ON MN. HWYS. 27 and 73 and climb a little along a paved shoulder that crosses railroad tracks at mile 0.7. (The depot to the south was built in 1910 and survived the fire of 1918.)

1.0 Shoulder ends as road levels off. The shoulder will be missed because there is a fair amount of traffic for the next four miles.

1.3 Pass Co. 12 coming in from your right.

5.3 BEAR LEFT (SOUTHWEST) ON MN. 27 as Mn. 73 goes straight.

6.2 Cross Kettle River. Note in season the rolled hay in the cleared fields.

10.9 TURN RIGHT (NORTH) ON CO. 12. St. Joseph's Catholic Church is on the northeastern corner. Co. 12 eventually heads east.

17.4 Cross **Kettle River** and enter town named after it. The road intersects Mn. 73, and at the north end of town on the west side of Mn. 73 is Nemadji Earth Pottery, a small pottery factory open to visitors. CONTINUE EAST ON CO. 12 as area opens up to more flat grazing lands.

18.8 The mix of fields and woodlands returns and the road begins to roll slightly. Co. 12 eventually heads south.

23.7 At T-intersection, TURN LEFT (EAST) ON MN. HWYS. 27 AND 73 and retrace your route back to Moose Lake Municipal Park trailhead at mile 25.

TOUR 6: *Moose Lake to Barnum Circle Trip*

Trailhead:	Same as Tour 4
Distance:	13 or 15 miles
Terrain:	Slightly to very rolling
Highlights:	Hanging Horn Lake, rolling farmland, and Barnum
Route:	(0.0) North on Birch Avenue; (0.4) East on Seventh Street; (0.7) East on Co. 27 which becomes Co. 8 after crossing under I-35; (4.0) North on Co. 13; (7.3) East on Co. 6 (Main Street) -- enter downtown **Barnum**; (7.7) Optional route south on Fire Trail; (10.8) South on Co. 15; (14.2) Moose Lake -- South on Mn. 73 (Arrowhead) and East on Third to trailhead at mile 14.6.

This route provides the shortest route and most hilly terrain of all the tours in this chapter. The somewhat lush rolling terrain during the first half of the trip contrasts with the scrubby flatlands and sparse farm sites along the second leg. There is plenty of tree cover, and in the fall, the turning leaves and blazing sumac give added color to the trip.

Midway through the tour is Barnum, a small community that sums up the history of the area as it evolved from an Indian village to a lumber town to the farm community it is today. Dawn-Marie Eller provides a warm and detailed account of Barnum's first 100 years in her book *Always Onward*. You can buy the book at the Northwoods Motel.

Log

0.0   From Moose Lake City Park. TURN RIGHT (NORTH) ON BIRCH AVENUE.

0.4 TURN RIGHT (EAST) ON SEVENTH STREET which soon circles north.

0.7 At T-intersection, TURN RIGHT (EAST) ON MN. 27 (paved shoulder) and cross Moosehead River.

2.0 Pass under I-35 at which point road becomes Co. 8.

4.0 TURN LEFT (NORTH) ON CO. 13 and climb reaching top at mile 4.4.

4.8 Chain link folk art holds up mailbox on your left.

5.1 Begin scenic roller-coaster descent leveling off at mile 5.4, as road passes between Hanging Horn Lake on your left (west) and Little Hanging Horn Lake on your right (east), and then resumes plunge reaching bottom at mile 6.2 for more shoreline views of the same lakes.

6.8 Pass Bear Lake on your right, cross over I-35, and enter outskirts of Barnum at which point Co. 13 also becomes Carlton Street.

7.3 TURN LEFT (WEST) ON CO. 6 (MAIN STREET) and cross Moose Horn River, which meanders through the municipal park on the north side of the road. Tall pines and outstretched elms provide a serene setting for this cozy park. Camping is available at the park.

7.5 Cross Co. 61 in center of town. A hardware store and the Rusty Diner are just to the north. To the south are the Carlton County fairgrounds, where a restored steam engine, Engine 27, lies in state. A side trip to the fairgrounds may be in order to visit the Little Red Schoolhouse and Railroad Museum located there. CONTINUE WEST ON CO. 6.

7.7 Pass extension out of Moose Lake of State Fire Trail and head west through flat scrubby terrain which opens up into more soothing farmland at mile 10.4. In the alternative GO SOUTH ON FIRE TRAIL 5 miles to Moose Lake.

10.8   TURN LEFT (SOUTH) ON CO. 15 (UNMARKED) as road begins to dip a little. Dense tree cover interspersed with a few small farm sites soon closes in.

13.0   Pass Soldiers Road coming in from your left (east).

13.8   Cross railroad tracks at right angle and descend a little as you enter outskirts of Moose Lake.

14.2   At T-intersection, TURN RIGHT (SOUTHWEST) ON MN. 73 (ARROWHEAD) AND LEFT (SOUTHEAST) ON ELM STREET.

14.4   TURN LEFT (EAST) ON THIRD STREET and go east three blocks to trailhead at mile 14.6.

LANESBORO TOURS

Flanked by high bluffs and shaped by the Root River, Lanesboro and the surrounding area offer some of the best bicycling in Minnesota. This quaint city is located in the heart of the so-called "driftless" area of southeastern Minnesota, the only portion of the state that was not leveled by the last glacier that advanced into Minnesota. The glacial drifts stopped short of the area. As the glaciers melted, the massive runoff carved deep valleys and gorges which have become the home of some of the state's last remaining hardwood forests. The forests, streams, small riverside towns, and cleared pastures in the valley combine with rolling farmland on the highlands above to make each bicycle tour out of Lanesboro a varied and scenic experience.

The Lanesboro area is ideally suited for either an easy-going weekend or a more extended stay. We offer five bicycle tours that provide plenty of opportunity for both the beginner and experienced bicyclist.

Each tour starts in Lanesboro. All of the tours take advantage of the Root River Trail -- a multi-use corridor developed by the state of Minnesota on the abandoned Milwaukee Railroad right-of-way. The paved portion of the trail runs for 28 miles from Rushford on the east to one mile east of Fountain on the west (with an extension to Fountain planned for construction in 1993). Lanesboro is located on the trail about 11 miles east of Fountain.

Tour 1: Fountain Hill Circle Trip -- 21 or 23 miles
Tour 2: Root River Valley Circle Trip -- 11, 27, or 36 miles
Tour 3: The South Rim Circle Trip -- 35 or 43 miles
Tour 4: The North Rim Circle Trip -- 38 miles
Tour 5: Two Day Trip: Forestville State Park Circle Trip -- 34 miles to park and 24 or 26 miles return trip

About the Area

How to Get There: About 115 miles and 2.5 hours drive south from the Twin Cities. Take U.S. 52 all the way to Fountain. From Fountain go east on Co. 8 to Lanesboro.

Wheat and flour milling and the railroad initially spurred growth in Lanesboro and the surrounding communities. By 1879, the village of Lanesboro had a stone school, three churches, five hotels, a warehouse, four general stores, two hardware stores, a harness shop, an implement store, eight saloons, three flour mills, and many residences. Still standing and in operation is a power dam erected in 1868 at a total cost of $15,000. The flour mills operated around-the-clock on water power from the dam.

All in all, 13 mills once flourished along the Root River Trail. Then soil erosion and depletion took its toll. As the farmers returned to crop rotation and more livestock, and competition from the larger mills in Minneapolis increased, demand for local flour milling diminished. In time, Lanesboro and the nearby communities ceased to be boom towns. Instead, they settled into what they are today -- comfortable small towns serving the surrounding farm community and visiting city folk.

Lanesboro no longer has any hotels. In their place, however, are several pleasant bed and breakfast establishments:

- Mrs. B's Historic Inn (507/467-2154), 10 rooms, gourmet dinners on Thursdays, Fridays, and Saturdays, with each room having its own bath and access to a balcony.

- Scanlon House (507/467-2158), a charming old victorian house with five guest rooms and a comfortable outdoor patio. Just across the street from the Scanlon House is the Victorian House of Lanesboro, which is a superb French restaurant (507/467-3457).

- Cady Hayes House (507/467-2621) owned and operated by one of Lanesboro's newest residents, Duke Addicks, master storyteller and bicycle tour guide, and his wife, Peggy.

Also in town are the Knotty Pine Cabins (507/467-3779; Historic Lodge Inn (507/467-2257) (3 bedrooms); Old Drug Store Hotel (507/467-2104) (3 bedrooms); Riverside Homestead (507/467-2104) (whole house rental on the Root River); Cottage House (507/467-2577) (6 rooms); Galligan House (507/467-2299) (Bed and Breakfast - 2 rooms); Guest Hus of Lanesboro (507/467-3512) (5 rooms); and Bue Studio Suite (507/467-2555 - 1 room).

In addition, for country lovers, just outside of Lanesboro is the Carrolton Country Inn (507/467-2257), a pre-1882 farm home, completely restored with four guest rooms and available for whole house rental. The Inn is situated on a rounded hill surrounded by lush pasture land and overlooking the south branch of the Root River below. Another farm house retreat is Birch Knoll Ranch Bed & Breakfast (612/475-2054), three bedrooms, a one to two mile bike ride to the trail.

For campers, Sylvan Park, a well-kept city park (507/467-3722), with camping facilities (showers and running water) is nestled next to the bluffs and two small trout ponds. Another campground (80 sites) is the Old Barn Resort (507/467-2512), which includes the Old Allis Barn converted into a 60-bed hostel and restaurant. This place was once the site for the now-vanished mill town of Clear Grit. The complex is located five miles west of Lanesboro just off Co. 17. The sponsors of this project also run a reservation service for host farms and cottages in the area (507/886-5392). Primitive camping facilities are also available at Isinours Unit about 1/4 mile off the trail at mile 5.2 in the log for Tour 1.

The number of saloons in Lanesboro has dwindled, but be sure to order some rhubarb wine at Scenic Valley Winery, Inc., or one of the other fruit wines made from locally grown fruits. Also, don't bother to pack a lunch. Stop at one of the two grocery stores where you can order your own sandwiches from assorted meats and cheeses. Or try a German style bratwurst with homemade mustard at Das Wurst Haus. Or at River Valley Cheese feast on a variety of fresh cheese processed on site from milk provided daily by the Amish farmers.

The whole downtown area of Lanesboro is listed on the National Register of Historic Places. The two- and three-story brick and stone buildings have changed very little since they were first built a century ago. Some of this history is captured in the exhibits at the Lanesboro Museum located above the Root River Trail Center next to the trail. For evening entertainment, take in the summer stock theater at the St. Mane.

For additional information about Lanesboro contact its tourist bureau at 1-800/944-2670.

On the outskirts of Lanesboro are three added attractions:

- The State Fish Hatchery, a mile west of town, is the largest trout hatchery in the state and one of the largest in the midwest. Weekday tours of the hatchery and adjoining laboratory facilities are available (507/467-3771).

- The Forest Resource Center (507/467-2437) is located on a bluff above the north branch of the Root River. The center provides 4.5 miles of hiking trails, woodland, a bat condominium, and shiitake mushroom demonstrations and workshops.

- The Amish farms south of town where black, horse-drawn carriages and non-motorized farm wagons join the wandering cyclist to slacken the pace of the roving automobiles. For bus tours of the area, contact Michael's Amish Tours (507/886-5382).

The tours out of Lanesboro take you into a number of surrounding communities. Each community, forged out of a common history of flour milling, farming, and railroading, has its own special attractions. To the east along the Root River Trail is Whalan, once the tobacco center of Fillmore County and now a small bedroom community with no business district. Overlooking the town is the stately white-steepled Whalan Lutheran Church with a glistening brass bell silhouetted in the belfry. The Overland Inn and Ice Cream Parlor (507/467-2623) - 3 rooms above parlor - is strategically located next to the trail. A block away from the trail is Besta's Hüs (507/467-2630), lodging and tea room.

Further east of Lanesboro is Peterson. Here you can find a ballpark next to the trail (a must stop when a game is in progress), the 1877 Peterson Station Museum (507/875-2503), open sometimes on weekends, and Bev's Country Cafe, a good place for a cup of coffee and homemade cooking. Lodging is available at Wenneson Hotel (507/875-2587), a restored 1904 hotel (5 rooms) and 413 Park Street Inn (507/875-2231), a bed and breakfast accommodation.

remaining two-store SMRC depot still on its original site. In town is the Mill Street Inn, once a hardware store built from quarried limestone in 1870 and now a restaurant. The city also provides home cooking at Carl's Cafe, a refreshing dip at the municipal pool, a bed and breakfast at River Trail Inn (507/864-7886) (ten rooms) and at Meadows Inn (507/864-2378). Free picnic and camping facilities are found at the Rushford North End park and Magelssen Bluff (no water and gravel road ascent) overlooking the city. East of Rushford, the Root River Trail continues as a hiking and horseback trail for an additional six miles.

To the west of Lanesboro, just beyond the end of the trail, is Fountain. This town has a grocery store (Willie's Grocery and Locker) and a small restaurant (White Corner Cafe) -- a must stop for great pies, and an ice cream parlor scheduled to open in 1993. Lodging in Fountain can be found at Main Street Inn (507/268-4454) -- whole house rental only, Cedar Street Inn (507/268-4454) whole house rental only, and Thriftway Inn of Fountain (1-800/437-1259), a bed and breakfast accommodation.

Fountain boasts the Fillmore County History Centre (507/268-4449), a haven for genealogy buffs looking for their roots. The center also exhibits artifacts and memorabilia dating back to when the Indians still roamed the area. The center is open Monday through Friday from 11:30 a.m. to 4:30 p.m. and Saturday and Sunday, summer only, from 12:00 noon to 4:00 p.m.

On Tour 5, you venture out even further from Lanesboro on a trip which passes through Preston and Wykoff, offers a side trip to Mystery Cave, and provides for an overnight at Forestville State Park. Preston remains a thriving community situated on the banks of the south branch of the Root River. In town, the old jail, elegantly restored in a Victorian motif, is now an 11 room country inn ("The Jail House," 507/765-2181). Two of the bedrooms are literally "behind bars." On the eastern edge of town Camp Hidden Valley (507/765-2467) provides shaded campsites along the Root River and three miles of biking trails. For more information about the area, call the Preston Tourism Commission (507/765-2100).

Founded in 1871 and flanked by two spiral churches, Wykoff is a friendly small town which should be savored. As stated in the *Historic Bluff County Journal*:

> An open invitation is extended to you to drive through our streets of the early 1900's. See our limestone gymnasium, one room brick jail built in 1913, The Dohs House built in 1876, the history of one man's life at Ed's Museum, the old creamery, and if you get lucky you may see the wild turkeys that sometimes roam our streets.

To assure a proper pause is made in this town, stop at The Forest Inn (closed after 2:00 p.m. Saturday and Sunday) for at least a cup of coffee at not breakfast or lunch.

Forestville State Park (507/352-5111) is one of the prettiest state parks in Minnesota. It is tucked into one of the sculptured valleys where the south branch of the Root River, Canfield Creek, and Forestville Creek converge. Most of the park is covered by various kinds of hardwood (oak, basswood, sugar maple, ironwood, elm, green ash, black walnut, bitternut, hickory, and aspen). The park has excellent camping facilities and more than 15 miles of hiking trails.

The park was once the site for the town of Forestville. In the 1850's it had two stores, two hotels, two sawmills, a grist mill, a cooper shop, a chair factory, a wagon shop, a distillery and a tavern. It thrived as a center for two stagecoach lines but all that changed when these routes were abandoned and the railroad by-passed Forestville.

Today the site is administered by the Minnesota Historical Society and is open to the public daily May 1 through Labor Day (weekends from September 7 through October 10) with costumed guides who portray actual residents and their daily activities in the late 1800's. You can visit the Meighen Store which closed in 1910 with its merchandise of side saddles, ox yokes, spinning wheels, a civil war drum, etc. still on the shelves. The Post Office, a granary, garden and the Meighen residence with a newly restored kitchen are open also. (507-765-2785).

Less than a mile east of the store on Co. 12 (gravel) is a farm that raises a variety of exotic fowl and provides bed-and-breakfast accommodations in a separate cottage called Sunnyside Cottages of Forestville (507-765-3357) -- three rooms and whole-house rental.

Just 0.5 mile south of Forestville State Park on Co. 5 is the turnoff to Mystery Cave (507/937-3251), a fascinating chain of underground caves and sinkholes recently acquired as part of the Forestville State Park system. Note that there are two entrances to the caves 1.5 miles apart providing two different underground tours. Both tours are well worth a visit. The caves are open June, July, and August.

TOUR 1: *Fountain Hill Circle Trip*

Trailhead:	Trail parking lot at junction of Co. 8 and Mn. 250 in downtown Lanesboro (restrooms in trail center across the street)
Distance:	23 miles or (if return on Co. 8) 21 miles
Terrain:	Painless gentle climb
Highlights:	Pastoral scenery along trail, Fillmore County Historical Centre, and stunning valley views along Co. 8.
Route:	(0.0) West on trail; (10.0) West on Co. 8; (11.4) **Fountain** -- turn around; (12.4) Southeast on trail to Lanesboro at mile 22.8 or West on Co. 8 to Lanesboro at mile 20.5

This tour is a pleasant, leisurely circle trip. Beginning at the Root River Trail Center in Lanesboro and heading along the Root River Trail west to Fountain, the tour follows the south branch of the Root River with the river on the left and the high bluffs on the right. The scenery is a patch work of pasture land, hardwood forests, limestone cuts, and inviting streams.

Half way through the trip, the trail begins a gentle climb at railroad grade up Fountain Hill finally ending a mile east of Fountain. On the return trip (after a visit to Fountain), take either the same route or (for a highland run and intermittent views of the Root River Valley below) stay on Co. 8 and swoop into Lanesboro for the last mile.

Log - Mileage from west to east is in parenthesis

0.0 (11.4) Trailhead: Northwest corner of junction of Co. 8 and Mn. 250 in Lanesboro just west of Mrs. B's. On right is the Root River Trail Center (with rest-room facilities and trail maps) at basement level and Lanesboro Museum on the first and second floors. (Parking across street on northeast corner next to trail.) HEAD WEST ON ROOT RIVER TRAIL across south branch of Root River on wooden bridge built on old iron-ribbed railroad trestle.

Before the bridge, the trail passes between two 30-foot poles. They once held between them a wire mesh (the "flycatcher" or "telltale") to alert the engineer (and the brakeman or any hobos on top) that the train is packed too high to pass under steel girders framing the bridge.

0.3 (11.1) Power dam on south side just before trail cuts through limestone rock. Watch out for the occasional rattlesnake sunning on the hot pavement or flat rocks nearby.

1.9 (9.5) Cross gravel road which leads to Carrolton Country Inn (0.5 mile southwest). (See narrative.) At this point, the trail follows the river which is about 30 feet below on the south side.

2.4 (9.0) Picnic table on south side on spot overlooking river.

2.5 (8.9) Another picnic table on south side. Trail soon parts from river.

3.7 (7.4)	Cross river. Small log cabin shelter on south side just before bridge. Lots of willow trees dipping into river north of bridge.
4.1 (7.3)	Cross river again over trestle bridge. Just beyond are two more of those telltale poles with the wire mesh still in place.
44.4 (7.0)	Trail cuts through more limestone rock creating miniature canyon effect and then crosses gravel township road. Old Barn Resort is just off this road to the south. Trail enters wider valley with lush pasture land on both sides.
5.2 (6.2)	Cross another gravel road (Co. 17). Connected to this road just south of the trail is another gravel road which parallels the trail for awhile, then crosses the trail, and leads to the Isinours parking and picnic area on north side at mile 5.7. The place once housed a depot to serve the citizens of Preston who were later linked to the Root River line by a branch line which connected a mile east. (Plans are afoot to restore the branch line as another paved trail that will eventually extend to Harmony.) Toilet facilities, interpretive displays on the Richard T. Dorer Memorial Hardwood State Forest, maps for a self-guided hiking tour through Isinour's "Demonstration Woodland," a log cabin shelter, and an artisan well are present. Primitive camping facilities are also available about 0.25 mile off trail.
5.9 (5.5)	Cross Watson Creek. At this point, the trail begins a gentle climb over what, in railroad days, was called Fountain Hill. For a train, the grade was considered steep enough to require a special engine, called the "Pusher," to push any heavy ladened train from the rear as the main engine pulled up front.
6.4 (5.0)	Cross Watson Creek again and bridge over township road.

6.6 (4.8)	Bucolic views of pasture, woods, and serpentine creek to the south.
7.3 (4.1)	Picnic table on west side of road.
7.6 (3.8)	As trail climbs, it passes through a tunnel of overhanging maples before finally entering clearing at mile 7.9.
8.3 (3.1)	False top of Fountain Hill with pastoral panoramic views to north and south.
8.6 (2.8)	Wind through working farm on north side. Cross gravel road. Trail cuts through another exposed limestone bluff on the north side and resumes its gentle climb.
9.0 (2.4)	Picnic table on north side of road.
10.2 (1.2)	Log cabin shelter and parking on north side as trail ends at mile 10.3. (Plans have been made to extend the trail to Fountain in 1993.)
10.4 (1.0)	TURN LEFT (WEST) FOR FOUNTAIN ON CO. 8. Fountain Lutheran Cemetery on south side.
11.0 (0.4)	TURN RIGHT (NORTH) ONTO RESIDENTIAL ROAD.
11.1 (0.3)	At T-intersection, TURN LEFT (WEST).
11.4 (0.0)	Impressive stone church on south side. Intersection with White Corner Cafe on northwest corner. (See narrative.) Small business district one block further west. Visit the Fillmore County History Centre. (See narrative.)

Return to Lanesboro on same route or by way of Co. 8. If Co. 8 is taken, use log for Tour 5, Option A, at mile 50.4.

TOUR 2: *The Root River Valley Circle Trip*

Trailhead:	Same as Tour 1
Distance:	Option A: 11 miles to Whalan and back
	Option B: 27 miles to Peterson and back
	Option C: 36 miles to Rushford and back
Terrain:	Level
Highlights:	Sights along the Root River Trail, Whalan, Peterson, and Rushford
Route:	Take trail both ways; (5.3) **Whalan**; (13.6) **Peterson**; and (18.0) **Rushford**.

This trip sticks to the Root River Trail all the way to Rushford and back in the comfort of the Root River Valley. For a shorter trip, turn around at Whalan or Peterson. (See narrative about communities.) Along the trail, the alluring Root River intermittently comes into view as it winds through the valley. Sightings of wild turkey, white-tailed deer, red-tailed hawks, and turkey vultures are common. Like the route west, high bluffs hug the trail on the north for most of the way.

Log - Mileage from east to west is in parenthesis

0.0 (14.4)   Trailhead: Junction of Co. 8 and Mn. 250 in Lanesboro just west of Mrs. B's. Parking lot on northeast corner next to trail. HEAD EAST ON ROOT RIVER TRAIL FOR RUSHFORD.

OPTIONS A, B, and C: On to Whalan

0.1 (18.0)   Cross road and back onto trail.

0.3 (17.7)   Cross Root River (south branch) on wooden bridge.

1.5 (16.5)   Trail begins to parallel river on the south side.

1.7 (16.3)   North branch of Root River begins following trail on the north side.

1.9 (16.1)   Cross wooden bridge where both branches of Root River converge. After crossing, trail parts from the river for a while.

3.0 (15.0)   After winding around a farmer's pasture, trail returns to river (picnic table on north side) and for the next mile follows river located on the south side 40 feet below. Great views of the river.

4.0 (14.0)   End (or beginning) of mile-long traverse along river embankment.

4.5 (13.5)   Enter **Whalan.**

4.7 (13.3)   Reach center of town. The Overland Inn and ice cream parlor is adjacent to the trail. The Whalen County Store also abuts the trail. To the northeast up a hill 0.15 mile is Whalan Lutheran Church (see narrative).

5.3 (12.7)   Small rest area/parking area on north side (satellite toilet). Picnic table on south side. If Option A is taken, turn around and return on same route. Otherwise continue east on trail.

OPTIONS B and C: On to Peterson

5.4 (12.6)   Enter thick stand of hardwood.

6.5 (11.5)   Trail follows river again for 0.5 mile of churning water. Picnic table at beginning and end of this stretch.

7.5 (10.5)   Trail passes between red barn and outbuildings on south side and pretty white farm house with red trim on north side.

8.0 (10.0)   Rustic view of farm tucked in snug valley to the north Creek crossing.

9.1 (8.9)	Horseshoe view of river on south side. Perfect picnic spot next to river as it turns away from trail. Log seats already in place. Across the river is a campsite for canoeists.
9.9 (8.1)	After cutting through cornfields, cross small creek. Be on the lookout for wild turkeys.
10.1 (7.9)	River parts. Picnic table on river side as trail turns north.
10.7 (7.3)	Cross Big Spring Creek. Good place to wet your feet. River soon returns to trail. Note abandoned highway bridge upriver (future site for park).
11.4 (6.6)	River soon turns away from trail for last look before Peterson.
12.6 (5.4)	Picnic table on south side.
13.3 (4.7)	Co. 25 begins to parallel trail on the north side as trail enters **Peterson**. Bridge crossing. Ballpark on south side.
13.5 (4.5)	Pop machine on south side.
13.6 (4.4)	Cross Main Street and Co. 25. Interpretive display on history of Peterson. Next to the trail are the old Quickstad Wagon Works building (once a blacksmith shop where wagons and sleighs were built), an 1876 mill chimney (on Mill Street), and further ahead, the old Peterson trout farm owned by the town's namesake (no trout farming here today). A turn south leads to downtown Peterson (see narrative). If Option B is taken, turn around and return on same route. Otherwise continue east on trail.

OPTION C: On to Rushford

14.2 (3.2)	Trail begins to crowd the hillside to the north as tree cover returns. Intermittent views of river resume for next 1.5 miles.
14.9 (3.1)	River appears. Look for signs of beaver.
15.0 (3.0)	River bends south for last view.
15.4 (2.6)	Picnic table.
15.9 (2.1)	Trail emerges from tree cover and parallels Mn. 16 as area opens up and northerly slopes recede. Well-kept farm to the north.
17.9 (0.1)	Red building on north side. Owner plans to open it up for bicyclists with showers and rooms.
18.0 (0.0)	Rushford Depot on north side (see narrative). Public rest rooms inside. To get into center of town, cut between grain elevators just to the east. (See narrative). Return on same route.

TOUR 3: *The South Rim Circle Trip*

Trailhead:	Same as Tour 1
Distance:	Option A: 35 miles (Peterson shortcut) Option B: 43 miles (full circle)
Terrain:	Varied but only one significant climb
Highlight:	State Fish Hatchery, buffalo farm, spectacular views along ridge, a winding highland ride, Highland Prairie Church Park and sights along Root River Trail.

Route: (0.0) South on Mn. 259; (9.05) West on Mn. 16; (0.9) South on Co. 21; (6.9) East on Co. 12; (8.3) North on Co. 23; (10.0) Northeast on Co. 10; (14.0);

Option A: North on Co. 25 (20.6) North on Mn. 16; (21.0) West on Co. 25; (21.4) South then West on trail; (30.3) **Whalan;** (35.0) **Lanesboro** -- trailhead.

Option B: East on Co. 10; (17.0) Southeast on Co. 37 to Highland Prairie Church Park and back; (19.0) North on Mn. 43; (24.7) West on Mn. 16 and North on next road to Rushford Depot; (24.9) West on trail; (29.3) **Peterson;** (38.4) **Whalen;** (42.9) **Lanesboro** -- trailhead.

This is a must trip for the venturesome bicyclist. The tour takes the southern route to Rushford and returns to Lanesboro by way of the Root River Trail. It also provides a two-mile diversion to the State Fish Hatchery just out of town. The climb out of Lanesboro is a gradual, winding ascent up a narrow forested vale. Upon reaching the top, you are rewarded with breathtaking views of rolling farmland in the valleys below.

The route continues south along a ridge past grazing buffalo and then turns east for a delightful winding upland ride that eventually leads to Highland -- a small town with an all-purpose country store. Soon afterwards, the trip can be shortened by turning north and taking the plunge back to Peterson or can be extended by way of a winding road through more high farm country (with a side trip to a unique church park) and, after reaching Bratsberg, a pretty valley descent north into Rushford. In either case, the route returns to Lanesboro by way of the Root River Trail.

Log

0.0 Trailhead: At junction of Co. 8 and Mn. 250 in Lanesboro. HEAD SOUTH FROM MRS. B'S THROUGH TOWN ON MN. 250.

0.2	Sylvan Park is on your left, and Power Dam Falls is on your right.
0.5	TURN RIGHT (WEST) ON MN. 16. Road climbs a little and has a small paved shoulder.
0.9	Junction with Co. 21. **Decision Point:** Either (a) take a side trip to the State Fish Hatchery by continuing west on Co. 16 for about 0.75 mile and turn left on road leading to hatchery about 0.25 mile away or (b) TURN LEFT (SOUTH) ON CO. 21. The rest of this log assumes that the left on Co. 21 has been taken. Road continues to climb gradually out of valley as it winds its way upward through a somewhat narrow cut surrounded by overhanging maple and oak trees. Quite spectacular in the fall.
2.9	Road continues to climb as the cut expands into rolling hills and the trees disappear finally reaching top side at mile 3.5. On the way up note on your left an abandoned one room school house (No. 33) followed by an excellent example of contour farming. From mile 3.5 to mile 3.9, there are spectacular views of distant farm land in the valley below to the west interspersed with similar vistas to the east.
4.2	Road climbs a little more topping off at mile 4.9 with more spectacular views on both sides. Road dips a little.
5.9	On your left is Horner's Corner, another one room school house converted into a private residence.
6.5	Pass Co. 12 coming in from your right to join Co. 21.
6.7	Buffalo farm on your left.
6.9	Co. Roads 21 and 12 split. BEAR LEFT (EAST) ON CO. 12 for slight downhill. Amish farms in the area.
8.3	TURN LEFT (NORTH) ON CO. 23. Road roller coasters a little.

9.0	Note on your left standout view of red brick church 1/2 mile to the west.
10.0	Co. 23 makes sharp left becoming gravel. BEAR RIGHT (NORTHEAST) ON CO. 10 INSTEAD as road snakes through scenic farmland.
11.2	Highland Store (groceries/snacks) on right along with small gasoline station.
14.0	Road forks with Co. 25 coming in from your left and Co. 10 bearing right. **Decision Point:** Either (a) turn left (north) on Co. 25 and return to Peterson (Option A) and save 8 miles or (b) bear right (east) on Co. 10 and proceed to Rushford (Option B).

OPTION A: Proceed to Peterson

14.0	GO LEFT (NORTH) ON CO. 25. Road climbs a little reaching the top at mile 12.3 then roller coasters.
16.9	Nice panoramic view to west.
17.8	Descent into Peterson begins.
19.3	Pass Co. 107 coming in from your right.
19.4	Peterson Fish Hatchery on your right. State is fixing it up for public.
20.6	At T-intersection, TURN RIGHT (NORTH) ON MN. 16.
21.0	TURN LEFT (WEST) ON CO. 25 into Peterson crossing bridge which spans Root River. Follow Main Street/Co. 25 into middle of town. (See narrative).
21.3	Peterson Station Museum on your right and Bev's Country Cafe on your left.

21.4 Junction with Root River Trail. TURN LEFT (SOUTH) ON TRAIL for Lanesboro 13.6 miles away. (Pick up east-to-west log for Tour 2 at mile 4.4.)

OPTION B: Proceed to Rushford

14.0 BEAR RIGHT (EAST) ON CO. 10. Road winds a lot.

17.0 TURN RIGHT (SOUTHEAST) ON CO. 37 and go 2/10th mile to Highland Prairie Church Park. Note the natural amphitheater, sculptured "Folk art" and scale model of the original church. Nice spot for a picnic - pavilion, toilets and water. Double back to Co. 10.

18.3 Restored 19th Century limestone house on your left.

19.0 At T-intersection, TURN LEFT (NORTH) ON MN. 43. Just after turn is a gasoline station with a pop machine. This small community is called Bratsberg. Road roller coasters a little.

20.2 Long, gliding descent through narrow valley begins.

21.6 Road levels off somewhat as valley opens up.

23.9 Road merges with Mn. 16 coming in from right. CONTINUE STRAIGHT ON MN. HWYS. 43/16 towards downtown Rushford.

24.3 Cross Root River.

24.7 TURN LEFT (WEST) ON MN. 16 AND AT MILE 19.9 TURN RIGHT (NORTH) ON ROAD HEADING FOR DEPOT. (Alternatively, head straight into center of town and look around. See narrative.)

24.9 Arrive at Rushford Depot and eastern trailhead for the paved portion of Root River Trail. HEAD WEST ON TRAIL for Lanesboro 18.0 miles away. (Use the east-to-west log for Tour 2 at mile 0.0.)

TOUR 4: *The North Rim Circle Trip*

Trailhead:	Same as Tour 1
Distance:	38 miles
Terrain:	Varied with only one significant climb
Highlights:	Sights along the Root River Trail, two sentinel churches in high farm country, and plunge into Root River Valley
Route:	(0.0) East on trail; (4.7) **Whalan**; (13.6) **Peterson**; (18.0) **Rushford** Depot -- East one block and North on Mill Street; (18.2) West on Mn. 30; (29.2) South on Mn. 250; (38.3) Lanesboro -- trailhead.

This trip takes the Root River Trail to Rushford and then returns by way of a northerly route first up a tree-lined hill out of Rushford and then over high country farmland. Midway back you may either turn south and proceed downhill to Peterson or keep heading west. The westerly route soon passes two white Lutheran churches, situated like sentinels, only a mile and a half apart in the midst of open farm country. Eventually the route turns south and, after a roller-coaster dip, makes a two mile descent into the Root River Valley leading to Lanesboro.

Log
Use the log for Tour 2 for trip from Lanesboro to Rushford

18.0   Rushford Depot. (See narrative.) HEAD EAST BETWEEN GRAIN ELEVATORS AND TURN LEFT (NORTH) ON MILL STREET.

18.2   TURN LEFT (EAST) ON MN. 30.

19.5   Cemetery on your left.

22.0	Road climbs gradually at first, getting steeper from mile 22.4, as you travel through a thicket of hardwood trees, and finally break into the open and reach the top at mile 23.5. We are now in high farm country.
25.4	Cross Co. 25. (Peterson is a three mile downhill plunge south.) Arendahl Cemetery is at northeast corner.
26.2	See first of two standout white Lutheran churches 1.5 miles further west.
27.2	Gasoline station with pop machine.
27.6	Arendahl Lutheran Church (beautiful white steepled church) on your right. Road roller coasters a little.
28.2	Lovely tree-lined cemetery with second white church (North Prairie Lutheran) on your right.
29.2	Junction with Mn. 250 (south) and Co. 32 (north). Turn left (south) on Mn. 250. Road roller coasters.
34.5	Steep descent into Lanesboro in valley below bottoming out at mile 35.3.
35.4	Cross north branch of Root River.
35.8	Gravel road on right leads to Southern Minnesota Forest Resource Center. See narrative.
37.9	Cross Root River. Parking near to Root River Trail on other side of bridge.
38.2	At T-intersection, turn left on Parkway Avenue and head into Lanesboro business center.
38.3	Junction with Co. 8 and Mn. 250. On left is Mrs. B's. Parking lot across the street.

TOUR 5: *TWO DAY TRIP: Forestville State Park Circle Trip*

Trailhead:	Same as Tour 1
Distance:	34 miles to park and 26 miles return trip if Root River Trail is taken out of Fountain (or 24 miles if Co. 8 instead of trail is taken)
Terrain:	Varied
Highlights:	Spectacular views along ridge, wide open farm country, Mystery Cave, Forestville State Park (Meighen Store), Wykoff, and gliding descent down Fountain Hill along Root River Trail.
Route:	(0.0) South on Mn. 250; (0.5) West on Mn. 16; (0.9) South on Co. 21; (6.5) West on Co. 12; (10.4) Northwest on U.S. 52; (13.5) West on Co. 12; (14.1) **Preston**; (16.5) Southwest on Co. 14; (28.4) North on Co. 5; (31.5) East on Co. 12; (33.7) **Forestville State Park** - turn around. West on Co. 12; (35.8) North on Co. 5; (40.9) **Wykoff**; (41.8) East on Mn. 80; (49.0) North on U.S. 52; (49.1) East on Co. 8 -- **Fountain**; (50.4) Root River Trailhead.
	Option A: Continue east on Co. 8 to Lanesboro at mile 58.5.
	Option B: Go southeast on trail to Lanesboro at mile 60.4.

This trip initially follows the same route taken in the South Rim Circle Trip to Rushford (Tour 3) but instead of heading east, turns west, at the crest of the hill, for Forestville State Park. After a roller-coaster ride into a broad valley cut by the south branch of the Root River below, the route enters Preston. (See narrative.) From there a manageable climb out of the river valley follows. Half way up, a 6.5 mile shortcut, mostly on a gravel road, may be taken to the park. Once out of the valley, the route zigzags over high farm country, eventually reaching the turn off to Mystery Cave (see narrative) and soon afterwards makes a gentle winding descent into a wooded vale, which is home for Forestville State Park. (See narrative).

The return trip backtracks out of the park and resumes a gently rolling meander through high farm country. After passing through Wykoff (see narrative), the route heads east over flat farmland. Eventually the tour enters Fountain (see narrative) and then concludes with either a delightful gliding descent along the Root River Trail back to Lanesboro or a highland run (with intermittent views of the Root River Valley below) followed by a one-mile plunge into Lanesboro.

Log

0.0	Trailhead: Junction of Co. 8 and Mn. 250 in Lanesboro. HEAD SOUTH FROM MRS. B'S THROUGH TOWN ON MN. 250. Follow the same route as Tour 3 as far as mile 6.5 where Co. 21 meets Co. 12.
6.5	TURN RIGHT (WEST) ON CO. 12. Road roller coasters in downward swoop for next six miles. Look for Amish farms on your right.
7.5	Climb for 1/2 mile, then down again through more pasture and farmland.
10.4	At T-intersection, TURN RIGHT (NORTHWEST) ON U.S. 52.
11.9	U.S. 52 merges with Mn. 16 coming in from your right. Keep going straight on U.S. 52/Mn. 16.

13.5	Just before cement bridge, TURN LEFT (WEST) ON CO. 12. Opposite the turnoff is the road leading to Hidden Valley Campground one-quarter mile from U.S. 52/Mn. 16. (See narrative.)
13.6	Cross creek with small roadside park with a couple of picnic tables just beyond, as road enters Preston.
14.1	Cross Root River and at mile 14.3 enter downtown **Preston**. (See narrative.) KEEP GOING STRAIGHT ON CO. 12 (FILLMORE STREET) past the IGA food market.
14.7	Cross Root River again at which point CO. 12 PICKS UP CO. 15 and begins to climb reaching the top at mile 14.9 with Fillmore Cemetery on your left.
15.5	Road splits with Co. 15 bearing left and Co. 12 turning right. BEAR RIGHT (WEST) ON CO. 12. More climbing.
16.5	Road continues to bear left (southwest) as Co. 14 or turns right as Co. 12. (Co. 12, which later becomes Co. 118, is a shorter route to Forestville State Park, 11 miles to Information Bureau, instead of 17 miles, but is gravel after 1.2 miles.) BEAR LEFT (SOUTHWEST) ON CO. 14 and keep climbing finally leveling off after a few dips at mile 19.1. For next five miles, road travels through high farm country on relatively level terrain.
24.0	Co. 9 comes in from your left and joins Co. 14. STAY ON CO. 14.
24.8	Co. 14 turns right (west) while Co. 9 goes straight (north). TURN LEFT (WEST) ON CO. 14 and climb a little. Road begins to roller coaster.
26.1	Beginning of steep down and up past quarry.
28.4	TURN RIGHT (NORTH) ON CO. 5. Road continues to roller coaster somewhat.

29.9	Gravel road for Mystery Cave 1.5 miles away coming in from your left. (See narrative).
30.1	Co. 5 descends for a mile, crosses bridge, and then climbs reaching top and turn off on Co. 12 to Forestville State Park at mile 31.5.
31.5	TURN RIGHT (EAST) ON CO. 12, which is compact gravel.
32.2	Begin descent to park at river bottom, reaching a paved road at mile 33.4 and the State Park Information Station at mile 33.7. RETURN WEST BY SAME ROUTE TO CO. 5.
35.8	TURN RIGHT (NORTH) ON CO. 5.
36.0	Road climbs, then roller coasters with a few steep dips during next four miles.
40.0	CROSS CO. 16 AND PICK UP MN. 80.
40.9	Enter Wykoff. (See narrative.)
41.8	TURN RIGHT (EAST) ON MN. 80 (instead of going straight on Co. 5), pass Wykoff Farm Store (hardware) on your right and head into open farm land. Relatively flat open farmland for next seven miles. Sinkholes to the north closer to Fountain easiest to identify by a clump of trees and brush in the middle of a farm field.
49.0	At T-intersection, TURN LEFT (NORTH) ON U.S. 52.
49.1	Junction with Co. 8 just after Standard Station. TURN RIGHT (EAST) ON CO. 8 which passes through Fountain.
49.3	Fillmore County Historical Center on your right. (See narrative.) TURN LEFT (NORTH) INTO FOUNTAIN BUSINESS DISTRICT where Willie's Grocery and Lockers Store is located, THEN RIGHT (EAST) JUST BEFORE FIRST STATE BANK. At next intersection is the White Corner Cafe on your left. Good place to stop for pie. TURN RIGHT (SOUTH).

49.5	Fountain United Methodist Church is on your right. At T-intersection, TURN LEFT (EAST) BACK ONTO CO. 8.
50.0	Road descends with Fountain Cemetery on your right at mile 50.3.
50.4	Root River Trailhead on your right.

TWO OPTIONS: First Option - County Road 8 Option

       Continue east on Co. 8. For next six miles, road dips and climbs a little with intermittent sweeping panoramic views to your right (south) of Root River Valley below.

53.0	Cemetery on your left.
56.4	Descend into Root River Valley gradually at first and at mile 57.7 rapidly, with magnificent view of Lanesboro half way down at mile 58.2.
58.5	Cross Root River. Mrs. B's on your left and parking lot across the street at junction of Co. 8 and Mn. 250.

SECOND OPTION: Root River Trail Option

50.4	Turn right onto Root River Trailhead. Use the west-to-east log for Tour 1 starting at mile 1.2 and east to Lanesboro 10.2 miles away. The first four miles are all downhill!

NOTES

MISSISSIPPI RIVER BLUFF COUNTRY TOURS

The Mississippi River Bluff Country Tours offer something for everybody. They originate out of either Winona, Minn., or Fountain City, Wisc., with a shorter option on the Minnesota side beginning in Nodine. The common features are the high bluffs overlooking the Mississippi River on both sides. The first tour consists of three short "warm up" trips in and around Winona. The second tour, a circle trip, begins in Winona, climbs up one valley, and plunges down another past historic Pickwick Mill. The third trip begins in Nodine (or Winona for the super fit) and features the Apple Blossom Scenic Drive along the crest of the bluffs and a lush farm valley for circling back. The fourth tour tackles the high bluffs on the Wisconsin side in a circle trip which starts in Fountain City and explores narrow valleys and high plateaus.

> **Tour 1:** The Winona Warm Up -- 18.4 miles (divided into three mini-trips of 5.8, 3.8, and 8.8 miles)
> **Tour 2:** Pickwick Mill Circle Trip -- 32 miles
> **Tour 3:** Apple Blossom Drive Scenic Trip -- 61, 33, or 25 miles
> **Tour 4:** Fountain City Circle Trip -- 36 or 38 miles (with several shortcuts saving up to 12 miles)

About the Area

How to Get There: About 120 miles and 2.5 hours drive southeast of the Twin Cities.

To Winona: Take either U.S. 61 or U.S. 52 (crossing over to U.S. 61 on Mn. 50) all the way to Winona. (Alternatively, stay on U.S. 52 to Rochester and then head east on U.S. 14 to Winona.)

To Fountain City: Take either U.S. 61 or U.S. 52 (crossing over to U.S. 61 on Mn. 50), cross over to Wisconsin side of Mississippi at Wabasha, and take Wisc. 35 southwest 5.5 miles to Fountain City. (From Winona, follow Wisc. 43 across river and take Wisc. 35 northeast five miles.)

Amtrak Alternative: Catch a crack of down train ride from St. Paul to Winona (small charge for packing bike) and return on evening run that gets into St. Paul just before midnight.

Viewed from above, Winona appears like a flat floating island awash in the bottomlands of the Mississippi with high bluffs rising beyond. On the ground, it is a pretty, bustling city framed by the waters of the Mississippi to the northeast and Gilmore Creek feeding into Lake Winona to the southwest. Once a thriving lumber town, today Winona draws its strength from a diverse economy and the locally based higher educational institutions.

The city's Indian roots are deep. The city was named for We-no-ah, daughter of Sioux Chief Wa-pa-sha. Overlooking Winona to the southwest is Sugar Loaf Mountain, called Chief Wa-pa-sha's cap by the Sioux Indians.

When white settlors moved west, steamboats began to ply the Mississippi, and soon, Winona became the last stop for disembarking immigrants in search of rich farmland to the west. In time, the surge of settlers subsided. Flour milling then took hold, only to be replaced by the lumber industry.

A major attraction in Winona is the Julius C. Wilkie Steamboat Center, an actual size replica of a steamboat, "moored" permanently on the Mississippi in the heart of town. The center houses a museum full of river memorabilia and includes a pilot house on the third deck and an elegantly decorated, Victorian-style saloon where lunch is served (507/454-6880).

Another attraction is the Winona Farmers' Market located under the Interstate Bridge between Second and Third Streets. A large variety of vegetables, flowers, herbs, and fruit are sold each Saturday from 7:30 a.m. to 2:00 p.m., June through October.

Winona offers you two restful, town parks: Levee Park located on the banks of the Mississippi River in the heart of town and Lake Park found on the east and north sides of Lake Winona (swimming, canoe and paddle boat rentals, concerts in the band shell, and picnic and restroom facilities). Maps and tapes of downtown walking tours of historic "Prairie School" architecture are available at the Armory Museum.

Winona has a number of motels serving the area. For a listing call the Winona Visitors Bureau (800/657-4972). For a throw back to the turn of the century, the Carriage House Bed and Breakfast

(507/452-8256) offers an authentic three-story carriage house with four guest rooms plus a four-season porch. Complimentary bicycles are available for guests. For a taste of the old railroading days, a meal at Zachs On The Tracks (a converted railroad depot) is a must. For seafood delights, try either Finn & Sawyer's Bar and Grill or the Hot Fish Shop.

Complete with an enclosed deer park, Prairie Island Campground (507/452-4501) next to the river is the nearest camping area. Tucked in the bluffs overlooking the Mississippi is O. L. Kipp State Park (507/643-6849). The park is located 16 miles southeast of Winona and is an alternative trailhead for the Apple Blossom Trail Circle Trip. It has 31 rustic campsites and six miles of nature trails featuring prairie wildflowers, migrating birds, and sweeping bluff-top views. (Bike campground in park at bottom of bluffs off U.S. 61.) Finally, situated in a small ravine at the bottom of the bluffs is the Winona KOA Campgrounds (507/454-2851). The campgrounds are located six miles south of Winona on the Pickwick Mill Circle Tour (campground store, outdoor pool, free hot showers, and Laundromat).

Bike shops are Adventure Cycle and Ski (507/452-4228) in downtown Winona, Kolter Bicycle Store (507/452-5661) at east end of town, and Cj Robinson (507/452-8566) on Co. 17 outside of town. Pick up a bike map for an in-town bike route either at the bike shops or at the Tourist Information Bureau on Huff Street next to Lake Winona.

Located along Tour 2, five miles south of Winona, is the Bunnell House (507/454-2723), a cottage built in the 1850s where fur trader and explorer Willard Bunnell and his family settled. This house provides a living reminder of the past as tour guides recreate various domestic crafts essential to life in the wilderness (fee charged).

On the Wisconsin side and named for the numerous springs in the bluffs, Fountain City clings to the hillside, providing a picturesque river town setting. The Swiss architecture of the bank and a number of other buildings serves as a reminder of the largely Swiss heritage of the town's early settlers. For a "pick me up," try homemade ice cream at the Kwik Trip. For something more substantial, dinner at the Fisherman's Inn next door (river views in back dining room) provides a nice end to the day. North of Fountain City is Merrick State Park (608/687-4936), a beautiful place to camp and alternative trailhead for the Fountain City Circle Trip. The park abuts the marshy backwaters of the Mississippi River and has 73 campsites.

TOUR 1: The Winona Warm Up

Trailhead:	Holiday Inn parking lot on southeast corner of junction of U.S. 61 and Mn. 43 south of Winona.
Distance:	5.8 miles first leg, 3.8 miles second leg, and 8.8 miles third leg for total of 18.4 miles
Terrain:	Level for the first leg, steep ascent for the second leg, and gentle climb up the valley for the third leg
Highlights:	Winona Lake, rose garden, Garvin Heights Park, and bucolic valley
Route:	Winona Lake Leg -- (0.0) North on Mn. 43 and West on Parks Avenue; (0.4) South on Winona Lake bicycle path and clockwise around Winona Lake Garvin Heights Leg -- From Information Bureau -- (0.0) South on Huff Road; (0.2) East on Lake boulevard; (0.4) South on Garvin Heights Road and High Road to park (1.9) and back
	East Burns Valley leg -- From Holiday Inn -- (0.0) South on Mn. 43/Co. 17; (0.2) West on Co. 43; (0.3) South on Sugar Loaf Road; (0.5) Southwest on East Burns Valley Road (Co. 105); (4.4) End of pavement -- return

This trip gives you a nice taste of Winona. The trip starts with a leisurely six-mile circle trip around Winona Lake on a bicycle trail. For those wishing to tackle the second leg, an invigorating climb to Garvin Heights Park for a sweeping overlook of the city 500 feet below is in store. The final leg provides a sample of one of the scenic valleys that work their way up through the bluffs to the southwest. The trip up the valley is a gentle meander through inviting pasture land. When the road becomes gravel, the route returns the way it came.

Winona Lake Leg -- Log

0.0 Trailhead: Outskirts of Winona. Holiday Inn parking lot on northeast corner of junction of Mn. 43 and U.S. 61. TURN RIGHT (NORTH) OUT OF DRIVE ONTO MN. 43 AND LEFT (WEST) ON PARKS AVENUE AND HEAD STRAIGHT FOR WINONA LAKE, which is divided into West Lake and East Lake.

0.4 BEAR RIGHT JUST BEFORE LAKE, TURNING LEFT AT EAST END FISHING PIER, AND THEN LEFT AGAIN AT MILE 0.7 ONTO WINDING BICYCLE TRAIL which circles lake and also serves as a walking/jogging trail. Keep a sharp eye for wood ducks and mallards.

1.0 Dead ahead is full view of Chimney Rock on top of Sugar Loaf Mountain. This rock formation is what remains of a large bluff which was Chief Wa-pa-sha's Cap, so-called by the Sioux Indians. The rock around Sugar Loaf was removed in 1890 by quarrymen. Scattered along the southeast side of the lake are several picnic tables.

1.3 Head west on south side of East Lake through a tunnel of trees.

2.3 Tourist Information Bureau with outdoor pop machines on your left at west end of East Lake. (At this point, the Garvin Heights leg of the tour provides an invigorating side trip. See "Garvin Heights Leg" below.)

2.5 TURN LEFT ON TRAIL AND CROSS HUFF STREET. CONTINUE WEST ON TRAIL on south side of West Lake.

3.1 Reach west end of West Lake and circle north and head east along trail on north side of West Lake.

3.6 Lake Winona Fishing Pier on your right.

3.9 East end of the second half of lake (East Lake). Cross Huff Street and continue east.

4.1 On your right is a sandy beach running about one-half mile with a swimming area and bathing facility -- Lake Park Lodge at mile 4.2.

4.3 Outdoor band shell with summertime concerts on your left and canoe and boat rental shop on your right. Ample parking facilities next to band shell.

4.5 Well-kept rose garden on your left. Worth a stop and stroll. Stately residences just to the north of rose garden and gazebo at east end. Good view of Chimney Rock.

5.5 Cross creek at the east end of East Lake and circle south.

5.6 Trail forks. TAKE THE LEFT FORK, cross a driveway, and keep going straight through the Community Memorial Hospital parking lot winding your way back out to Mn. 43.

5.8 Just west of the hospital building, TURN RIGHT (SOUTH) ON MN. 43 AND LEFT JUST BEFORE THE PHILLIPS 66 STATION, arriving at Holiday Inn at mile 5.9.

Garvin Heights Leg -- Log

0.0 Trailhead: Tourist Information Bureau on Huff Street at west end of East Lake. HEAD SOUTH ON HUFF STREET and cross U.S. 61.

0.2 At T-intersection, TURN LEFT (EAST) ON LAKE BOULEVARD AND RIGHT (SOUTH) ONTO GARVIN HEIGHTS ROAD. Begin steep, twisting climb.

1.2 Garvin Heights Road turns right while High Road bends left. BEAR LEFT ONTO HIGH ROAD (a sign directing you to the park is on a pillar) and keep climbing.

1.7 Top is reached. Turn left (a sign directing you to the park is on a pillar).

1.9 End of road. Garvin Heights Park. Great views of Winona below and river beyond. Hiking trails. Turn around and return by same route.

East Burns Valley Leg -- Log

0.0   Trailhead: Outskirts of Winona. Holiday Inn parking lot on northeast corner of junction of Mn. 43 and U.S. 61. TURN LEFT (SOUTH) ON MN. 43, CROSS U.S. 61, AND HEAD SOUTH ON MN. 43/CO. 17.

0.2   TURN RIGHT (WEST) ON MN. 43 (Co. 17 goes straight).

0.3   TURN LEFT (SOUTH) ON SUGAR LOAF ROAD.

0.5   Cross bridge and TURN RIGHT (SOUTHWEST) ON CO. 105 (EAST BURNS VALLEY ROAD).

1.7   Reach top of gentle climb. Lush valley views to your right.

2.5   Cross stream and enter East Burns Valley, which is drained by West Burns Valley Creek. This is a picturesque narrow valley with some farming on both sides of road.

4.4   Pretty white barn on your left. Pavement ends and gravel begins. Turn around and return to trailhead on same route. (Gravel road continues up gorge reaching Co. 12 in 2.9 miles.)

TOUR 2: Pickwick Mill Circle Trip

Trailhead:	Same as Tour 1
Distance:	32 miles
Terrain:	Varied with one significant hill
Highlights:	Pretty valley, high farm country, thrilling plunge, Pickwick Mill, and Bunnell House.

Route:	(0.0) South on Mn. 43/Co. 17; (0.2) South on Co. 17; (7.7) East on Co. 12; (13.7) North on Co. 7; (10.1) **Ridgeway;** (18.0) **Pickwick;** (20.1) West on U.S. 61; (27.7) West on U.S. 61 frontage road which later becomes Co. 15 and is even later joined by Mn. 43/Co. 17; (32.0) Cross U.S. 61 to Trailhead

This trip climbs out of the river bottom up through a pretty valley (aptly called Pleasant Valley) which narrows towards the end. On top, the road winds through high farm country before taking a plunge down a gorge cut through the bluffs. Towards the bottom is Pickwick, where a stop at Pickwick Mill and Pickwick Inn is a must. Upon reaching the bottom, the route circles back along the Mississippi, passing Bunnell House on the way.

Log

0.0   **Trailhead:** Outskirts of Winona. Junction of U.S. 61 and Mn. 43. (Park in Holiday Inn parking to on northeast corner.) Cross U.S. 61 and HEAD SOUTH ON MN. 43/CO. 17.

0.2   Mn. 43 turns right. CONTINUE STRAIGHT ON CO. 17.

0.7   Co. 15 veers left while Co. 17 turns right. FOLLOW CO. 17 TO THE RIGHT.

1.7   Winona Country Club on your left. Road descends in a gentle fashion leveling off and then descending some more before reaching bottom at mile 2.8. For next four miles, meander through broad valley with some gradual climbing.

6.0   Steeper climb up winding road for next 1.2 miles.

7.2   Top is reached. Pass Co. 15 coming in from left. Witoka is dead ahead.

7.4	Road runs into Co. 12 coming in from your right. GO STRAIGHT (SOUTHEAST) ON CO. ROADS 17 AND 12.
7.7	Co. 17 turns right. KEEP STRAIGHT (EAST) ON CO. 12 which parallels Interstate 90 for next six miles.
9.5	Enter Ridgeway. A ball park and Ridgeway School on your left.
10.1	Center of Ridgeway with Flip'n Jons, a friendly corner bar and grill, on your left. Co. 12 dips a little for next 3.5 miles.
13.7	TURN LEFT (NORTH) ON CO. 7. This is a downhill run beginning at mile 13.9 and levelling off at mile 15.9.
18.1	Pass Pickwick Mill on your left, CROSS BRIDGE, AND TURN LEFT. The mill, built in 1856, is Minnesota's oldest mill. The six-story building was constructed of pale yellow limestone and is being restored for operation on a limited basis.
18.3	Pickwick Inn on your left. (Open at noon on weekends and 3:00 p.m. on weekdays.) This place has a nice bar and restaurant with a large picture window that captures the tumbling falls of a small creek with Pickwick Mill beyond. Must stop.
20.1	TURN LEFT (WEST) ON FRONTAGE ROAD just before junction with U.S. 61. Follow Mississippi River upstream for next seven miles.
20.5	TURN RIGHT ONTO U.S. 61 THEN LEFT HEADING WEST ON U.S. 61.
20.7	Nice pullover; Great views of river.
21.8	Pass Co. 9 coming in from your left.
22.6	Attractive KOA campground is on your left. (See narrative.)
27.6	TURN LEFT ONTO FRONTAGE ROAD WHICH BECOMES CO. 15.

28.1   Co. 15 comes in from left. STAY ON FRONTAGE ROAD WHICH PARALLELS U.S. 61.

28.2   Homer Grocery Store is on your right.

28.5   Bunnell House is on your right (see narrative).

31.3   Co. 17 comes in from your left and joins Co. 15. STAY ON CO. 15.

31.8   Mn. 43 comes in from your left and joins Co. Roads 15/17.

32.0   Cross U.S. 63. Holiday Inn and parking lot are on northeast corner.

TOUR 3: Apple Blossom Drive Circle Trip

Trailhead:	Same as Tour 1; alternative trailheads; (1) O. L. Kipp State Park -- reached by following the Winona Option bike route to junction of Co. Roads 12 and 7. At this point, Co. 12 turns right for Nodine. Instead, go straight on Co. 3 to O. L. Kipp State Park, which is two miles away. (2) Nodine -- reached by following the Winona Option bike route to Nodine.
Distance:	61 miles (or 33 miles from O. L. Kipp State Park or 25 miles from Nodine)
Terrain:	Varied with two (or only one if alternative trailheads are used) significant hills
Highlights:	Glorious blufftop views of Mississippi River, apple orchards, high farm country, and lush farm valley(s)

Route: (0.0) South on Mn. 43/Co. 17; (0.2) South on Co. 17; (7.7) southeast on Co. 12; (18.1) **Nodine** -- East on Co. 12; (20.0) Southeast on Apple Blossom Scenic Drive (Co. 1); 28.5(**La Crescent** -- East on Main Street, South on Walnut Street, and Southwest through town; (29.7) West on Seventh Street which becomes Co. 6; (37.5) Co. 6 becomes Co. 5; (43.4) **Nodine** -- return to Winona or O. L. Kipp the way you came; (61.0) Winona -- Trailhead

For those of you who thrive on physical challenges, the Apple Blossom Drive Circle Trip should start in Winona. The muscles can then be limbered by making an early morning climb out of the river valley along Pleasant Valley Creek. Otherwise, use the alternative starting points at either O. L. Kipp State Park (if you are camping there) or, preferably, Nodine.

The circle trip from Nodine initially follows the Apple Blossom Scenic Drive along the crest of bluffs overlooking the Mississippi. This leg of the trip provides one spectacular panoramic view after another of the Mississippi River below and an opportunity to drink a little cider at one of the apple orchards along the way.

After a swoop down the hill to La Crescent and perhaps a refreshing yogurt at Corky's, a different but equally rewarding experience is the return trip through a lush, serpentine valley drained by Pine Creek. The final climb of the day out of that valley back to Nodine is a little wearing but well worth the effort. Whether or not the tour ends in Nodine, we recommend taking a break at K's Corral in Nodine to celebrate the day.

Winona Option -- Log

Trailhead: Same as Tour 2. Take the same route as Tour 2 to junction of Co. Roads 7 and 12 -- 13.7 miles away.

Log

13.7   Junction of Co. Roads 7 and 12. CONTINUE EAST ON CO. 12.

16.5   Junction with Co. 3. Co. 12 turns right and Co. 3 goes straight to O.L. Kipp State Park two miles away. TURN RIGHT (SOUTH) ON CO. 12 AND CROSS I-90.

16.8   Truck stop (Phillips 66) on your right.

17.6   Hiler Cemetery on your left.

18.1   Road enters **Nodine**. At T-intersection, Co. 12 turns left and Co. 5 comes in from your right. Small grocery store on your left. TURN LEFT (EAST) ON CO. 12.

18.3   Reach Winona County Highway Department on your right, the starting point for the Nodine Option.

O.L. Kipp State Park Option -- Log

Take gravel state-park road one mile to T-intersection with Co. 3. TURN LEFT (SOUTH) ON CO. 3. Follow Co. 3 to where it intersects Co. 12. TURN LEFT ON CO. 12 and pick up the Winona Option route described above at mile 16.5. The distance from the park to Nodine is 3.8 miles.

Nodine Option -- Log

0.0   Trailhead: Start at Winona County Highway Department at east end of Nodine. HEAD EAST ON CO. 12.

0.7   Magnificent panoramic view of undulating farmland and wooded vale to the south. The scenery becomes more and more spectacular both to the north and to the south. Look for goats chained on side of bank.

1.7   TURN RIGHT (SOUTHEAST) ON CO. 1. This is called the Apple Blossom Scenic Drive. Road follows the bluffs' southeastern axis for the next six miles with magnificent

	interspersed views through parted valleys of the Mississippi River valley below.
5.8	Great view of Lock and Dam No. 6 to Southeast and LaCrosse beyond.
7.1	Yet another great view of the river through an apple orchard to east. Stop at Leidel's Orchard to buy apples.
7.6	Pull over for a spectacular, 140-degree view of LaCrosse across the river to the east.
7.8	Descent begins.
8.2	Lautz Orchard is on your right. A lush offering of apple products. The descent is a beautiful winding ride to the bottom at mile 9.4.
9.6	United Methodist Church on your left as road enters La Crescent on Elm Street.
10.0	TURN LEFT (EAST) ON MAIN STREET.
10.2	La Crescent City Hall on your right next to an IGA grocery store.
10.3	Enter the downtown district at junction of Main and Walnut Streets. Corky's (at southeast corner of Main and Walnut Streets) is a nice clean restaurant with great frozen yogurt cones. Next door is a tempting Country Gift and Antique Store. TURN RIGHT (SOUTH) ON WALNUT (hardware store on right). GO SOUTHWEST OUT OF TOWN -- A RIGHT ON SECOND STREET, A LEFT ON MAPLE STREET, A RIGHT ON FOURTH STREET, A LEFT ON HILL STREET, AND A RIGHT ON SEVENTH STREET. You are now heading west. A municipal swimming pool and park are located on the east side of Hill Street.
11.3	Begin short climb on Seventh Street which turns into Co. 6. This is a four-lane highway with the outside lane serving as a paved shoulder.

12.3	Road becomes a two-lane highway with no shoulder.
12.7	Pass North Pine Tree Road coming in from your right. STAY ON CO. 6 and immediately afterwards cross Pine Creek, which generally parallels Co. 6. Road follows a broad valley mostly planted in corn. When the corn ripens, watch out for corn bangers that periodically pop off along the way. They fire to scare off crows, not bicyclists. Some climbing while road traverses southern slope of valley.
15.5	Nice view to your right of large chicken farm overlooking a pretty, expansive valley with more farms in background.
16.2	Pass Co. 16 coming in from your right.
19.0	A mailbox converted into a Holstein cow marks the farm on your left. Co. 6 soon becomes Co. 5 at Winona County line.
21.9	Co. 5 turns right while Co. 8 goes straight. TURN RIGHT (NORTH) ON CO. 5.
22.7	Cross creek. On opposite side, Co. 125 comes in from your left while Co. 5 goes straight. Stay on Co. 5. Steep one-mile climb out of the valley beings.
24.8	Enter Nodine. K's Corral, a cozy tavern that serves food, is on your left.
24.9	Co. 12 comes in from your left and joints Co. 5.
25.1	Winona County Highway Department Maintenance Facility on your right.

TOUR 4: *Fountain City Circle Trip*

Trailhead:	Municipal park on southwest side of Wisc. 35 next to City Meat Markets just southwest of Fountain City downtown area (alternative trailhead: parking lot next to south campgrounds in Merrick State Park)
Distance:	36 miles (or 42 miles from Merrick State Park) with shortcuts of 20 (18) miles, 26 (30) miles, and 29 (33) miles
Terrain:	Varied with two significant hills
Highlights:	Beautiful views of marshland and distant bluffs along remote country road, hidden valleys, top-of-the-world farm country, and exhilarating descents.
Route:	(0.0) Northwest on Wisc. 35; (2.8) North on Waumandee Creek Road (unmarked); (7.2) North on Wisc. 88; (8.3) Northeast on Oak Valley Road (unmarked); (11.0) South on Canada Ridge Road; (16.7) South on Waumandee Creek Road; (18.7) East on Lower Eagle Valley Road; (21.8) South on Co. G; (23.4) East on Wisc. 95; (25.0) South on Co. Roads P and M; (25.2) South on Co. M; (30.9) West on Wisc. 35; (36.4) Trailhead

Though challenging, this tour offers magnificent back-road scenery as soon as it leaves Wisc. 35. On Waumandee Creek Road (called "lovers lane" by the locals), you can ride close to craggy slopes that look out on a sequence of floodplain forests, marshland, and patches of open water, with the distant Mississippi River bluffs beyond.

Eventually, the route connects to a more travelled road which winds its way up through a wider valley along Waumandee Creek before turning once more onto a remote country road. This road passes through a narrow coulee before making a twisting climb to the high plateau farm country above. Once on top, the route follows the crest of the high bluffs with sweeping panoramic views in all directions. Finally, the road descends into a narrow gorge and rejoins Waumandee Creek Road.

The balance of the trip initially follows another back road which leads to a hidden valley lying east of Fountain City behind a hilly fortress. This road eventually climbs out of the valley after which you may return to Fountain City by one of three routes through openings to the west.

Log

0.0   Trailhead: Parking area next to City Meat Market on west side of Wisc. 35 south of downtown Fountain City. The parking lot is next to a small municipal park (rest rooms and water). TURN LEFT ON WISC. 35 AND HEAD NORTHWEST (wide shoulder).

0.6   Approaching center of town with houses terraced on hillside.

0.8   Yankee Craftsmen, gift shop, on your left.

0.9   Folk Art shop on your right. Road forks. BEAR LEFT ON WISC. 35.

1.0   Pass Wisc. 95 coming in from your right.

2.8   TURN RIGHT (NORTH) JUST BEFORE BRIDGE onto Waumandee Creek Road, a narrow, unmarked back road. Red barn on right side of road.

3.0   Road passes brick house on your right and red outhouses on your left and then forks. BEAR LEFT ON LOWER ROAD. Floodplain forest and small stream on your left for the next 0.2 mile followed by marshland as road begins to hug hillside on your right.

4.6   Pass Semling Road coming in from your right.

4.8	Marsh opens into large body of water on your left. Views get better and better for next two miles as slough lake and distant bluffs across the Mississippi loom.
5.0	Road forks. BEAR LEFT ON LOWER ROAD.
6.0	Road forks. BEAR LEFT ON LOWER ROAD.
6.7	Cross slough creek over narrow bridge and climb a little.
7.2	At T-intersection, TURN RIGHT (NORTH) ON WISC. 88. Road winds between cow pastures as it follows broader valley drained by Waumandee Creek.
8.3	TURN RIGHT (NORTHEAST) ON OAK VALLEY ROAD (UNMARKED EXCEPT FOR STOP SIGN) and cross a small stream. This road winds up through narrow valley.
8.9	Climb steepens reaching first level at mile 9.1.
9.6	Road starts to climb again reaching second level at mile 9.8. Scenic views of valley on your left.
10.0	Road starts final ascent up a gorge. Climb is steep but not unmanageable.
11.0	Reach top. At T-intersection, TURN RIGHT (SOUTH) ON CANADA RIDGE ROAD, another narrow, unmarked road and begin top-of-the-world traverse along somewhat desolate Canada Ridge high above the bluffs. Little to no traffic.
11.2	Pass paved road coming in from your left and cut through a sheep farm.
12.8	Massive chicken building on your left. Road winds a lot and dips a little.
15.3	Steep descent begins.
15.5	Pass paved road coming in from your right.

16.7 At T-intersection, TURN LEFT (SOUTH) ONTO WAUMANDEE CREEK ROAD from where you came.

18.7 TURN LEFT (EAST) ON LOWER EAGLE VALLEY ROAD which is not marked at this point and begin steep 0.3-mile climb. (**In the alternative**, for a shortcut back to the trailhead, go straight the way you came and reach municipal park three miles away or state park 2.7 miles away. This shortcut will save 16 miles (or 24 miles if the Merrick State Park trailhead is used).

19.0 Road levels off as it enters another lovely valley fed by Eagle Creek. The road traverses the hillside as it dips into the valley, follows along the lowlands, and then climbs a little.

21.8 At T-intersection, TURN RIGHT (SOUTH) ON CO. G (which is not marked at this point) as road levels off and then begin gradual, 1.3-mile climb.

23.4 At T-intersection, TURN LEFT (EAST) ON WISC. 95 and climb a little. (**In the alternative**, for a shortcut back to the trailhead saving 10 miles (or 12 miles if Merrick State Park trailhead is used), turn right on Wisc. 95 and return downhill into Fountain City, where Wisc. 95 T-intersects Wisc. 35 approximately 1.7 miles away. From this point the municipal park is an additional mile away and the state park is an additional 3.3 miles away.)

23.8 Pretty cemetery on your right with ornamentally pruned trees.

25.0 TURN RIGHT (SOUTH) ON CO. ROADS P AND M.

25.2 Co. P bears left while Co. M bears right. FOLLOW CO. M past Hilltop Bar and Ballroom (open evenings only) through high farm country for next 4.6 miles along Buffalo Ridge.

26.6 Pass Co. YY coming in from your right. (**In the alternative**, for a shortcut to the trailhead saving seven miles (or nine miles if Merrick State Park trailhead is used), turn right on Co. YY and return to municipal park 2.5 miles away or state park 6.8 miles away. See description of "Co. YY Spur" below.)

27.4	Mini-tractor mailbox on your right.
29.9	Road begins winding descent.
30.6	Pretty valley opens up with road leveling off at mile 30.8.
30.9	At T-intersection, TURN RIGHT (WEST) ON WISC. 35. Nice paved shoulder.
31.3	Pass Wisc. 43 coming in from your left from Winona (1.6 miles away).
31.9	Paved shoulder narrows to 1.5 feet.
33.1	Lock and Dam No. 5A comes into view to your left.
35.6	Pass Co. YY coming in from your right.
36.4	Trailhead (municipal park) on your left. If the trailhead is at Merrick State Park, continue straight on Wisc. 35 and follow it through Fountain City to state park trailhead 4.3 miles away.

Merrick State Park Spur - Log

The Merrick State Park trailhead is located about 3.5 miles north of downtown Fountain City, a mile off Wisc. 35 on the river (west) side.

0.0	Start at parking lot for southern campgrounds.
0.1	Boat landing parking area on your left.
0.6	Ticket office and main entrance on your left. Slight climb follows topping off at mile 1 as road passes over railroad tracks.
1.1	TURN RIGHT (SOUTHEAST) ON WISC. 35. Soon shoulder gets broader.
1.5	Just after crossing a creek, TURN LEFT ONTO WAUMANDEE CREEK ROAD (UNMARKED). Red barn on right side of unmarked road.

Co. YY Spur -- Log

0.0   Junction of Co. Roads M and YY. HEAD SOUTHEAST DOWNHILL ON CO. YY for Fountain City through narrow wooded gulch.

0.4   Road levels off as pretty gullied pasture opens up on your right.

1.2   Road begins gradual descent

1.7   At T-intersection, TURN RIGHT (NORTHWEST) ON WISC. 35.

2.5   Trailhead (municipal park) on your left. If the trailhead is at Merrick State Park, continue straight on Wisc. 35 and follow it through Fountain City to state park trailhead 4.3 miles away.

CARLTON COUNTY--MUNGER TRAIL TOURS

Often overlooked in route to destinations further north, Carlton County has attractions of its own. From the spectacular river gorge scenery of Jay Cooke State Park to its wilderness of woods and lakes and its prosperous farms, Carlton County is a thoroughly enjoyable area. Our bike route south of Carlton goes through a cross section of topography and the other route follows the paved Munger Trail through gorges and by rivers. This state trail (officially designated The Carlton--West Duluth segment of the Willard Munger State Trail) is an abandoned railroad right-of-way and is pretty enough to recommend taking both ways.

Tour 1: 30 miles
Tour 2: 23, 37, or 40 miles

About the Area

How to Get There: Take I-35 from the Twin Cities approximately 130 miles and 2 1/2 hours north to Mn. 210. Turn east on Mn. 210 two miles to Carlton.

Nestled among the evergreens is the clean and friendly town of Carlton. It is the county seat, and the courthouse is the largest building in town. For food try Charlotte's Restaurant, which is noted for its flamboyant owner and good food, or try the Cozy Cafe or Fran's Bakery. The S & A Market has water, yogurt and ice cream, and rents bikes. The Trolley Station at the trailhead has fast food and snacks. Three and a half miles west of town are the Stagestop Lounge and Restaurant, the American Grill, and the Unocal Station, which also has a restaurant. There is lodging at the Royal Pines Motel (218/384-4242) or the AmericInn (218/384-3535) both at the junction of Mn. 210 and I-35 just west of Carlton. Camping is available at Jay Cooke State Park (218/384-4610).

Just west of Carlton is a sign which states, "At this point February 15, 1870 construction of the Northern Pacific Railway was commenced." This was a landmark in opening up the area to commerce.

Jay Cooke State Park is located three miles east of Carlton on Mn. 210. Hardwood forests, steep valleys, river gorges, and huge rock formations are park attractions. There are hiking and mountain bike trails in the park. This is an area of early fur traders and the Dakota and then the Ojibwa Indians. Deer, black bear, timber wolf, and coyote are found in the park, and it is an important wintering area for the white-tailed deer. Pileated woodpeckers, marsh hawks, and great blue herons are among the more spectacular birds that may be seen there.

The park has a camping area with 80 regular sites, backpack camping, shelters, and picnic areas. Fishing is good in the river. Rangers and naturalists conduct activities in the park throughout the summer.

The village of Thompson is just outside the park. A tiny community which looks as though time forgot it, it has a backwoods charm. There is one small store with snacks and information on professional guided raft tours, horseback riding, and trail information.

The Lake Superior Zoological Gardens (sometimes known as the Duluth Zoo) are at the Duluth end of the Munger Trail and are actually in West Duluth. Set among the rocks and hills at the foot of Spirit Mountain, the zoo is well worth a visit. The nocturnal house is a special treat. Tap-A-Keg Bar and Restaurant is also at the end of the trail. The side door leads to the restaurant which serves American or Italian food. If you want instead to picnic or camp, turn right and head for Indian Point Park. Just off the trail, is the Willard Munger Inn (218/624-4814), an attractive motel with dining facilities open from 7 a.m. to 2 p.m.

At the other end of our county road bike route is Mahtowa. T.J.'s Country Store bills itself as "One of the best in downtown Mahtowa." No matter that there are only three other places of business in the whole town. T.J.'s does have everything one would need. Don't miss the local attractions of the weather vane and mileage signs on the side of the building. Perhaps the same person with a sense of humor put them up, as put in the parking meter, fire hydrant, and water tower; all in this town with no parking problems and no city water.

TOUR 1: *Carlton to West Duluth*

Trailhead:	Parking lot in Carlton one block south of Mn. 210 on Co. 1. Parking and portable toilet facilities there.
Distance:	15 miles one way; 30 miles round trip.
Terrain:	The trail is level sloping slightly downward toward Duluth. It is not so much downhill as to make the return trip difficult.
Highlights:	River gorges, view of Lake Superior, Duluth Zoo.
Route:	Stay on Munger Trail all the way. Cross Grand Avenue to zoo in West Duluth, if desired. Return on trail.

A spectacular trip through rocky out-croppings, along a rushing river and over the viewpoint of Duluth and Lake Superior. This trip could be taken several times with new discoveries each time. For a day trip, begin in the morning, bike to West Duluth for lunch and the zoo, and return in the afternoon. The return trip is a little slower but the grade is not at all steep.

Log

0.0 Begin at parking lot in Carlton.

0.5 Rock outcroppings and a view of Otter Creek before you cross the water-eroded gorge of the Saint Louis River at mile 1. The flow of water in the river is regulated by the Thomson Dam just upstream from the bridge.

2.0   Trail passes by Forebay Lake, a 40 acre holding pond which controls the water flow to the hydroelectric power plant 375 feet below. Stop at the kiosk midway along the lake to learn more about this manmade feat. Tours of the power plant are available through Jay Cooke State Park.

3.5   Pass Hemlock Ravine Scientific and Natural Area. This is an example of a hardwood conifer forest containing Eastern Hemlock at its westernmost growing range. People are requested to stay off these slopes because the Eastern Hemlock grows on steep, highly erodible slopes and they are easily damaged by human activity. There are stands of sugar maples, yellow birch and red and white pine on this trail also. The trail continues through these woodlands and crosses Mission Creek.

6.0   Half-way stop (toilet) at Stenman Road.

9.5   Pass around Ely's Peak cutting through the rocky hillside, then swing back around Bardon's Peak at mile 10.5. Spectacular views of the Saint Louis River and Duluth and Superior from this area.

11.5 From here the trail gradually descends for about 3 miles passing through the neighborhoods of Smithville and Riverside.

15.0 The trail ends at Tap-A-Keg Restaurant and Bar 2/10ths of a mile west of the parking lot. The zoo is across the street. The underwater viewing of the zoo's two frolicking polar bears is well worth the price of admission. Stop to rest and then retrace the trail back to Carlton. The round trip is 30 miles.

TOUR 2: *Carlton-Mahtowa*

Trailhead:	Same as Tour 1.
Terrain:	Level with slightly rolling small hills.
Distance:	Main Route: 37 miles. Douglas Road Option: 23 miles. Chub Lake Park Option: 40 miles.
Highlights:	Woods, lakes, farms, pleasant uncrowded countryside, Mahtowa.
Route:	(0.0) South on Co. Roads 1 and 3; (1.0) South on Co. 3; (2.0) West on West Chub Lake Road; (8.0) West on Co. 4; (11.5) South on Co. Roads 4 and 5; (12.5) West on Co. 4; (16.5) South by Lutheran Church; (17.2) **Mahtowa** -- turn around; (18.0) East on Co. 4; (22.0) North on Co. Roads 4 and 5; (23.0) North on Co. 5; (29.0) East on Mn. 210; (37.0) Carlton.

This tour is a biker's dream: long, level stretches; some hills for variety; a few lakes; and lovely views. Chub Lake Park is available as an option, and Mahtowa offers a chance to see a small, small town operating as a viable community center.

Log

0.0 Begin in the parking lot in Carlton. TAKE CO. ROADS 1 AND 3 SOUTH BY OTTER CREEK.

1.0 TURN RIGHT (SOUTH) ON CO. 3. Good shoulder for biking.

2.0 TURN RIGHT (WEST) ON WEST CHUB LAKE ROAD. Narrow, but not busy. Hilly around the lake with summer and year-round homes along the way. Pretty views of Chub Lake and woods. (Option A: Chub Lake Park Option. Continue south on Co. 3. Turn right (west) on East Chub Lake Road for one mile and stop at Chub Lake Park. The park is free on weekdays and has a $1 charge on weekends and holidays. There are picnic grounds, swimming beach, and boat-launching area. The road into the park is 0.8 mile long and is paved. Continue on East Chub Lake Road to join West Chub Lake Road and Hay Lake Road at mile 6. This adds 3.5 miles to the tour.)

5.5   Hill top vista of Hay Lake to the south. Descent follows.

6.0   West Chub Lake Road joins Hay Lake Road and East Chub Lake Road. This is a level road and passes Hay Lake, a marshy lake often populated with water fowl.

7.5   Watch for sod-roofed house on your left.

8.0   TURN RIGHT (WEST) ON CO. 4. A little climbing in store.

11.0   Pass Finke's Berry Farm on your right as route enters level farmland drained by the Blackhoof River.

11.5   At T-intersection, Co. 4 joins Co. 5. TURN LEFT (SOUTH) ON CO. ROADS 4 AND 5. (Douglas Road Option: At T-intersection with Co. 4, turn right (north) on Co. 5. Wooded area, rolling hills. At mile 15.5, turn right (northeast) on Mn. 61. Ride single file as there is no shoulder and there may be some traffic. At mile 18.5, turn right (east) on Douglas Road. Hay fields and two substantial hills. At mile 21.7, turn left (north) on Co. 3 back to the trailhead. This shortens the ride to 23 miles. Mile 23 is trailhead in Carlton).

12.5   Co. 4 separates from Co. 5. TURN RIGHT (WEST) ON Co. 4. Some climbing.

14.5   Road crosses over freeway.

16.5   TURN LEFT (SOUTH) BY THE RED BRICK LUTHERAN CHURCH into downtown Mahtowa. 29 Pines Golf Club is further south on this road.

17.2	Downtown Mahtowa. T.J.'s Country Store has plenty of food, snacks and drinks. The Mahtowa Bar and an auto parts store are the only other stores in this town. After a stop, retrace route to the freeway overpass.
19.5	Road crosses over freeway. Continue east on Co. 4.
22.0	TURN LEFT (NORTH) ON CO. ROADS 4 AND 5.
23.0	Co. 4 separates from Co. 5. STAY ON CO. 5 GOING NORTH. (Co. 4 goes east) Wooded area, rolling hills.
27.0	Junction with Mn. 61. (See mile 11.5 for Douglas Road Option.) FOLLOW SIGN FOR CO. 5, TURN LEFT (WEST), GO UNDER FREEWAY, IMMEDIATELY TURN RIGHT (NORTH).
29.0	TURN RIGHT (EAST) ON MN. 210. Busy, but a wide shoulder.
31.5	Go under freeway. At this junction are two motels and several restaurants (see narrative). The wide shoulder continues into Carlton.
33.0	Note the sign regarding the beginning of the Northern Pacific Railway. (See narrative).
34.0	Wayside rest, picnic tables, shelter, toilets.
37.0	Junction of Mn. 210 and Co. 1. Main intersection in Carlton. One block south is the parking lot. End of trip.

NOTES

TREMPEALEAU, WISC. TOURS

Discovering the Trempealeau area along the Mississippi bluffs is like finding the prize at the bottom of the cracker-jack box. A gem of a town amid scenic hills, it asks to be explored. Our bicycle routes do just that and take you on many of the back roads as well as on the Great River Trail, a Wisconsin State trail.

Tour 1: Trempealeau to Onalaska Trail and Lowlands Trip--30 miles
Tour 2: Perrot State Park, Wildlife Reserve, and Hill Country--18 or 32 miles.
Tour 3: Trempealeau to Galesville Circle Trip--19 miles
Tour 4: Trempealeau River Valley and Dodge Loop--18 miles

About the Area

How to Get There: About 140 miles and three hours south of the Twin Cities on the Mississippi River. Take the Great River Road (Wisc. 35) south. At the intersection of Wisc. 35 and Wisc. 93 at Centerville, turn right (south) on Wisc. 35 and go four miles to Trempealeau.

The romance of the river town of Trempealeau, the locks, and the ambiance of the old Hotel Trempealeau are the reasons for choosing this small town as the headquarters for our tours in this area. The combination of rivers, good farmland, and beautiful hills makes for productive and pleasant land.

The town was settled in 1851 as Reed's Landing. It was renamed in 1856 after Trempealeau Mountain. The name means "mountains soaking in the water" and refers to the reflection of beautiful Trempealeau Mountain in the bay near Perrot State Park.

Perrot State Park has excellent camping facilities, good scenery, and miles of hiking trails. This park is on the Mississippi River as well as the Great River Bicycle Trail and is just a few miles northwest of Trempealeau.

The Trempealeau National Wildlife Refuge, adjoining Perrot State Park, is administered by the U.S. Department of Interior--Fish and Wildlife Service. It contains 5,600 acres of marshes, bottomland hardwoods, upland grasslands, and forest, and a one-mile, self-guided nature trail. Bicycling is allowed on the wildlife drive and on all refuge roads that are closed to public motorized vehicle traffic.

The Great River Trail, a 22.5-mile multi-use recreational trail, links the park and refuge area with Trempealeau and other points southeast of Trempealeau. The trail follows an abandoned railroad line that traverses the floodplain along the Mississippi. The trail is well-groomed and is very firm for a crushed limestone surface. Trail fees are charged. Permits may be purchased at the Trempealeau Hotel or at the park.

You can choose from several lodging places in Trempealeau. The Hotel Trempealeau (608/534-6898) is charming with a turn-of-the-century atmosphere. In 1993, the price per room was $25.20 a night. The seven rooms share one bathroom across the hall. The bar downstairs has live entertainment on Friday and Saturday evenings, and you will hear the music in your room. Just behind the hotel is the Riverview House, a one bedroom suite (with pullout each), available for $50.00 a night.

Other lodgings include the Pleasant Knoll Motel (608/534-6015) and the Riverview Motel (608/534-7784). The Pleasant Knoll Motel has kitchenettes.

Regardless of where you stay, you simply must eat at the Hotel Trempealeau. The food is excellent, prepared from fresh ingredients, and home-cooked. The walnut burgers are a "must try"; the chili is good; the vegetable stew and chicken noodle soup are excellent. Sitting on the porch of the hotel and eating Swedish apple pie, oat fudge bars, or poppy seed cake, while watching the Delta Queen cruise by on the Mississippi, is a treasured experience. We like to plan our bike trips so we can have lunch on the porch. Bicycle and canoe rental provided at the hotel.

Galesville is located near Trempealeau in an area called the "Garden of Eden." This refers to the Reverend David O. Van Slyke's lifelong campaign to convince the world that the area was indeed the biblical Garden of Eden. Visitors and locals may not agree with the theory, but no one doubts the beauty of the area. The town is on Marinuka Lake, which is formed by Beaver, Dutch, and Silver creeks. The lake is named for the Princess Marie Nounka, the granddaughter of the great Chief Decorah. There are four parks in town, one featuring a "Wedding Gazebo."

Three special times to visit Galesville might include SummerFest, the second week in June; the Trempealeau County Fair, the third week in July; and the Apple Affair, the first Saturday in October. Be sure to eat at the Mill Inn for special natural foods and sometimes live music. About 3 miles southeast of town on Wisc. 53 is Pow Wow Campground (608/582-2995), a full service, mostly wooded campground with 148 sites.

In town is The Clark House (608/582-4190), a bed and breakfast in a 1906 Queen Anne Victorian home (2 rooms). The Sonic Motel (608/582-2281) is located at the intersection of Wisc. 93 and Wisc. 54, with a nice restaurant (Jeffreys) next door.

TOUR 1: *Trempealeau to Onalaska Trail and Lowlands Trip*

Trailhead:	Trempealeau Hotel
Distance:	To Onalaska and back: 30 miles Option B: 23 miles Option C: 25 miles
Terrain:	Level, old railroad bed
Highlights:	Floodplain forests, teeming marshland, Lake Onalaska (a national wildlife and fish refuge), and spectacular views of the fertile floodplain and bluffs.

> **Route:** (0.0) East on 1st Street, North on next street, and East on 2nd Street; (0.6) North on Fremont Street and East on Wisc. 35; (1.2) East on trail; (11.2) **Midway**; (14.6) **Onalaska**--turn around; (17.2) West on Co. Z; (19.2) West and North on Co. ZB; (22.9) Northwest on Co. Z; (23.3) North on Lytles Road and West on trail; (30.0) Trailhead.

You will find easy biking along this route with views of the bluffs from below. The trail is mostly shaded and pleasant. The alternate roads are level and cross the floodplain through farmland, wildlife areas and a lakeside residential development. The trail once ended in Onalaska but now continues on to LaCrosse and the Sparta Elroy trail beyond.

Log

0.0	Leaving from the Trempealeau Hotel, GO TOWARD THE RIVER AND TURN LEFT (EAST) ON 1ST STREET, LEFT (NORTH) A BLOCK LATER, AND THEN RIGHT (EAST) ON 2ND STREET.
0.6	TURN LEFT (NORTH) ON FREMONT STREET and go up the hill. TURN RIGHT (EAST) ON WISC. 35, which passes Tremplo Bike shop on your left just before the trail.
1.2	TURN RIGHT (EAST) ON GREAT RIVER TRAIL.
2.7	Bench overlooking marsh.
3.8	Trail crosses bridge.
6.8	Trail crosses Black River. Bench on east side. Road and a parking lot for trail access a little further east.
9.6	Bench overlooking the swamp on the Wisconsin side. The bluffs are about five miles away.
10.1	Trail crosses bridge. Swift shallow river below.

11.1	Town of **Midway**. Kerry Corner Bar with outside pop machine.
	Option B: Turn right (west) on Co. ZN for the ride back to Trempealeau. Ride west 1.2 miles to T-intersection, turn right (north) on Co. Z, and turn right (north) on Lytles Road at mile 23.3 on the log.
12.1	Intersection with Co. Z.
	Option C: Turn right (west) on Co. Z and pick up main route at mile 17.2 of the log.
14.6	**Onalaska.** Paul's Pantry store. Just to the west is the La Crosse Airport. Turn around for return trip.
15.6	Bench overlooking the river.
17.2	TURN LEFT (WEST) ON CO. Z.
17.6	Cross the double railroad track at right angles.
18.0	Grandpa's Bar and Antiques and God's Green Acres.
18.2	Mossey public boat landing.
18.6	Lake Onalaska on your left. This is a large, shallow lake with good fishing that borders the airport. For next 4 miles the road passes a string of lake homes.
19.0	GO STRAIGHT ON CO. ZB instead of following Co. Z, which turns right (north).
20.8	Park and playground on your right. Toilet facilities.
21.1	At T-intersection, TURN LEFT (WEST) AND STAY ON CO. ZB.
21.9	TURN RIGHT (NORTH) AND STAY ON CO. ZB (Shore Drive goes straight).

22.9   At T-intersection, TURN LEFT (NORTHWEST) ON CO. Z.

23.3   TURN RIGHT (NORTH) ON LYTLES ROAD for one block.

23.4   TURN LEFT (NORTHWEST) ON TRAIL.

30.0   Back at Trempealeau Hotel.

TOUR 2: *Perrot State Park and Hill Country*

Trailhead:	Trempealeau Hotel
Distance:	18 or 32 miles
Terrain:	The lowland portion is level. The hill portion has easy to moderate rolling hills.
Highlights:	Perrot State Park, Trempealeau National Wildlife Refuge, Great River Trail, Trempealeau River Valley, and the unglaciated hill country.
Route:	(0.0) North on Main Street which becomes Wisc. 35; (0.8) Northwest on trail; (5.5) Southwest on Refuge Road; (5.7) Refuge--Northwest on Wildlife Drive; (10.0) Repeat one mile of Wildlife Drive; (11.0) North on bike/footpath; (12.5) Cross Wisc. 35 and North on Co. P; (18.2) **Dodge**--Cross Co. J and river and turn South on Co. J; (19.9) South on Co. G; (23.9) East on Wisc. 35; (24.2) South on Prairie Road; (25.4) Southwest on West Prairie Road; (28.1) South on Lehman Road; (28.6) South on Park Road; (32.5) South on Main Street to Trailhead.

This route follows the trail along the lowlands past Perrot State Park to the Trempealeau National Wildlife Refuge and then heads north into the surrounding hill country. The climb out of the river valley is moderate as the road works its way up one side of a water drainage cut by the Trempealeau River and returns down the other side to Perrot State Park and a scenic ride along the Mississippi River.

The shorter route goes only as far as the wildlife refuge. This trip could be used as a half-day warm up or be done as a leisurely day trip. There are ample opportunities to linger at both the refuge and the park.

Log

0.0 Leaving the Trempealeau Hotel, GO NORTH ON MAIN STREET which becomes Wisc. 35 two blocks later.

0.8 TURN LEFT (UPSTREAM) ONTO THE GREAT RIVER TRAIL.

4.0 Beautiful view overlooking a swamp with hills in the distance.

5.5 The end of the trail segment. TURN LEFT (SOUTHWEST) ON REFUGE ROAD.

5.9 TURN RIGHT (NORTHWEST) ON WILDLIFE DRIVE.

6.1 This area appears to be in the process of being converted from sand dunes and grassland to woodland.

6.9 Bypass the trail to the north and continue (counterclockwise) around the circle route of the Wildlife Drive.

7.8 Stop here for the nature trail. A good view of the estuary and pond from the wooden lookout.

10.0 Back at the sign that shows the park trails. (For a shorter trip of about 18 miles, return to the trail and head southeast on Prairie Road where you join the main route at mile 25.4 on the log.) For the main route, TURN LEFT (NORTHWEST) AND REPEAT ONE MILE OF WILDLIFE DRIVE.

11.0 TURN RIGHT (NORTH) ON A BIKE AND FOOT TRAIL.

12.0 Gate. Parking lot for autos and access from the north. (A shorter trip could begin here. Follow this log until mile 23.9 and then return to this wayside.)

12.5 Cross Wisc. 35 and TAKE CO. P NORTH.

13.1 At a Y in the road, BEAR RIGHT ON CO. P. Follow the Trempealeau River with steep banks on your left.

14.2 A small bridge to the right crosses the river and is a nice place to stop and snack or just look. The ascents here are gradual as are the descents. This area has many nice views of the valley and pleasant contours of hay and corn fields.

16.2 Beautiful valley with oak, sumac, ash mixed forest.

18.2 **Dodge.** Cross the river into Trempealeau County and enter the town. TURN RIGHT (SOUTH) ON CO. J (first road after bridge) past an International Harvester machinery dealer. A "tubes for rent $2.00" sign is next to the Bucket Bar. Servais Groceries opens at 7:00 a.m. Closes Sundays at noon.

18.7 Two parks on the right. Dodge Sportsman Park and the public park, which has toilet facilities.

19.1 Top of the hill. Gentle rolling area between the valley to the right and the higher hills to the left. This is a fairly level area and has an abundance of good farmland.

19.9 At T-intersection, TURN RIGHT (SOUTH) ON CO. G.

20.2	You are now riding in the middle of the plateau between the Trempealeau Valley and the high hills to your left. A beautiful panoramic view of the valley to your right.
20.7	Cross Co. NE (An extra 10-mile loop could be added here. Bear left at each intersection. The route includes: Schmiele Valley Road, Bear Coulee Road, Pine Creek Ridge Road, and Dodge Hill Road. At Pine Creek, turn left onto Peplinski Road (Co. G) until you find yourself back at mile 19.9 where the road T-intersects Co. G.)
22.9	Stop to see the herd of North American bison in a pasture close to the road on your right.
23.9	TURN LEFT (EAST) ON WISC. 35. This part has a narrow shoulder. Up a gentle hill to Prairie Road. (Turn right (west) on Wisc. 35 to return to the wayside at juntion with Co. P. Approximately 1½ miles.)
24.2	TURN RIGHT (SOUTH) ON WEST PRAIRIE ROAD. A small park with water pump on your left. No toilets.
25.4	TURN LEFT (SOUTHEAST) ON WEST PRAIRIE ROAD back toward Trempealeau.
28.1	TURN RIGHT (TOWARD THE RIVER) ON LEHMAN ROAD.
28.6	At T-intersection after crossing trail, TURN RIGHT (SOUTH) ON PARK ROAD to ride through Perrot State Park. Look for hawks.
29.8	Swimming area.
30.7	Indian mounds on your right. Perrot Ridge Trail on your left.
31.6	Leaving Perrot State Park. Ed Sullivan's Supper Club on your right. Magnificent views of river.
32.5	Back at Trempealeau Hotel.

TOUR 3: *Trempealeau to Galesville Circle Trip*

Trailhead:	Trempealeau Hotel
Distance:	19 miles
Terrain:	Quite level with no major climbs
Highlights:	Galesville history, gazebo park, and Mill Inn.
Route:	(0.0) East on 1st Street, North on next street, and East on 2nd Street; (0.6) North on Fremont Street which becomes Co. K; (7.0) East on Wisc. 93; (7.5) Northeast on Mill Road; (8.5) **Galesville**--turn around, head south on Ridge Street and follow signs to Co. K; (9.5) Cross Wisc. 35 and stay on Co. K; (12.0) South on Co. M; (15.0) West on 5th Street; (19.0) South on Co. K; (19.5) Trailhead.

Galesville is known as the "Garden of Eden" because of the confluence of three rivers and other characteristics noted by an early minister. The area certainly has beauty and charm. The ride is an easy one, traversing pleasant farmland and allowing for plenty of exploration in Galesville.

Log

0.0   From the Trempealeau Hotel, GO TOWARD THE RIVER AND TURN LEFT (DOWNSTREAM) ON 1ST STREET. TURN LEFT (NORTH) ONE BLOCK LATER AND THEN TURN RIGHT (EAST) ON 2ND STREET.

0.6   TURN LEFT (NORTH) UP THE HILL ON FREMONT STREET, WHICH LEADS TO CO. K. Co. K takes you out of town on a fairly level route through a flat farmland and some wooded areas.

6.0	Pass Co. M coming in on your right. Stay on Co. K.
7.0	TURN RIGHT (EAST) ON WISC. 35 AND LEFT (NORTH) 0.5 MILE LATER ON MILL ROAD which leads into Galesville. Follow this road to the Main Street.
8.5	**Galesville** -- town square and park. Historical photos and information are posted on the sides of the information kiosk. Across the street, overlooking Lake Marinuka, is a gazebo where weddings are often performed. The gas station next to the park has rest-room facilities.
8.5	Return trip. TAKE THE RIGHT TURN SOUTH OF THE GAZEBO ON RIDGE AVENUE AND FOLLOW THE SIGNS FOR CO. K THROUGH TOWN AND BACK TO WISC. 35. Note the traditional old homes and neat, tree-lined streets.
9.5	CROSS WISC. 35, STAYING ON CO. K.
12.0	TURN LEFT (SOUTH) ON CO. M.
15.0	TURN RIGHT (WEST) ON 5TH STREET (BULAWA STREET).
19.0	TURN LEFT (SOUTH) ON CO. K on the north edge of Trempealeau and follow it back into town.
19.5	Trempealeau Hotel

TOUR 4: *Trempealeau River Valley and Dodge Loop*

Trailhead:	Wayside on Wisc. 35 about 2.5 miles east of the Winona cutoff and 1.3 miles west of junction with Co. P. Toilets and water available.
Distance:	19 miles (optional 10-mile loop can be added.) A 16-mile shortcut is noted.
Terrain:	Mostly level with some moderately rolling hills.
Highlights:	Trempealeau River valley, rolling farm country, Dodge, grazing buffalo, and wildlife refuge.
Route:	(0.0) East on Wisc. 35; (1.3) North on Co. P; (7.0) **Dodge** -- Cross Co. J and river and South on first road; (8.7) South on Co. G; (12.7) East on Wisc. 35; (13.0) South on Prairie Road; (14.2) **Refuge** -- West on Refuge Road; (14.6) North on Wildlife Drive; (15.6) North on bike/foot path; (17.3) West on Wisc. 35; (18.4) Trailhead.

This route includes the northern half of Tour 2. It is offered because the trailhead provides an attractive and convenient starting place for a one to three hour bike ride if the trip from Trempealeau seems too long.

Log

0.0   Ride east from wayside on Wisc. 35.

1.3   TURN LEFT (NORTH) ON CO. P. At this point, pick up the route on the log for Tour 2 at mile 12.5 and follow the trip on that log to mile 23.9 (junction of Co. G and Wisc. 35).

12.7	Junction of Co. G and Wisc. 35. **Decision Time:** Either turn right (west) and return to wayside three miles away for a total of 16 miles or turn left (east) for a loop into the Trempealeau National Wildlife Refuge for a total of 18.5 miles. The rest of this log assumes you TURNED LEFT (EAST) ON WISC. 35.
	Head up gentle hill on paved shoulder.
13.0	TURN RIGHT (SOUTH) ON PRAIRIE ROAD. A small park with pump but no toilet is on southeast corner.
14.2	TURN RIGHT (WEST) ON REFUGE ROAD and head for Trempealeau National Wildlife Refuge.
14.6	TURN RIGHT (NORTH) ON WILDLIFE DRIVE.
15.6	TURN RIGHT (NORTH) ON A BIKE AND FOOT TRAIL.
16.7	Parking lot for autos and access from the north.
17.3	TURN LEFT (WEST) ON WISC. HWYS. 35 AND 54. Across the road is Co. P.
18.6	Back at the wayside.

NOTES

RIDES BY DISTANCE

Rides 50-70 Miles in Length   Page

Pepin to Plum City Circle Trip/Option A	51 miles	175
Pepin Tour/Stockholm Spur	52 miles	183
Fire Trail -- Hinckley to Moose Lake and Back	66 miles	216
Finlayson to Banning State Park/Option C	56 miles	222
Forestville State Park Circle Trip	60 miles	255
Winona -- Apple Blossom Drive Circle Trip	61 miles	270

Rides 40-50 Miles in Length   Page

Cannon Falls River Valley Trip/Option C	41 or 45 miles	42
Red Wing River Valley Trip/Option B	41 or 45 miles	56
River Falls to Diamond Bluff Circle Tour	47 or 52 miles	66
River Falls-Eastern Loop/Option D	47 miles	70
Spring Valley-Eau Galle River Loop/Option C	44 miles	87
Spring Valley-Rural Church Route/Main Route	47 miles	96
Osceola Circle Trip/Option B	41 miles	107
Red Cedar River Circle Trip/Option B-2	41 miles	150
Red Cedar-Western Highlands Route/Option A	48 miles	158
Red Cedar-Western Highlands Route/Option B	40 miles	158
Maiden Rock/Plum City/Pepin Trip	42 miles	171
West From Waterville	46 miles	207
Fire Trail -- Hinckley to Willow River and Back	46 miles	216
Lanesboro -- South Rim Circle Trip/Option B	43 miles	248

Rides 30-40 Miles in Length   Page

Cannon Falls to Welch Circle Trip	34 miles	47
River Falls - Eastern Loop/Option A	39 or 43 miles	70
River Falls - Round Barn Trip	38 miles	77
Spring Valley-Eau Galle River Loop/Option B	36 or 37 miles	87
Spring Valley - Rural Church Route/Option D	40 miles	96
Osceola Circle Trip/Option A	35 miles	107
Pine Island - Mantorville	35 or 40 miles	133
Annandale North Route/Option A	37 miles	141
Red Cedar River Circle Trip/Option B-1	32 miles	150

Red Cedar -- Eastern Farm Country Route/Option A	30 miles	156
Red Cedar -- Eastern Farm Country Route/Option B	32 miles	156
Pepin to Plum City Circle Trip/Option C	35 miles	175
Maiden Rock to Plum City Circle Trip	33 miles	180
Lake City to Wabasha Circle Trip/Option B	33 miles	189
Waterville -- Faribault Via Trail and Co. 12	34 miles	203
Waterville -- Faribault Via Co. Rds. 13 and 99	34 miles	205
West From Waterville/Option B	35 miles	207
Fire Trail -- Moose Lake to Finlayson and Back	40 miles	216
Finlayson to Banning State Park/Option B	36 miles	222
Root River Valley Circle Trip/Option C	36 miles	245
Lanesboro - South Rim Circle Trip/Option A	35 miles	248
Lanesboro - North Rim Circle Trip	38 miles	253
Winona - Pickwick Mill Circle Trip	32 miles	267
Fountain City Circle Trip/Long Route	36 or 42 miles	275
Carlton - Mahtowa/Main Route	37 miles	285
Carlton - Mahtowa/Chub Lake Park Option	40 miles	285
Trempealeau - Perrot State Park and Hill Country	32 miles	294

Rides 20-30 Miles in Length   Page

Stillwater to White Bear Lake	22 or 24 miles	4
Houlton - Willow River State Park	25 or 28 miles	12
Stillwater - Lake Demontreville to Lake Elmo	24 miles	24
Stillwater to Afton	23 miles	27
Stillwater - High Bridge Tour/ Main Route	29 miles	31
Stillwater - High Bridge Tour/Second Shortcut	22 miles	31
Stillwater to Marine	27 miles	34
Cannon Falls River Valley Trip/Option B	21 miles	42
Cannon Falls Back Country Tour	28 miles	49
Red Wing to Welch Circle Trip	28 or 32 miles	51
River Falls Eastern Loop/Option E	28 miles	70
River Falls - Round Barn Trip/Shortcut	23 miles	77
Trimbelle Circle Trip	24 miles	80
Spring Valley - Rural Church Route/Option C	28 miles	96
Osceola Circle Trip/Option C-2	26 miles	107
Interstate Park Circle Trip/Option A	28 or 33 miles	114
Interstate Park Circle Trip/Option B	21 or 26 miles	114
Taylors Falls - Center City - Lindstrom	25 miles	124

Wild River State Park Circle Trip	26 miles	127
Annandale North Route/Option C	21 miles	141
Red Cedar Trail and return	30 miles	150
Red Cedar - Canoe to Durand and Bike Back	28 to 30 miles	162
Menomonie North/Option A	21 miles	164
Lake City to Wabasha Circle Trip/Option A	26 miles	189
Red Wing to Lake City Trip	20 or 23 miles	194
Lake Pepin Ramble/Option B	21 miles	197
West from Waterville/Option A	21 miles	207
Fire Trail -- Hinckley to Finlayson and Back	26 miles	216
Hinckley to Grindstone Lake	30 miles	221
Finlayson to Banning State Park/Option A	21 miles	222
Moose Lake to Sturgeon Lake Circle Trip	21 miles	227
Moose Lake - Kettle River Loop	25 miles	230
Lanesboro - Fountain Hill Circle Trip	21 or 22 miles	241
Root River Valley Circle Trip/Option B	27 miles	245
Nodine -- Apple Blossom Drive Circle Trip	25 or 33 miles	270
Fountain City Circle Trip/First Shortcut	20 or 18 miles	275
Fountain City Circle Trip/Second Shortcut	26 or 30 miles	275
Fountain City Circle Trip/Third Shortcut	29 or 33 miles	275
Carlton to West Duluth	30 miles	283
Carlton - Mahtowa/Douglas Road Option	23 miles	285
Trempealeau to Onalaska	23, 25 or 30 miles	291

Rides 10-20 Miles in Length   Page

White Bear Lake Circle Tour	14 miles	10
Somerset Route	8 miles	16
Stillwater to Withrow	16 miles	18
Scandia -- Marine	14 or 16 miles	21
Stillwater - High Bridge Tour/First Shortcut	16 miles	31
Red Wing - The Poets Route	19 or 23 miles	54
Red Wing River Valley Trip/Option A	20 or 24 miles	56
River Falls Eastern Loop/Option C	19 miles	70
Spring Valley - Eau Galle River Loop/Option A	18 miles	87
Spring Valley Rural Church Route/Option B	17 miles	96
Hatchville and Weston Circle Trip	20 miles	102
Osceola Circle Trip/Option C	19 or 26 miles	107
Annandale - South Route	19 or 26 miles	139
Pepin to Plum City Circle Trip/Option B	16 miles	175
Lake Pepin Ramble/Option A	18 miles	197

Fire Trail - Moose Lake to Willow River	20 miles	216
Moose Lake to Barnum Circle Trip	13 or 15 miles	232
Root River Valley Circle Trip/Option A	11 miles	245
Trempealeau - Perrot State Park	18 miles	294
Trempealeau to Galesville Circle Trip	20 miles	298
Trempealeau River Valley and Dodge Loop	16 or 20 miles	300

Rides Under 10 Miles   **Page**

Cannon Falls River Valley Trip/Option A	9 miles	42
Tour of River Falls	5 to 9 miles	64
River Falls -- Eastern Loop/Option B	10 miles	70
Spring Valley Rural Church Route/Option A	10 miles	96
Annandale North Route/Option B	6 miles	141
Menomonie In Town Tour	5 to 18 miles	148
Menomonie North/Option B	10 miles	164
Waterville - Faribault - Waterville Trip/Shortcut	8 miles	203
Winona Warm Up/Winona Lake Leg	6 miles	264
Winona Warm Up/Garvin Heights Leg	4 miles	264
Winona Warm Up/East Burns Valley Leg	9 miles	264

BUYING A BICYCLE

Buying a bicycle is a difficult procedure. Difficult because unless you have actually ridden a bike for several days you can't be sure if it is just what you want.

It helps to know what type of bicycling you will be doing: touring, city cycling, off-road cycling, or racing. Plan to spend enough money to get a quality bicycle that won't break down or require frequent adjustment. Generally, a better bicycle gives you a lighter weight frame and better quality components.

Try to patronize a local bike shop. Many good reasons exist for doing this, including:

1. The employees have a wealth of knowledge and experience at biking;

2. You are likely to need the services of a competent bike shop before 1,000 miles are up; and

3. The competent shop will custom outfit your new bike when you buy it at very little additional cost. (See discussion on "Custom Gearing" which follows.)

To ensure satisfaction with the purchase of a bicycle, spend some time planning and evaluating before buying. Read reviews and articles in cycling magazines. Talk to people who bike to get their ideas. Visit several bicycle shops, talk to personnel, and listen to what they have to say. Try out as many bicycles as possible. Don't focus on a single brand name of bike and expect it to be significantly better than another. All builders tend to select components from the same manufacturers.

The general classifications of bicycles are:

- racing bikes - the fastest and possibly the best performance bicycles. They are also more fragile, may need more adjustment, and may not give the most comfortable ride.

- touring bikes - more comfortable and generally the most popular with the average biker. They provide more comfort for long rides, low gearing for hills, better brakes, and can carry some load.

- mountain or all-terrain bikes -- very popular in recent years with smaller wheels and wider tires. They are steady, strong, and can carry a heavier load. They are also heavier and slower.

Be sure to get a third chain wheel (the "granny gear") for lower gearing. It makes exploring those hills and valleys so much easier. Purchase the attachments for carrying a water bottle, a tire pump, and panniers. It is possible to buy an all-terrain bike with a frame geometry for touring and an extra set of wheels and tires for road touring. Consider whether you want dropped or upright handlebars.

Check with a competent salesperson to fit the bicycle to your size as proper size is vital to comfortable biking. This is especially true for women. Most manufacturers still size most of their frames to be compatible with the male anatomy.

CUSTOM GEARING

Although this book tends to be fairly non-technical, we have included this short section on custom gearing for three simple reasons:

- almost no other source tackles the subject;

- good shifting can make a significant improvement in your riding pleasure; and

- it is a very low cost improvement when specified with the purchase of a new bike or new gear cluster.

In recent years, most bicycles have been geared with the athlete in mind. For those of us who are a little too old, fat, or have a tendency to knee soreness, the lower gearing made available by a third chain wheel can make the difference between fun biking and hurting.

For a discussion of gearing, you should understand that bicycle gearing is notated in "gear inches." This is the distance in inches that the bicycle will travel with each revolution of the crank (pedals) times 3.14 (pi). It is calculated by making a ratio between the number of teeth on the front chainwheel and the number of teeth on the rear sprocket times the diameter on the wheel in inches. Many sport bikes have a gearing range from about 35-40 to 98-105. For climbing hills with some touring gear on board, the low gearing needs to be in the range of 22 to 27. In order to get the gearing available in the more often used lower ranges, it may be advisable to give up some top range gearing. If your top speed on a flat surface is 25 mph, you can manage that with a top range gearing of about 90. The 90 top range will still allow you to pedal up over 40 mph down hills if that is something you wish to do.

Most touring bicyclists find shift patterns that go 1 through 5 on each chain wheel easier to work with than the split shifting popular on most touring bikes and racing bikes. To become familiar with the practical meaning of various gear inches, calculate the gear inches of your current bike, write them on a small card which is then taped to the bar on your bike for reference while riding. A gearing example that has been used for easy shifting patterns and close gears is given here.

Chain rings of 26, 38, and 48 teeth with a seven-speed sprocket cluster of 14, 15, 16, 17, 19, 24, and 30 teeth give the following shifting patterns.

- the 26 tooth chainring equals 23, 29, 37, 41, 47 and 50;

- the 38 tooth chainring equals 34, 42, 54, 60, 64, 68, and 73;

- the 48 tooth chainring equals 43, 54, 68, 76, 81, 86, and 93.

This combination gives the granny gearing to climb steep hills with ease and a good assortment of road and trail gears. The gear shifts are close enough that you can always keep your cadence up around 90 for low knee strain.

BICYCLE MAINTENANCE

Safe and happy bicycling demands bicycle maintenance. It is no fun to have a flat tire 10 miles away from the car or to go downhill and have a brake or wheel failure.

Several options are available to bicyclers for bicycle maintenance:

- have a shop do it;
- find a competent and soft-hearted friend; or
- do it yourself.

The first two categories will take care of themselves, but do-it-yourselfers still have more options.

1. buy a book and tools and learn by reading;
2. take a course at a bike shop and learn by watching;
3. get that competent and soft-hearted friend to teach you and learn by direction; or
4. experiment and try to learn by your mistakes.

Any of these methods will be a plus for a problem on the road.

Elementary maintenance should include:

1. Periodic overhaul to clean and lubricate bearing surfaces. Once a year is probably often enough for most cyclists. If you put in lots of miles, more frequent overhauls may be advisable.
2. Periodic checks of wheel trueness, headset tightness, and cable tightness. It is best to do this right after a ride and then fix any problems right away so that you are ready to go on the next ride without any worry.

3. Strange noises are a sign of trouble. Try to isolate the noise by testing and then fixing it or having it fixed.

4. Everyone should be able to change a tire and fix a flat. That is the most common problem and not difficult to learn how to do. Don't depend on someone else to come by and rescue you. At least one rider in a group should have the tools necessary.

A bicycle tool kit to take along might include the following items:

Basic:

- tire pump
- patch kit
- tire levers
- adjustable wrench
- chain tool

Optional:

- innertubes of correct size
- tire
- extra brake pads
- bicycle nuts
- two-ounce squeeze bottle of Tri-Flow
- set of three Allen wrenches (or vice grips)
- a bit of wire
- roll of black electrical tape
- screwdrivers

TRANSPORTING BICYCLES

Unless you plan to take bicycle trips only within close proximity to your house, it is necessary to transport your bicycle to the tour starting point. The three main ways to transport your bike are in the car, on a rear car rack, or on a rack on top of the car.

For those whose bicycles have quick release wheels, it is possible to take off the wheel and store the whole bicycle inside the car. This method is cheap and keeps the bike safe from theft, weather, dust, mud, and road hazards. However, it also severely limits the space inside the car and requires reassembly before biking. Certain cars will not accommodate bicycles at all. For a van, station wagon, or truck, however, that is not a problem. If the bicycles are layered on their side, we recommend placing a chaise lounge cushion (or the like) between each bike to prevent scratching the bikes and entangling peddles and spokes.

Least expensive and most common are racks which hook onto the back of the car. Two bicycles can be transported this way and are easily put on the rack and taken off. The racks themselves are usually light, easily stored, and cheap. Disadvantages are that the bike is vulnerable to dust, dragging on the ground when going over dips or humps, and theft. It may be difficult to lock bicycles on securely and extra tie downs are needed. If you purchase this type of rack, make sure it fits your model of car and rests firmly on the back of the car. The straps should primarily position the carrier with the load being transferred directly to the car.

Car top carriers may allow four bikes to be transported and still have room for four people in the car. There is usually good theft protection as the bikes can be locked to the carrier. Some car top carriers can be used for skis or canoes also. However, they are usually more expensive than other types of carriers. The bicycles may be difficult to position, and you may need to climb on top of the car to do it. Bikes are out in the weather, and gas mileage will suffer. One hazard to watch out for is driving into your garage while the bikes are still on top of the car! It happens too often, once to one of the authors. To avoid this hazard, consider tying a ribbon or visible string from the bike to the front bumper of your car to remind you that a bike is there.

A trailer to carry bicycles and folding bicycles are other options.

As with other purchases, read and investigate to see what will fit your car and your habits before buying.

PACKING FOR A TRIP

Every participant in bicycle touring has compiled his or her list of what to take on a bike trip. The aim is to make the trip a happy, carefree experience. What one takes depends on the time of year, the length of the trip, and any other planned activities. Here is our list.

Essentials:

1. Your *Biking With The Wind* book.

2. Bicycle helmet. Wear one before the spill!

3. Rear-view mirror either attached to the bicycle or the helmet. Hint: Try mounting the helmet mirror on both sides before giving up as most of us have a dominant eye.

4. Water. One or even two water bottles are necessary. Drink water before you are thirsty to prevent dehydration.

5. Munchies or lunch. Part of the fun of a bicycle tour is the stop at the local bakery or home-town restaurant. However, some spots along the way are so pretty that a stop to view the scenery and to have a light snack is preferred. Munchies help keep the energy level up, too.

6. Repair kit. At least one person in the group should know how to use and should carry: a patch kit, tire levers, a bicycle pump, and an adjustable wrench. (See bicycle maintenance section for more on tools.) Find a happy medium between carrying nothing and being unprepared and carrying too much or too heavy equipment.

7. Sunglasses, chap stick, and suntan lotion (for obvious reasons).

8. First aid kit containing band-aids, antiseptic cream, pre-packaged moist toweletes, tape, and an ace bandage. Only one person in the group needs this.

9. Bicycle lock, for peace of mind while wandering overland or exploring town by foot.

10. A pannier, rack bag, or handlebar pack to put the gear in, with a little excess room to carry home an irresistible artifact acquired along the way. Include a plastic bag to protect all content from rain.

Optionals:

1. Padded cycling gloves to help cushion your hands even though padded handle bars are used.

2. Padded cycling shorts to help prevent soreness problems.

3. Rain gear. A jacket and pants are suggested as the jacket can double as a wind-breaker, if needed.

4. A storm sheet plastic or space blanket. It can serve as a sit-upon or picnic table when snacking or to provide additional protection in inclement weather.

5. Cyclocomputer. For those who like to know how far, how long, how fast, current speed, average speed, maximum speed, etc. Lots of fun.

6. Compass. Helps on the crossroads that are poorly marked.

7. "Halt" or an equivalent anti-dog repellent spray.

8. A dry shirt or sweater wrapped in a plastic bag.

9. Pant clips or elastic to prevent long pants from catching in the chain. Otherwise, it is necessary to roll them up if they are loose.

10. A flashlight - just in case.

11. A camera; to record the trip for posterity.

HINTS FOR BETTER BIKING

1. Soak in the scenery and take plenty of quality stops. Bicycle touring is to be enjoyed, not endured. We think that a stop at an antique store or eatery or on the bank of a hill with a great view is the hallmark of a good bicycle tour. Allow time for it.

2. Mileage logs in this book are not guaranteed to match another's bike odometer. Accept the numbers as being ballpark figures arrived at in good faith to give you an idea of how far points are apart and how far you have come. Odometers may vary, and if you do not have one, do not worry. The map and the log will tell you where you are.

3. Test brakes before descending a steep hill, especially if the weather is or has been rainy. A little pumping on the brake handles will help maintain control and help dry off the rim in the rain.

4. Plan ahead and line up your lodging for an overnight while on a two-day trip. Even 10 miles out of the way in order to find a camping spot or a motel can be difficult at the end of the day.

5. Enlist friends to bike with you, and shuttle cars so one is at the end of the trip if you are not taking a circle trip.

6. Don't over-extend yourself. Short trips to start with, building up to longer ones keep enthusiasm high. This also helps the breaking-in process for that part of the anatomy which spends long hours on the bike seat.

7. Be sure to wait for your biking companion and do not take off just as he or she arrives at the catch up point. (This behavior can turn off a friend or mate to bicycling touring if not to a happy relationship.)

8. Cross all railroad tracks at right angles or walk across. **Never** cross railroad tracks on the diagonal. A serious accident can occur if the bike tire gets caught in the groove of a railroad track.

9. Do not zigzag up a hill. It is dangerous and expends more energy. Go straight up and if you run out of steam, stop, straddle the bicycle, rest for 30 seconds, and then continue on. You will be amazed how quickly you will recuperate. Don't be embarrassed to walk up a very steep hill.

10. Finish your ride before dusk. Night riding can be dangerous if unprepared. However, you may consider installing lights for a pleasant and unusual experience on very lightly traveled roads.

11. Keep track of your companions. This doesn't mean keeping them in sight. It does mean, however, making certain that everyone has a clear, precise, unmistakable rendezvous spot and deadline for the next meeting in route. Sound familiar?

12. Go with a positive attitude! Enjoy!